Praise for *Beatleness*

"This fun and insightful study of pop music fandom is recommended both to older Beatlemaniacs who were there and to younger fans who want to know what it was like to be a part of the phenomenon."

—*Library Journal*

"A must-have for Beatles fans looking for new insight . . . Leonard uncovers fresh ideas [that] . . . six decades of Beatles literature passed over by shifting attention from the Beatles' personal and professional lives to their fans' stories. . . . Leonard's ability to mesh both a strong narrative style and her research adds concrete scenes readers can enjoy and picture throughout the book."

—Payton Davis, thespectrum.com

"A book like no other . . . Highly recommended to anyone who was alive when the Beatles rocked our world, or for those who came later that want to visit Beatle magic for the first time."

—Lauren Passarelli, guitar professor and Beatles expert, Berklee College of Music

"Explores a vital, yet overlooked aspect of the Beatles' phenomenon, and the many quotes from fans provide invaluable perspective on the band's impact on US teens during the sixties."

—*The Glass Onion Beatles Journal*

"For once, a book about the Beatles that differs . . . from the ones that have gone before. *Beatleness* is a look at the meaning of the Beatles to the 'first generation' . . . Told through numerous perspectives, it traces the five-year journey of these fans along with the Beatles from their debut, their progression and their end in May 1970. . . . A worthwhile and deeply interesting read . . . Highly recommended."

—Rob Ross, *Popdose*

"Candy Leonard explores new ground in this glorious examination of how the four lads from Liverpool changed our lives. *Beatleness* is the story of you, me, and millions of other baby boomers that grew up loving the Beatles."

—Chachi Loprete, host of *Breakfast with The Beatles*, WZLX Radio, Boston

"A fascinating study of the Beatles' resounding impact upon late-twentieth-century American culture. . . . While hundreds of Beatles books stake claims about being the definitive work, Leonard's *Beatleness* finally gets to the heart of the matter, offering readers new insights into the unusual and lasting nature of Beatles fandom."

—Kenneth Womack, author of
Long and Winding Roads: The Evolving Artistry of the Beatles
and *The Beatles Encyclopedia: Everything Fab Four*

"As a college-level Beatles instructor, I find Dr. Leonard's work accessible to students new to the fields of sociology and critical cultural studies. This text puts the 'popular' back in popular culture studies. What Howard Zinn accomplished in *A People's History of the United States*, Dr. Leonard achieves in *Beatleness*, a true People's History of The Beatles."

—David Gallant, Suffolk University, Boston

"There have been many books through the years about the Beatles, but Candy Leonard's *Beatleness* stands out. It's a wonderful analysis of the Beatles and Beatlemania that will make Beatle fans smile because they can relate to it and see themselves in it. There have been many attempts over the years to describe how the Beatles affected their fans and the world. Pick up *Beatleness* and discover the Beatles all over again."

—Steve Marinucci, *Beatles Examiner*

"Unique among Beatle books—and I've read just about all of them—*Beatleness* is a heartfelt exploration of the relationship between the lads from Liverpool and first-generation fans, showing how that relationship changed all of us. You will find yourself in these pages, and you will love what you read."

—Jude Southerland Kessler,
author of *The John Lennon Series*

"Leonard manages to find a new angle of approach to the study of the Beatles. . . . A welcome . . . sociocultural study for the Beatlemaniac bookworm."

—*Kirkus Reviews*

"Candy Leonard's focus on the way the Beatles' fans saw them—particularly as they changed, musically and otherwise, during the 1960s—is both innovative and revealing, and adds a new dimension to how we think of the Beatles and their accomplishments."

—Allan Kozinn, former *New York Times* music critic and author of
The Beatles: From the Cavern to the Rooftop

"Beatlemania was a singular force in the history of the world, and it has never been capably explained in all of its dimensions. But Candy Leonard's *Beatleness* gets us a little bit closer. This is a soulfully written, genre-defying book that should be of interest to Beatles fans and cultural historians alike."

—John McMillian, author of *Beatles vs. Stones*

"A new book that's bound to give even a modest fan a unique look at how the Beatles forever changed the world of music."

—*US Airways Magazine*

"*Beatleness* demonstrates that the Beatles are an important part of who we are as baby boomers."

—Paul Briand, *Baby Boomer Examiner*

"*Beatleness* taps into our generation's collective memory and evokes the sixties through our personal relationship with the Beatles. The Beatles were our troubadours who helped us make sense of a turbulent era, and *Beatleness* shows us how. . . . For those who want to see how the Beatles helped define a generation, this is the book to read."

—Leonard Steinhorn, author of *The Greater Generation: In Defense of the Baby Boom Legacy*

"Candy Leonard's evocative book is filled with striking insights into the experiences and sensibilities of the young who plunged into Beatlemania, and contributes much to a composite portrait of the sixties as they were lived."

—Todd Gitlin, author of *The Sixties: Years of Hope, Days of Rage*

"An accessible read and an often fascinating journey of how one generation has incorporated the Beatles' music into their lives. . . . Fills a knowledge gap in the band's vast history . . . First generation fans will appreciate this look back at a particular time in music history, while subsequent generations will enjoy learning why the band still plays a significant part in music and general history."

—Kit O'Toole, author of *Songs We Were Singing: Guided Tours Through the Beatles' Lesser-Known Tracks*

"Leonard connects Beatles fans' experiences with the tumult of the times, creating a rich and insightful study of what truly has to be one of the most significant phenomena of the twentieth century."

—William Routhier, *Boston Music Examiner*

"With the sheer number of Beatles-related books available, it seems a fool's errand to try to write one that offers a fresh perspective. Leonard's *Beatleness*, however, does just that, because she goes straight to a vital (and largely ignored) Fab Four source: the fans. . . . She builds a three-dimensional, completely human tale, the likes of which has never before been tackled by a Beatles author."

—Allison Johnelle Boron, *Goldmine*

"In producing *Breakfast With The Beatles* for 25 years, one of my greatest ongoing challenges is trying to describe what it was like when Beatlemania was actually happening. For first-generation and new fans alike, Candy Leonard's *Beatleness* is the go-to source for exactly that. It goes way beyond the simple chronology of events, explaining why we felt the way we did about The Beatles and their music, and why they were so important to us. In telling the story this way, *Beatleness* provides a clearer picture of how they changed the world."
—Dennis Mitchell, producer/host of the globally syndicated, award-winning Dennis Mitchell's *Breakfast With The Beatles*

"Candy Leonard was 'possessed' when she first heard the Beatles, and *Beatleness* is her story and ours. It's breezy, smart and openhearted, and everyone who grew up with the band—or wants to know what that was like—will appreciate its insights and feel its emotional impact."
—Anthony DeCurtis, contributing editor, *Rolling Stone*

"Very impressive. *Beatleness* not only describes what it was like to be a hardcore fan from the beginning (like me), but explains it in a historical and personal context. For forty years of The FEST we've been celebrating our love for the Beatles with thousands of fans. Now we have a word for it."
—Mark Lapidos, president, Mark Lapidos Productions and founder, The Fest for Beatles Fans

"A very intelligent and well-researched book on a phenomenon that has reached the half-century mark and is still evolving."
—Dave Schwensen, author of *The Beatles at Shea Stadium* and *The Beatles in Cleveland*

"From ex-employees to ex-lovers, we've seemingly heard from everyone associated with the Beatles. *Beatleness* finally lets us hear from another group: the fans whose lives were forever altered by rock's greatest band.

These are vivid snapshots of people who rode the wave—and suffered through the crash—of Beatlemania as much as anyone who worked for the band."

—David Browne, author of *Fire and Rain: The Beatles, Simon & Garfunkel, James Taylor, CSNY, and the Lost Story of 1970*

"I love this book! The beautifully written *Beatleness* will not only bring to life all the excitement for those that weren't living yet during the Beatle years, it will cause major goosebumps, all over again, to those who were there. It's an incredibly hip and astute account of all the Beatles' major happenings that affected so many people around the world who were riveted to their every move. I can't wait to read it again!"

—Will Lee, Grammy Award–winning bass player and studio musician, *Late Show with David Letterman* and *Fab Faux*

BEATLENESS

BEATLENESS

How the Beatles and Their Fans Remade the World

CANDY LEONARD

With a New Preface by the Author

Arcade Publishing • New York

First Paperback Edition

Arcade Publishing books may be purchased in bulk at special discounts for sales promotion, corporate gifts, fund-raising, or educational purposes. Special editions can also be created to specifications. For details, contact the Special Sales Department, Arcade Publishing, 307 West 36th Street, 11th Floor, New York, NY 10018 or arcade@skyhorsepublishing.com.

Arcade Publishing® is a registered trademark of Skyhorse Publishing, Inc.®, a Delaware corporation.

Visit our website at www.arcadepub.com.
Visit the author's website at www.beatleness.com

10 9 8 7 6 5 4 3 2 1

Library of Congress Cataloging-in-Publication Data

Leonard, Candy.
  Beatleness : how the Beatles and their fans remade the world / Candy Leonard. — First paperback edition.
      pages cm
  Includes bibliographical references and index.
  ISBN 978-1-62872-417-2 (hc : alk. paper); ISBN 978-1-62872-609-1 (pb : alk. paper); ISBN: 978-1-62872-455-4 (ebook)
  1. Beatles—Influence. 2. Popular music—Social aspects—United States—History—20th century. 3. Popular culture—United States—History—20th century. 4. Nineteen sixties—Social aspects—United States. 5. Popular music fans—United States—History—20th century. I. Title.
  ML421.B4L39 2014
  782.42166092'2—dc23
                                        2014009103

Cover design by Brian Peterson
Cover photo © AP Images

Printed in the United States of America

For Adam, Janna, Mason, and Harley,
who inspire me every day.

Beatleness /bē-tl-nəs, bē-tl-nis/

noun

1. the qualities or characteristics of the Beatles and their works; a manifestation of the essential qualities that define "the Beatles"

2. an emotional or spiritual state, condition, or feeling resulting from exposure to or thinking about the Beatles and their works

3. the cultural references and artifacts, tangible and intangible, that evoke the Beatles; artistic or commercial use of words and images associated with or evocative of the Beatles

Contents

Preface to the Paperback Edition

SINCE *BEATLENESS* WAS FIRST PUBLISHED IN 2014—marking the fiftieth anniversary of the band's arrival in America—I've received numerous emails and messages from readers of all ages, confirming that the book appeals to anyone interested in the Beatles, pop music, or mid–twentieth century history. It's deeply gratifying to know that people of all ages are learning from my book, and I'm delighted it is being used in high school and college classrooms.

Readers appreciate what many describe as the book's "fresh approach" to a very familiar story. By looking at the interplay of the Beatles' evolution, fan reactions, and contemporaneous events, *Beatleness* reveals aspects of the Beatles phenomenon that readers "had never thought about before." Lifelong fans familiar with decades of scholarship on the band told me they have a new perspective after reading the book. Younger readers say they now "get what all the fuss was about."

Beatleness shows how the band fueled the generation gap between baby boomers and the World War II generation in the sixties. But today, Beatles music is enjoyed by people of all ages; it's a bridge between boomers and their children and grandchildren. Millennials tell me they understand their parents in a new way after reading the book.

Many young people today are intrigued by the sixties, and it's not only the cool fashions and groovy music. They see it, correctly, as a time of optimism and idealism, when young people thought seriously about the issues of the day and genuinely believed they could make the world a better place. Young readers, some as young as twelve, tell me *Beatleness* feels like time travel back to the sixties. Older readers also tell me the book is "a wonderful journey back to that special time and place." *Beatleness* seems to rekindle the enchantment and the sense of boundless possibility that characterized middle-class boomer childhoods.

Several of the fans I interviewed for the book told me they found the interview "therapeutic." But readers are finding the book itself therapeutic, many saying they felt as if I was writing about them. Fans across the age range, male and female, told me, "You nailed it." They appreciated how it made them examine their own relationship with the Beatles and Beatles music. It triggered thoughts about old friends, old neighborhoods, brothers, sisters, and parents. Readers were able to revisit their youth; they thanked me for allowing them to look back at their young selves through grown-up eyes.

More than an analysis of Beatle fandom, *Beatleness* is a cultural history of growing up in the sixties—it revisits "that special time and place" referred to above. As I discuss, many historic events and developments defined and shaped this generation, but the Beatles were the only unifying focal point across the boomer age range. Their influence worked synergistically with other progressive cultural trends over those years, instilling in this generation a powerful belief in a happy future, filled with boundless possibility.

There are truths underlying boomers' belief that they, uniquely, grew up in an enchanted and optimistic time. The economy was healthy, the middle class was flourishing, higher education was affordable, there was progress on civil rights for African Americans, women, and gays, and efforts were being made to eradicate poverty. We started paying attention to the environment, and we were exploring new, more fulfilling kinds of intimate relationships. Though the Age of Aquarius never quite dawned, the generation that grew up with the Beatles has left its mark.

I look forward to hearing from more readers and meeting more fans at Beatle fan gatherings in the coming years. And if I'm still around in February 2064, at age 107, I'll be celebrating the Beatles centennial.

Preface to the Original Edition

BEATLENESS IS THE STORY OF FIRST-GENERATION American Beatle fans—the millions of children and adolescents who welcomed the Beatles into their lives in February 1964. It's about the young people who were in the right place at the right time at the right age to observe and participate in an unprecedented historical event that lasted for six years and left a permanent mark on them.

Beatlemania happened because a unique set of cultural and historical forces converged in February 1964. Fifty years later, many fans are genuinely puzzled about why the Beatles still mean so much to them. As one female fan (b. '56) explained, "I was seven years old and it had an effect on me I still don't understand." Some wonder about it quite a bit, some are even slightly embarrassed by it. *Beatleness* explains how that unique relationship was able to develop, its impact on fans, and its impact on the world.

First-generation Beatle fans believe they experienced something truly extraordinary. This book shows why that's true and how it happened.

Beatleness doesn't include the perspective of Beatle insiders, friends, or ex-lovers. It doesn't include opinion from the usual "Beatle experts." It does, however, include the perspective of people who possess authentic expertise about the Beatles' impact—the fans. It's not laden with

xvi • BEATLENESS

minutiae about the lives of the Beatles or their inner circle. Instead, it chronicles and captures the experience and the impact of growing up with the Beatles, from February 1964 through May 1970, watching them flower during a period of rapid social change, much of which the band and their fans brought about.

My purpose in writing this book is to fill three gaps in the vast Beatles literature. The fans have always been a main part of the Beatle story, yet the fan experience has not been looked at from a cultural or historical perspective. There are several books about Elvis fans, ranging from lighthearted to snarky to thoughtful cultural analysis. Similarly, the appeal of *Star Trek* has been explored from a variety of perspectives, including that of Trekkies. There are several books about fans of the Grateful Dead, and the fandom surrounding Bruce Springsteen has also been the subject of critical analysis. Surprisingly, there has been no focused effort to understand Beatle fans since the spring of 1964, when Dr. Joyce Brothers, godmother of celebrity shrinks, was asked to explain Beatlemania.

I've read many books about the Beatles over the years—starting at age twelve with the Hunter Davies authorized biography—and at some point I realized that, for the most part, Beatle scholarship is a conversation among male observers. It's ironic that the fan voice *and* the female voice are so underrepresented. It's not quite the same as an all male panel discussing reproductive rights, but it's similarly problematic. I knew that in-depth interviews with fans would enhance our understanding of the entire Beatle phenomenon, and I wanted to add my voice, and theirs, to the conversation.

At the same time, it has become commonplace to say the Beatles "changed everything," but *how* they actually accomplished this remarkable feat has not been closely examined or explained. There's been very little discussion of how the experience and involvement of the fans contributed to that process. By bringing the voices of Beatle fans into the conversation, *Beatleness* reveals how a musical group, a "mere" entertainment phenomenon, came to play such a unique cultural role and did, in fact, "change everything."

This book reflects the thoughts and feelings of fans born between 1945 and 1961—thoughts and feelings shared during hundreds of hours of phone and face-to-face interviews. I also communicated with fans through social media and through an open-ended online questionnaire.

Because the Beatles were so intertwined in the childhoods and adolescence of the men and women I interviewed, they often shared very personal information. Some interviews lasted several hours. Copious notes were studied, and themes emerged. These are not casual reminiscences—these are heartfelt testimonies elicited by a sociologist and professional interviewer—who is, of course, also a fan.

My Beatle Story

I was among the seventy-three million people who watched the *Ed Sullivan Show* on February 9, 1964. I was seven and a half years old. Like so many Americans, I can remember sitting with my family in front of the boxy black and white television set. Our interest and curiosity were aroused by the hype, and we were expecting something new and different—not just another Sunday evening with Ed, the little mouse, and the guy who frantically keeps the plates spinning.

I was young, but I remember the excitement in the days and weeks following that broadcast and the subsequent *Sullivan* broadcasts. Beatlemania seeped into our Queens apartment and my family seemed to welcome it.

A few months later I chose an article about the Beatles for my current events homework and my teacher made me do it over, explaining that the Beatles were "not newsworthy." "Not newsworthy?" Then why were their pictures in every newspaper and magazine that got cleared off the dining room table before dinner? Why were they always mentioned on the evening news? Why were more and more men and boys starting to look like them? I knew the Beatles were newsworthy then and I've known it ever since.

The Beatles didn't contribute to intergenerational conflict in my family like they did in the families of some of the fans I interviewed. For better and for worse, my parents were different from other parents. Though neither had formal education beyond high school, my parents were voracious readers and found outlets for their creativity in a variety of community projects. They were enthusiastic followers of the popular culture of their day, and they were liberal Democrats and civil rights advocates who called themselves "progressive."

I remember being taken to a Ban the Bomb rally when I was four. I remember walking in a huge crowd down a Manhattan street. I remember passing a building emblazoned with a big bunny head, with pointed ears and a bowtie, and I remember overhearing political discussions with neighbors that went on long after my head hit the pillow. My parents were members of SANE, one of the first anti-nuclear organizations. I remember hearing names like Paul Robeson, Lenny Bruce, and Woody Allen. My father was a vegetarian and a food label reader, and we were the only family I knew with whole grain bread and "yoghurt" in the kitchen; no Twinkies or Fruit Loops. I remember a lot of Frank Sinatra, Stan Getz, Steve and Eydie, and some Elvis Presley. We sang along with Mitch.

Current events were discussed and debated over our heads and through the night. My parents modeled a commitment to social justice, political awareness, and critical engagement with the pop culture landscape—a landscape on which, suddenly, the Beatles overshadowed everything else.

I remember the Kennedy assassination and the days of mourning that followed. I remember seeing Lee Harvey Oswald shot dead by Jack Ruby on national television, yet I didn't really understand these events and I certainly didn't understand what they had to do with me. But the Beatles were for me; they were the bolt of electricity that charged my cultural consciousness.

What the press called "Beatlemania" made me realize there was a big world out there and that I was part of it. It made me realize that what we hear on the radio and see on television connects us to strangers.

It made me see that many, many people around the world could share an experience even though they don't know each other.

My parents created an environment where pop culture and politics were front and center, but it became personally meaningful when the Beatles arrived. I was watching and thinking about the hoopla around them while experiencing and thinking about the hoopla they created in my own life.

By age seven, I came to understand that society is made up of individuals, individuals make up society, and that influence flows in both directions. Beatlemania sparked my "sociological imagination"—a concept I would learn about years later as a doctoral student reading C. Wright Mills. I knew for decades that I would someday write about the Beatles and their impact, but I didn't know the project would be set in motion by my first, brief trip to their birthplace.

A Trip to Liverpool

I spent less than two days in Liverpool but managed to see all the important Beatle sites. I felt the grandeur and vitality that centuries of travelers from all over the world must have felt as they entered this port. I walked through the canyon-like cityscape of massive Georgian and Victorian buildings. The ornate detail on the buildings—even where you can barely see it—tells you this was a proud gateway for many important comings and goings—everything from West Indian slaves to Little Richard records.

I sat on a bench on one of the docks and looked out at the Mersey River, a stone's throw from the Royal Liver Building, which I saw for the first time as the backdrop in Beatles trading cards. Forty-five hours after arriving, I took my seat on the train back to London, pulled out a notebook, and started writing about my surprisingly emotional experience. Several months later my essay was published in the *Boston Globe*.

Within days of the *Globe* article, fans from all over New England contacted me. Some wanted to ask me about my trip. Some wanted to tell me how lucky I was to have had this experience. But mostly they just wanted to connect with me. I affirmed something very important for them and they did the same for me.

This was when I learned about Beatlefest, now called The Fest for Beatle Fans, and the existence of the Beatle fan community. Though this might sound strange, it never occurred to me that so many other people had the same deep, powerful feelings of connection to the Beatles that I had. It wasn't something I talked about much because it's difficult to describe and many people don't understand it. It's easier to not talk about it than to try to explain it.

There's a statue on Liverpool's Matthew Street that pays homage to the Beatles, calling them "four lads who shook the world." Much in Liverpool was interesting and moving, but I was especially moved to see this statue because I vividly remember a photo and article about its installation in our local paper. I remember reading the caption and thinking this was something very important—and true—even at age eight. This odd little statue also figured in a dream I had, which further fueled this project.

My Paul Dream

I dreamed I got on a bus in London and saw Paul McCartney sitting there, as if waiting for me to board. He smiled at me in a way that confirmed his identity, and motioned me over to sit with him. I sat down on the empty double seat in front of him, my back to the window and my legs casually extended across both seats. I turned my head to talk with him.

We got into a spirited discussion about the impact of the Beatles, during which I expressed the opinion that much of the social change we saw in the sixties could be attributed to them. Paul was familiar with this perspective but didn't quite accept it. I reminded him of the words on the odd little statue. "Well, four lads who shook *your* world maybe," he responded. I pointed out that neither of these statements could be true without the other being true. Then I woke up.

My dream conversation with Paul reflected my thoughts about Beatle fans—including myself. Yes, neither one of those statements could be true without the other being true because all the "yous," as in "shook your world," comprise tens of millions of people. The world "shook" because the Beatles affected each one of us, individually.

I woke up with the realization that my background in developmental psychology and sociology gave me tools to understand a phenomenon that, since the age of seven, I've been not only observing but actively participating in and wondering about. I saw the "shook *my* world/shook *the* world" dichotomy in different terms: personal/cultural, biography/history, individual/society—and saw the same underlying concept, the same interactive process. All that shaking starts with each individual fan, in his or her room, gazing at an album cover and listening to music. *Beatleness* explains why fans are still so emotionally attached to the Beatles, and shows and tells, in fans' words, how their worlds were shaken and how they and the Beatles, collectively, shook the world.

Frameworks and Metaphors

An early sixties TV commercial for bread told us, "Wonder helps build strong bodies twelve ways," and while the Beatles were helping to build fans' psyches in more ways than we could count, age and gender determined how fans experienced the Beatles.

The three-year-old watching the *Ed Sullivan Show* while bouncing on a rocking horse, with enthusiastic siblings and bemused parents nearby, would have interpreted the experience differently from a teenager already into music, buying records, and beginning their dating years. Fans in the middle of that age range had a different experience as well. Yet, fans across a sixteen-year age range all believe they were at the best age to experience the Beatles in real time. How can this be? This conundrum, answered over the course of this book, is critical for understanding the Beatles' impact, then and now.

I've divided first-generation fans into three general age groups: early childhood (born 1959 to 1961), middle childhood (born 1953 to 1958), and teens (born 1945 to 1952). I do not mean to suggest that all fans of the same age experienced the Beatles in the same way. Children develop at their own pace, and there are many other individual differences. But there is a predictable sequence in how children learn to process the world. I wanted to understand how fans of different ages responded to the Beatles and their music during each Beatle period.

It's been said that Lennon-McCartney lyrics presented more egalitarian gender relationships than other pop songs of the day. But what are the implications of that? Did female fans listen more closely to the lyrics than male fans? Were boys and girls getting something different from the lyrics—or from the whole experience? These questions are explored throughout the book.

Similarly, there is the recurring observation that somehow the Beatles reduced inhibition in female fans, thus all the screaming. Another observation is that the Beatles were sexy but safe fantasy boyfriends because all they wanted to do was hold your hand. I explored these issues with female fans. And male fans of different ages told me about the various ways they identified with the Beatles and how that affected them.

Continuing to view the phenomenon through a child development lens, I reframe the experience of growing up with the Beatles as exposure to an alternative curriculum. This metaphor captures the experience of exposure to new ideas from a single authoritative source over a period of time. It was a "spiraling curriculum" in that fans would go back to earlier material and explore it more deeply when they were older and get something new and different out of it.

For the youngest fans, much in this curriculum was just outside their understanding, even "weird," but the Beatles seduced them out of their comfort zone again and again. Even those who said they were frightened by "Strawberry Fields Forever" were intrigued by it and listened to it repeatedly.

Many fans found the Beatles disturbing at times, but always compelling; many described them as "challenging." The Beatles kept young fans in what Russian psychologist Lev Vygotsky, writing in the nineteen thirties, called the "zone of proximal development," where children are presented with something just beyond their grasp but come to understand it with the help of older peers. Fans experienced the Beatles in that zone—in a frame of mind where learning is optimal, pleasurable, and fun.

Fandom Without Judgment

Several fans told me their friends and spouses don't understand how they can still be so passionate about the Beatles after all this time, or why they spend so much time participating in the Beatle fan community. And non-fans can be judgmental. Before getting into the meat of this book about fans and fandom, I would like to be clear about my perspective on these issues.

Conventional wisdom often assumes that extreme fans and people who participate in fan communities are missing something more meaningful in their lives. In addition, adult fans are often seen as immature, clinging to childhood and childish things.

Research into fans and how they relate to the mass media began with a small group of scholars fleeing Europe in the early days of Nazism. This group, known as the Frankfurt School, was concerned with the media's power to influence how people think and behave. They became critical of mass culture, which they believed contributed to "false consciousness," and saw fans as passive and easily manipulated. Another perception of fans is that they can become violent, especially in crowds. Beatle fans know all too well what a lone, deranged fan is capable of.

A new generation of fan researchers—all of whom actually grew up with mass media and are themselves fans of one kind or another—has rejected these stereotypes. In recent research, fans are mindful and discriminating consumers of "media texts." Fans see details and nuances that are invisible to non-fans, and develop specialized knowledge and expertise. When fans come together to share, discuss, and debate these meanings, face-to-face or through social media, they're engaging in "fandom." When Beatle fans do it, they're Beatleing.

No one would look at a gathering of Shakespeare scholars and call it a fan convention. Yet there is really no difference between Abe Lincoln "buffs" and John Lennon fans who passionately discuss the minutiae of the latest biography. When Beatle fans compare and contrast bootlegs with official recordings, drawing on a wide range of knowledge, it is no different in kind or any less worthwhile than presidential scholars debating drafts of speeches that were never delivered, or when classical music "aficionados" argue over the definitive rendition of a musical score.

I view fandom simply as a hobby or leisure activity—a fun pastime. Looked at in this way, fandom is no more deviant than golf, bridge, gardening, or any other cultural interest or pursuit. Similarly, we can understand fandom as play—which a growing body of research shows is important throughout the lifespan, not only in childhood. Play promotes creativity, sharpens the mind, and reduces stress—and playfulness is associated with happiness. For fans, the Beatles remain an endless wellspring of intellectual and emotional stimulation, still providing the raw material of play.

A Map of the Book

America's over-the-top reaction to the Beatles in 1964 and the complexity of the fan experience can only be understood by first looking at the broader historical context. Chapter one ("Setting the Stage") provides a brief review of the Kennedy era, focusing on the cultural elements that were especially resonant with what the Beatles represented when they arrived, only seventy-nine days after the assassination.

Although there are many ways to define the different Beatle periods, I've divided the Beatle timeline in a way that reflects how American fans experienced the band's evolution as it happened. That timeline begins in chapter two ("Something New: February 9, 1964–July 1964") with the early days of Beatlemania, from the *Sullivan* broadcasts up to the release of *A Hard Day's Night*. Chapter three ("British Boys: August 1964–November 1965") focuses on *A Hard Day's Night*, the Beatles' first and second American tours, and their second film, *Help!* Chapter four ("The Embodiment of Cool: December 1965–January 1967") looks at the period from *Rubber Soul* up to the release of "Penny Lane" b/w "Strawberry Fields Forever" after *Revolver*. Chapter five ("I'd Love to Turn You On: February 1967–December 1967") covers the psychedelic period. Chapter six ("We All Want to Change the World: January 1968–December 1968") begins with the release of "Hey Jude" b/w "Revolution" and ends with the release of *Abbey Road*. Chapter seven ("The Last Leg: January 1969–May 1970"), the final piece of the timeline, looks at the period after *Abbey Road* through the release of the *Let It Be* album and film.

Finally, chapter eight ("Beatleness Abounds") synthesizes the major themes that emerged from the fan narratives and offers a fresh perspective on the entire phenomenon and the Beatles' place in American history.

I hope the story you're about to read will transport you to that brief moment in time when fans watched and listened with delight as the Beatles went through their many phases, and that it enhances your understanding of the Beatles and your own fan experience. Most of all, I hope it inspires you to celebrate the Beatleness around us.

Acknowledgments

I WANT TO THANK EVERYONE who took time out of their busy lives to share their stories and answer my questions. I couldn't have told this amazing story without their enthusiastic support, encouragement, and patience:

Al Sussman, Andre Gardner, Andy Gordon, Archer Dublason, Barbara Joy Mullen, Becky Pazdon, Beth Harrington, Betty Taucher, Brett Milano, Brian Pike, Britt Boughner, Carolyn Paulk, Chachi Loprete, Cheryl Garner, Chris Fitzgerald, Craig G., Dale True, David Fisher, David Gelfand, Dana Teton, Debbie Stern, Debra Hess Norris, Diana Sabella, Diane Casara, Denise Benoit, Donnie Lyons, Eddie Deezen, Emily Prince, Estelle Babey, Frank Secich, Gary Berman, Greg Panfile, Harold Montgomery, Ira Sonin, Jeff Onore, Jerry Gordon, John Berke, John Covello, John Haberstroh, John Van Horn, Joanne LaRiccia, Jude Southerland Kessler, Judith Reed West, Katharine Whittemore, Kathy Buda, Kenneth Langlieb, Kevin Trudell, Lauren Passarelli, Laurie Schloff, Lenny Scolletta, Linda Andriot, Linda Cooper, Linda Robbins, Linda G., Liz Burns, Lori Freckelton, Luna Collins, Mara Witzling, Marcia Merritt Hauenstein, Mary Kinneavy, Michael Versaci, Michelle Kerman, Nancy Kopfhammer, Patti C., Patti Trudell, Paul Comerford, Paul Zullo, Randy Deutch, Renee Gold, Richard Courtney, Richard Riis, Rob White, Robert Leh, Sheryl Garner, Stan Stein, Steve Brodwolf, Steve Davidson, Steve

Johnson, Stew Williams, Susan Banco, Susan Franzosa, Susan Ratisher Ryan, Susannah Blachley, Susie Davidson, Teresa Izzo, Terri Morris, Tim Jackson, Tom Blachley, Tom Frangione, Tricia Unger, and Vicki Williams.

There are two other members of the siblinghood of Beatle fans whom I need to thank: Bill Trudell and Nico Detourn. Both of these wise, trusted advisors, each with unique talents and perspectives, made the book better with each reading and each conversation. Their multifaceted support and assistance brought out the best in me, and they were there for me at those moments when the process brought out the worst. I can't thank them enough.

And finally, I must thank Cal Barksdale and Arcade Publishing for believing in the project and for allowing me to stay true to my vision and voice.

BEATLENESS

CHAPTER ONE

Setting the Stage

A UNIQUE CONFLUENCE OF FORCES was in play at the end of the Kennedy era that maximized the impact the Beatles would have on the United States, making it possible for them to become the unique phenomenon they were. This is not to say it was all luck or timing, but our immediate response to the Beatles and their overall impact, up through today, was enhanced by events and circumstances at the moment of their arrival.

There were about fifty million young people in the Beatles' potential core fan base when they came to America—more potential fans than any previous performers could possibly have had in their lifetimes. And the Beatles were able to reach this biggest-ever audience on a scale no previous performer enjoyed. When Elvis appeared on the *Ed Sullivan Show* in 1956, 65 percent of American households had television; seven years later, when the Beatles appeared in that same time slot, they could be seen in 90 percent of American households.

During that same seven-year time span, the transistor radio had become cheap, ubiquitous, and essential to even the youngest music fans. With the little white earplug, for one ear only, it was the first in a long line of personal music devices that have been necessities for every generation since. Future Beatle fans were the first young people who could go into a drugstore or appliance shop, spend a few judiciously saved allowance dollars, and transform their music into an on-the-go companion.

Not only did the Beatles have more powerful and effective channels to reach their huge audience but the particular consciousness of this audience made them especially receptive to the band and what they seemed to represent.

Throughout the brief Kennedy era, American sensibilities were continually challenged and disrupted by innovation of all kinds. The pace of technological and cultural change had been increasing since the Industrial Revolution, but by the mid-twentieth century, wartime R&D and postwar prosperity led to a quantum leap in the pace of change. Events demanding that we rethink old assumptions, recalibrate the realm of possibility, and consider new ideas were commonplace. Emerging social trends were reflected back to us through popular culture, hastening the pace of change.

In order to understand how the Beatles were both a disruption and a continuation of Kennedy-era trends, we need to take a brief, Beatlecentric and youthcentric look at the cultural landscape on which they landed. How did this dazzling array of newness—and the cultural cognitive dissonance it caused—set the stage for the Beatles arrival?

The New Frontier and the Power of Youth

The election of 1960 gave America its youngest President, a man who embraced change and asked his country to do the same. He took time during his numerous press conferences to explain how this or that policy or scientific achievement would enrich American lives. He was competent, forward-looking, and made us believe everything would be okay.

With Hollywood looks and charm, Kennedy was a sharp contrast to Eisenhower, the bald old man who had occupied the White House for the previous eight years. The twenty-seven-year age gap between them—the largest ever between an incoming and outgoing president—created a new national vibe of youthful optimism and possibility. Though Kennedy, like his predecessor, was a war hero, he was a *new* kind of hero for a *new* decade—inviting us to value the arts, reach for the moon, and embrace the moral imperatives of freedom and justice. The young husband and father, frolicking with his beautiful family, seemed to have a stake in the future that transcended politics.

Kennedy's vision was of a New Frontier, a concept that especially resonated with young people. Foreshadowing the sentiment Bob Dylan would express three years later in "The Times They Are A-Changin'," Kennedy said "our concern must be with the future" because "the world is changing" and "the old ways will not do."[1]

Understanding the broad implications of unprecedented change, Kennedy asked all Americans to be pioneers on this New Frontier, with a special call to the "young in heart, regardless of age." Kennedy talked about the need for courage and strength, especially with regard to the USSR, and reminded us that mankind has "the power to exterminate his species seven times over." First-generation Beatle fans were the first generation to grow up in a world where this was possible, when reality had become this absurd.

In office less than two months, Kennedy went on television to introduce the Peace Corps, a new initiative that would send young Americans abroad not as warriors with guns and bombs but as ambassadors with slide rules and books. This idealistic effort, seeking peace instead of war, recognized and sought to harness the power of youth to promote positive social change on a global scale—the same youth power the Beatles would tap into in a few short years. The ascendancy and energy of youth, embodied in Kennedy himself, was a strong cultural current in the early sixties and would only intensify throughout the decade.

Young people were becoming aware of their growing power, but were not always in perfect sync with their youthful president. In June 1962, Students for a Democratic Society adopted the *Port Huron Statement*, a manifesto offering a vision of a new, participatory democracy and a thoughtful, scathing critique of the military-industrial complex. The youth movement, both on and off campus, embraced many of that document's themes, such as racial equality, reduced militarism, and humanity's "unfulfilled capacities for reason, freedom, and love."[2]

These youth movement concerns would soon be reflected in the lyrics of Lennon-McCartney, whose band, that very same month, had their first recording session in the London studio they would in time make legendary.

Good Rockets, Bad Rockets

On April 12, 1961, Soviet cosmonaut Yuri Gagarin became the first human launched into outer space, rekindling America's fear of losing the space race. In response, Kennedy asked Congress for nine billion dollars to fund the Apollo program, saying, "I believe that this nation should commit itself to achieving the goal, before this decade is out, of landing a man on the Moon and returning him safely to the Earth." Nine months later, John Glenn became the first American to orbit the earth and a hero to many young Americans. The mission was hailed as a great achievement despite the fact that two Soviets had already done this.

Americans of all ages were completely sold on the space program's wow factor; we were proud of it and paid attention to each televised launch. Toys such as Mr. Mercury and Saturn Rocket appeared. The space race seemed to suggest that science would solve all our problems.

But not all rockets were friendly. We were asked to envision a future of peace and prosperity, with technological wonders for all, while living with the real possibility of annihilation at the hands of the Soviet Union. And while the Soviet Union was far away, Cuba was a lot closer to home.

In April 1961, a US paramilitary brigade invaded Cuba's Bay of Pigs, only to be defeated three days later. This misadventure in Cuba was one of many US attempts to overthrow the Castro regime, which, as Americans were constantly reminded, was a Soviet proxy and Communist presence a mere ninety miles from Florida.

Four months later, East Germany began constructing the Berlin Wall with the stated purpose of keeping out Western "fascists," but the real goal was ending defections to the West. This powerful symbol of

East-West tensions heightened the public's anxiety about an eventual confrontation with the Soviets. Americans who were nine or ten at the time still remember hearing news reports of people killed attempting to escape East Germany.

These were the days of "duck and cover"—a ritual performed by schoolchildren all over America. There was something vaguely scary about the drill, but it was also fun in that it broke up the routine of the school day, much like the more mundane fire drills. But fire drills were practice for an emergency kids could understand; lining up in the hallway and crouching under desks were preparation for something much more amorphous and scary. Yellow and black fallout shelter signs suddenly appeared on buildings across America, making that amorphous threat a real part of daily life.

Just as duck and cover was being phased in, an older, more familiar ritual was eliminated when the Supreme Court declared officially sanctioned prayer unconstitutional. The 1962 ruling was widely—and correctly—seen as a step toward a more secularized society, and led some to see greater urgency in a Cold War against "godless communists."

Though children across America would no longer begin their school day by engaging with an invisible authority figure, they would, beginning in February 1964, begin their day huddled in joyful conversation about the Beatles.

October 1962 brought a significant Cold War update: Soviet missiles capable of hitting the US were discovered in Cuba. Normalizing Cold War anxiety, Kennedy said, "American citizens have become adjusted to living daily in the bull's eye of Soviet missiles located inside the USSR," but missiles ninety miles from the US were an "unjustified change in the status quo to which we had to respond."

Along with some saber rattling, Kennedy called upon Khrushchev to "move the world back from the abyss of destruction" and to search for permanent solutions. The situation was soon defused, but the sense of impending annihilation was driven deeper into the American psyche.

American children who would become Beatle fans sixteen months later didn't fully understand the Cold War but lived with a vague sense of potential, ultimate danger. A woman who was ten at the time recalls, "Any time an airplane flew by we thought it might be the Russians or Cubans coming to bomb us. My friends and I played out our fears by joking about airplanes being missiles, but we were scared." Another woman who was nine at the time said, "I remember seeing Khrushchev and Kennedy on TV. I thought they were saying 'the key to Khrushchev' instead of 'Nikita Khrushchev'; I always wanted to know what the key was but never asked."

Origins of a Quagmire

While Cold War anxieties over nuclear annihilation were periodically triggered by dramatic, singular events, an ongoing war of the more conventional kind, but generating far fewer headlines, was steadily escalating below the radar of America's increasingly fragmented attention. Following through on commitments made by his predecessors, Kennedy continued sending advisors to help the South Vietnamese fight the communists to the north. By the summer of 1963, the US had sent fifteen thousand "advisors" in the form of US servicemen, and one hundred had been killed.

American boys suddenly faced the frightening prospect of actually fighting the evil communists they'd been hearing about for years, and were increasingly aware that they had no say at the ballot box. Two years later, that awareness would reach the *Billboard* charts via Barry McGuire's "Eve of Destruction." For the time being, the previous year's chart-topping "Soldier Boy" by the Shirelles continued to provide a romantic and timely cultural script.

The Cold War and the Vietnam "conflict" made the world look chaotic and uncertain, but Kennedy seemed to have it all under control. Children too young to understand but old enough to sense tension could put world affairs out of their minds, with Guerrilla Poncho Gun Sets and Easy Bake Ovens. Grown-ups could keep their anxiety at bay with Valium, "a little yellow pill" two and a half times more potent than the suddenly old-fashioned Librium, introduced only three years earlier. Hooray for science, always offering something new to improve our quality of life.

Freedom and Liberation

Four months into the Kennedy administration, young Freedom Riders went south to challenge segregated travel facilities and met with so much resistance that Attorney General Robert Kennedy had to send four hundred federal marshals to protect them. After much violence and many arrests, travel facilities were desegregated. And while this was more evidence of the arc of the moral universe bending toward justice, it was a new and disorienting change from "the way things had always been," especially in the South.

Protests erupted again in the fall when the University of Mississippi violated a federal court order by refusing to allow James Meredith, a black student, to register for classes. After two people died and dozens were injured, Meredith registered for classes and segregation came to an end at Ole Miss. Another victory in the struggle for civil rights, but more change to absorb. That same week, Bob Dylan appeared at Carnegie Hall, performing "A Hard Rain's A-Gonna Fall" and other songs of "protest" and social justice, in evidence of a new social consciousness bubbling up within popular youth culture.

Emboldened by victories and undeterred by violence, bigotry, or defeat, Martin Luther King Jr. launched a series of protests in Birmingham, Alabama, in the spring of 1963. He was arrested, not for the first time, and spent a week behind bars, writing the now famous "Letter from Birmingham Jail." The protests of Birmingham's black youth were met with police dogs and high-pressure water hoses.

Americans of all ages, the vast majority of them white, watched this violence on television from the comfort of their living rooms, dens, and rumpus rooms. These televised riots were stunning and suggested a tipping point had been reached. President Kennedy was deeply disturbed by what he saw and sped up the drafting of a comprehensive civil rights bill.

Young America was watching the civil rights movement gain momentum and become increasingly violent, trying to make sense of it while listening to The Crystals' "He's a Rebel" and doing "The Loco-motion," many of them unaware that these were black artists they were enjoying. These were Nat King Cole's "Lazy Hazy Crazy Days of Summer." Daily exposure to black artists and the activism of widely popular celebrities such as Harry Belafonte, Sidney Poitier, and Louis Armstrong helped raise the consciousness of white audiences. Enjoying the Marvelettes, Mary Wells, Sam Cooke, and Sammy Davis Jr. in prime time after watching black students get attacked by dogs and water hoses on the evening news only added to young people's uneasiness about the world they were living in.

The civil rights movement gained enormous momentum throughout the spring and summer of 1963. In April, Kennedy again addressed the nation, reaffirming his commitment to civil rights on both moral and legal grounds. He announced that major civil rights legislation would be submitted to Congress that summer. The morning after outlining his plans, Medgar Evers, a US veteran and civil rights activist, was assassinated by a white supremacist.

Things like this aren't supposed to happen in America, and the murder brought new urgency and outrage to the civil rights struggle. In late August, more than two hundred thousand Americans of all races participated in the March on Washington for Jobs and Freedom, where Martin Luther King Jr. delivered his "I Have a Dream" speech from the steps of the Lincoln Memorial. The three television networks sent more than five hundred cameramen and correspondents to cover the march—more crew than covered the Kennedy inaugural.[3]

The struggle for black civil rights was unrelenting—and nationally televised. Those old enough to understand the chaos saw daily reminders of the cruel contradiction between America's enshrined belief in freedom and equality and how those beliefs were put into practice. People of all ages, but especially the young, were becoming increasingly uncomfortable with the hypocrisy they saw around them.

Gender and the Status of Women

The first oral contraceptive was marketed to physicians in 1961; the IUD soon followed. These advances are often cited as kick-starting the "sexual revolution"—something of an overstatement considering that married couples didn't have direct legal access to contraception until 1965. That said, women, married or single, with sympathetic doctors, had access to birth control throughout the Kennedy era.

With motherhood now a conscious choice, women had more control over all aspects of their lives, including the freedom to explore their sexuality and professional aspirations. Women's ability to consider new possibilities for their futures, and the empowerment that went with it, was a genuine threat to the status quo.

A new sexual morality was starting to emerge among young people. According to a Harvard University dean, "the pleasant privilege of allowing girls to visit boys' rooms" has now become "a license to use the college rooms for wild parties or sexual intercourse." The dean went on to say that 90 percent of the students have high moral standards, to which one student responded: "Morality is a relative concept projecting certain mythologies associated with magico-religious beliefs."[4] The times they were a-changin'.

In the 1962 bestseller *Sex and the Single Girl*, author Helen Gurley Brown encouraged women to become financially independent and explore their sexuality, with or without marriage. Brown advised young women in the workplace to use their sexuality for professional advancement.[5] One year later, Betty Friedan's *The Feminine Mystique* added a new dimension to the cultural conversation about the role of women by exposing the unhappiness and lack of fulfillment felt by American housewives, which Friedan called "the problem with no name."[6]

These books by Brown and Friedan, though different in tone, style, and message, are both widely credited with disseminating new ideas and new ways of understanding male-female relationships, thus "raising consciousness" and sparking the women's movement of the 1960s.

For all the forward-thinking ideas found in these bestsellers, older, more conventional ways of understanding male-female relationships remained in evidence on the era's pop charts. Songs like "Johnny Angel" by Shelley Fabares, and "I Will Follow Him" by Little Peggy March modeled passive female protagonists and conflated love and romance with female subservience. Leslie Gore, asserting her right to cry at her party, was relatively bold.

Friedan's prominence led to her participation in Kennedy's Presidential Commission on the Status of Women. Established in 1961 as a campaign debt to Eleanor Roosevelt, the commission's October 1963 report documented widespread discrimination against women in the workplace. The very creation of the PCSW announced to the country that women's traditional role was changing and that women's status and rights were a serious, national concern.

The modern women's movement began demanding change—in bedrooms, kitchens, workplaces, and the halls of Congress. It was called "Women's Lib" because it was about liberation and freedom from social rules and norms that were not only unfair, but had also lost whatever rationale they might have had in the distant past.

With the gender genie out of the bottle, traditional conceptions of masculinity would be challenged next. An invasion of longhaired boys, in heeled boots and collarless jackets, would provide a backbeat to that challenge. But it wasn't through their appearance alone that the Beatles offered an alternative proposition about gender. Their music, words, and attitude amplified and added nuance to changes already emergent in America when they touched down in 1964.

Cold War Pop Culture

Kennedy-era popular culture reflected the contradictions and anxieties of the day. Novels like *Advise and Consent, Seven Days in May*, and *Fail-Safe* focused on Communism and Cold War concerns. *Catch-22* captured the absurdity of war and coined a phrase to describe a no-win situation. *To Kill A Mockingbird* and the nonfiction *Black Like*

Me explored racism in the segregated South and resonated with the ongoing racial tensions Americans saw on the nightly news. All these books were later adapted for film and reached an even wider audience.

Americans became aware of a serious threat other than Communism with the 1962 publication of Rachel Carson's *Silent Spring*. The bestseller provoked widespread concern about the environmental impact of pesticides on animals, birds, and humans, raising questions about the side effects of science. Maybe there was a downside to all this progress.

Other books asked readers to question taken-for-granted assumptions about the way society and its institutions are organized. Ken Kesey's *One Flew Over the Cuckoo's Nest* explored the very definition of sanity and the controlling power of institutions, and Robert Heinlein's utopian critique of American society, *Stranger in a Strange Land,* added "grok" to the vocabulary of the young people who read it. J. D. Salinger's *Franny and Zooey* were two privileged, quirky young people who disdained phoniness and grappled with the meaning of life. Though not necessarily new, these themes had never before been disseminated on such a mass scale to such an impressionable audience.

Henry Miller's sexually explicit *Tropic of Cancer,* written in 1934 but published for the first time in the US in 1961, was the subject of an obscenity trial, but paved the way for the taboo-busting steaminess of Harold Robbins's *The Carpetbaggers* two years later. Other sexually explicit books would follow. Mary McCarthy's bestseller, *The Group,* chronicles intimate details in the lives of six women friends and includes frank discussions of sexual relationships, workplace discrimination, child rearing, homosexuality, and extramarital affairs.

Movies were also getting more boldly sexually explicit, with Vladimir Nabokov's mid-fifties novel, *Lolita,* almost as controversial on film in 1962 as when first published. Featuring Beatles fave and former Goon Peter Sellers, the dark comedy deals with a middle-aged man's obsession with a teenage girl. Another fifties novel, Ian Fleming's *Dr. No,* was initially deemed by Hollywood not only "too sexual" but also "too British" to merit film adaptation. However, more pecuniary minds prevailed and its 1962 release was followed a year later by

From Russia with Love. Both films injected the Cold War into popular entertainment and whetted America's appetite for the "with it" and "now." So much for "too British."

Like the Bond films, *The Manchurian Candidate*, released in 1962 and starring former teen idol Frank Sinatra, appealed directly to Cold War paranoia. Less noted in the US than the Bond films was *The Mouse on the Moon*, a 1963 British Cold War spoof that paired director Richard Lester with producer Walter Shenson, who the following year would together oversee the Beatles' cinematic debut.

Early sixties America had only three television networks, all piping similar fare directly into the nation's living rooms. Westerns helped viewers escape to the "old" frontier, trading modern anxieties in the face of accelerating change for a mythologized world where all decisions were black and white, gender roles were clear, and the good guys always won. Shows like *The Outer Limits* and *Twilight Zone* took us to other frontiers as well, the latter in a more sophisticated, cerebral way, often with stories involving futuristic technology, robots, or extraterrestrials, that spoke to our often uneasy relationship with the technological present.

Sitcoms often focused on children and teens learning valuable life lessons as they extricated themselves from predictable scenarios of mistaken identity, communication breakdowns, embarrassment, and bad timing. These TV kids—Timmy, Opie, Patty, Cathy, Dobie, Maynard, Zelda, Jethro, Ellie May—spanned the same age range as their baby boomer audience and offered younger viewers, still in single digits, a glimpse into the lives of older kids and teenagers.

These family-oriented sitcoms often ended with a "lesson" of some kind, but they also revealed to kids a secret about parent-child relationships they may not have known before: parents, it seems, are not always sure how to manage their kids' behavior. TV parents strategized behind closed doors before falling asleep in their twin beds.[7] The first TV generation saw adult fallibility previous generations had not, empowering them and giving further license to question adult authority, priming them for the Beatles arrival and all that would follow in their wake.

But young people also got inspiration from two other subversive forces, one covert, one overt.

Kennedy-era children spent a lot of time with Theodor Geisel, under his pen name, Dr. Seuss, whose stories and illustrations in books like *The Cat in the Hat* were more compelling than those in the Dick and Jane books and other early readers. Geisel's political views, which he himself described as "subversive as hell," were expressed in the silly, dynamic verse of these now–classic children's books, which reflected more democratic, New Frontier parenting styles and gently mocked adult authority.[8]

While little kids read Dr. Seuss, older kids were consuming the much more subversive *Mad* magazine, whose editorial mission statement was "Everyone is lying to you, including magazines. Think for yourself. Question authority."[9] *Mad* cartoonist Art Spiegelman claimed, "*Mad* was more important than pot and LSD in shaping the generation that protested the Vietnam War."[10] *Mad* often turned familiar aspects of children's culture into sharp, rude, commentary about adults and authority figures. The magazine had a forbidden quality to it—yet it was not forbidden, and it helped prepare young Americans for Beatle "cheekiness."

Kids of all ages, and their parents, watched *The Rocky & Bullwinkle Show*, an animated Cold War–themed satire in which the moose Bullwinkle and flying squirrel Rocky tangled with the Russian-like spies Boris Badenov and Natasha Fatale. Two other animated prime time shows, *The Flintstones* and *The Jetsons*, offered soft commentary on consumer culture and family life, the former in the "stone age," the latter in "the future."

Countless variety shows offered Americans stand-up comedy, from the best and worst of the borscht belt to the cerebral and edgy, including Mort Sahl, Jonathan Winters, Woody Allen, and Lenny Bruce. *Time* dubbed this group, especially Bruce and Sahl, "sick comedians" for taking on gritty, taboo topics.[11] Phyllis Diller and Joan Rivers were also charting new territory by bringing a female perspective on gender politics into stand-up comedy.

Kennedy-era entertainment in general was quickly becoming more satirical, referential, and thoughtful. Increasingly, within this brief period of time, entertainment not only reflected the issues of the day but also commented on them, thereby reflecting and abetting the equally if not more important *attitude* of the day. That new attitude had not yet reached popular music, but young music fans were ready for something new.

Pop Without the Pop

The pop music of the early sixties has a reputation for bland vapidity that is not entirely undeserved. But what it may have lacked in artistic quality, it made up for in ubiquity. Transistor radios allowed music fans to bring their music anywhere and everywhere, while television brought the dance party into the living room.

Young music fans could find the latest records and dance moves on Dick Clark's *American Bandstand*. Like *Mad, Bandstand* brought young people into a cool space where adults were increasingly irrelevant—which is not to say adults were invisible. Along with children and teens, adults were unable to resist "The Twist" after Chubby Checker sang the catchy song and demonstrated the anyone–can–do–it dance on Clark's highly rated, influential show. Thanks to Chubby, kids who would soon be the youngest Beatle fans were already excited about pop music.

ABC's *Hootenanny* was a family variety show that specifically targeted the "youth market" with a somewhat sanitized version of the folk music suddenly popular with older teens and students who rejected the vapid pop of the day. Ironically, before the show's debut, its producers blacklisted left-wing folk singer Pete Seeger, the man largely responsible for the folk revival that made *Hootenanny* possible. As a result, several important folk acts boycotted the show, including Bob Dylan and Joan Baez.

But there were other opportunities for Americans to see the suddenly hot Mr. Dylan on television. In March 1963, one month before *Hootenanny* went on the air, he sang to the nation's conscience, performing "The Ballad of Hollis Brown" and "Blowin' in the Wind" on a Westinghouse

Special. Dylan was scheduled for *Ed Sullivan* later that spring, but chose to walk rather than comply when CBS, looking out for its sponsors, requested he not sing the controversial "Talkin' John Birch Paranoid Blues."

Censorship in the name of quelling dissent was too little too late. By the time Peter, Paul and Mary joined Dylan, Mahalia Jackson, and Joan Baez at the Lincoln Memorial, along with Martin Luther King Jr. and 250,000 other Americans, their cover of Dylan's "Blowin' in the Wind" was number two on the *Billboard* charts—and the fastest selling single Warner Brothers had ever released. Its compelling message, delivered in sweet, three-part harmony, spoke to a generation's realization that something had to change. Folk music was rapidly going pop.

Under the validating influence of Dylan, Baez, and other folk artists, older teens and students were sensitized to the issues of the day and were increasingly critical of the "establishment." The status quo was being questioned at every turn, and Cold War anxieties fueled young people's sense that something was fundamentally wrong with the world they were destined to inherit.

With most households having only one TV, programming was designed to appeal to all ages, but it was especially important to grab the kids. An increasingly sophisticated advertising industry gleefully figured out how to turn even the youngest viewers into eager consumers. As a Chicago advertising executive told *Time* in October 1963, "Once children become impressed they are very successful naggers."[12] Perhaps 1962, when 90 percent of American households had television, was the moment we transitioned from citizens to consumers.

Despite resistance from sponsors and networks, agents of change, such as folk singers, "sick" comics and political satirists, were moving from late night to prime time, from coffee houses to the top of the charts, and getting more access to the national megaphone—a megaphone that had never been larger or as technologically capable—and were speaking to a young audience that had never been as big, with as much disposable income, and with as much potential social leverage.

Young people's eyes had been opened to adult fallibility, hypocrisy, and phoniness, and the call to question authority was coming in loud and clear from many sources. Entertainment that didn't reflect the changing times, or have that knowing sensibility, would seem not "with it." Although the stage had been set, no single force embodied this new sensibility and spoke for the Seuss readers and the *Mad* readers; for the Colorforms crowd and the "co-eds."

All the novelty and transformation of the Kennedy era—the struggle for civil rights, the changing role of women, fear of nuclear annihilation, fear of environmental poison, enthusiasm for space exploration, growing involvement in Vietnam, youth empowerment, the rapid modernization of the media—happened in *less than three years*.

Yet despite the pace and magnitude of these disruptive changes, Americans of all ages were optimistic about the future. The economy was expanding. *Newer, bigger, faster, improved*—became values. We had science and gadgets and a New Frontier. We had rockets and wrinkle-free fabrics, crescent rolls, and snap-open beer cans. We had Dictaphone machines, Polaroid cameras, and electric toothbrushes. We had color TV. And we had Kennedy. Until we didn't.

And That's the Way It Is

On Monday, November 18, NBC's *Huntley-Brinkley Report* ran a four-minute story on the Beatles, an oddly curious rock and roll band, little known in the US but creating quite a stir in their native England. On Friday morning, November 22, the *CBS Morning News with Mike Wallace* also did a piece on the Beatles and planned to air the feel-good segment again that night on the *CBS Evening News with Walter Cronkite*.

In the UK, whose clocks run five hours ahead of New York, *With the Beatles*, the band's second British LP, was being eagerly snapped up by fans who just had to own it on this first day of its release.

Around that same time, President Kennedy and his wife were traveling from Fort Worth to Dallas, where he was scheduled to give speeches and do the kind of things presidents do on trips like this, heading into an election year.

The cool constant amid all this change, the man with the plan, was violently removed. Americans of all ages were shocked and numbed. We liked Kennedy and trusted his steady hand and quick mind. We wanted him at the helm as we sped into a scary but promising future.

Young Kennedy supporters were heartbroken to see LBJ stand in his place—he was old and unattractive, and he wasn't cool. Though only nine years apart in age, LBJ seemed like someone from yesterday; not like someone from today, for tomorrow. A female Beatle fan, age seven at the time, recalls: "A familiar voice on the PA system told us we were being dismissed early but didn't say why. I had Brownie meetings on Friday afternoons, and I remember being in the meeting room with a few of my friends after we'd been told what happened. There was contemplative stillness. Everyone was glued to the TV all weekend and we saw Oswald get shot."

This was the first generation to see a live murder on television. It was a dramatic, foreboding moment that, along with the event of the previous day, made all Americans, especially young people, realize that the world was more harsh than we thought it was, only days before.

For many grown-ups, it strained credulity, from the get-go, that Oswald acted alone. A future male Beatle fan, age ten at the time, recalls, "I was forced to watch the funeral when all I wanted to do was go play basketball. After Oswald was shot, my dad commented, 'There's more going on here than we know.'" A boy of fourteen at the time had a very different reaction: "The teacher turned on the TV. School was dismissed early, but I stayed in my seat watching the coverage long after the other kids left. I missed my bus and walked the two miles home that day. I felt disconnected somehow. There was nothing in my life I could relate such a monumental event to. I had no context for it. I just knew the world was radically different."

Between Two Eras

Between the Kennedy era, which ended in November 1963, and the Beatles' arrival in February 1964, is a seventy-nine day corridor; a connector period linking "the Kennedy sixties" with "the Beatles sixties."

Of course the close proximity of these two events is historical accident, but hindsight suggests they are somehow connected and may be yet another way the moment favored the Beatles.

Many writers have put forward what I call the "Kennedy Rebound Theory of Beatlemania," suggesting that the Beatles, with their youthful, positive energy, were a fun diversion that helped us recover from the assassination, thus explaining the public's and the media's early infatuation with the "moptops from Liverpool." But this doesn't account for the shift in consciousness that occurred in those brief thousand days before the assassination. The events of the Kennedy sixties gave birth to a new sensibility, a new consciousness, at odds with the conformity and stifling constraint of the era. The assassination added to the already heightened sense of dissonance in the culture.

The brief moment between the Kennedy sixties and the Beatles sixties was thus an uneasy mix of dulled optimism and fear; a void between "before" and "after."

That Was the Month That Was

In its January 3, 1964 issue, *Time* named Martin Luther King Jr. "Man of the Year" for 1963, the first black person to receive this honor. Though King had mixed feelings about the cover story, he recognized its significance and thought it symbolized an important turning point in the movement. "The fact that *Time* took such cognizance of the social revolution in which we are engaged is an indication that the conscience of America has been reached and that the old order which has embraced bigotry and discrimination must now yield to what we know to be right and just."[13]

Later that month, NBC launched *That Was the Week That Was*, a weekly half-hour, not of "variety" but of pointed political satire. The controversial show accelerated the rapid rise of irreverent comedy and commentary, with regulars such as Alan Alda, Gloria Steinem, Tom Lehrer and Calvin Trillin. Also in January, talk show host Jack Paar aired a clip of the Beatles performing "She Loves You" and told viewers the British group would be on the *Ed Sullivan Show* the following month. By that time, many American kids had heard the Beatles or were at least aware of them.

The following week, LBJ declared "unconditional war on poverty in America" and the government, through the surgeon general, reported for the first time that smoking may be hazardous to health. Meanwhile, cigarette commercials featuring the rugged Marlboro Man cowboy fit seamlessly among the glut of prime-time Westerns.

On January 10, Vee-Jay Records released *Introducing . . . the Beatles*; ten days later, Capitol released *Meet the Beatles*. Music followers were starting to get acquainted with these four young men and their unusual image. Their long hair and highly styled suits—courtesy of Hamburg friend Astrid Kirchherr and closeted gay manager Brian Epstein— made for a strange yet compelling, androgynous look, though few people even knew that word at the time. Instead, the common reaction was "They look like girls."

Many fans first saw the Beatles in three black-and-white Dezo Hoffman photos.[14] No angular, pointy lapels here, but suits with round collars, making them seem softer somehow; sweet and approachable. They were mysterious but not at all frightening, and seemed to be looking right at us in every photo, inviting us in. By late January, the Beatles had entered young people's consciousness, but had not yet become a consuming passion.

Sandwiched between the two Beatle releases was Bob Dylan's third studio album, *The Times They Are A-Changin'*. Featuring all original compositions and focusing on issues of war, poverty, racism, and social change, the album entered the US charts at number twenty, completing Dylan's rapid transformation from folk singer to protest singer to "voice of a generation." In the now anthemic title track, Dylan warned the older generation that it had no choice but to accept the inevitability of change.

Dylan was singing about all-encompassing change; change that required an openness to change itself. Like King's letter quoted above, "The Times They Are A-Changin'" calls for the old order to "yield to what we know to be right and just." Dylan snarls earnestly as he tells parents their sons and daughters are beyond their command—thus crossing the *t*'s and dotting the *i*'s on the cultural power shift toward youth.

The question on many young people's minds, "How many times can a man turn his head and pretend that he just doesn't see" pointed a finger at the establishment's denial of the contradictions that were getting harder to ignore. At this moment, with the nation teetering on the cusp of change, the Beatles appear.

Meet the Beatles

Moments after stepping off the plane the Beatles were ushered into a room with over two hundred reporters present, many of whom had a bemused "what's all the fuss about" attitude. They had heard about Beatlemania in the UK, but they didn't think it would happen in the US. They soon saw what all the fuss was about as the Beatles effortlessly kibitzed for fifteen minutes, their sassy scouse humor winning the hearts and minds of a predominantly Jewish and Irish New York press corps. The word "cheeky" entered the American vocabulary.

The group's "performance" at the airport that Friday afternoon was probably more important to their success in America than their performance on Sunday night. But as America would soon discover, it was no performance. This is who they were. Beatle intelligence, humor, charisma, and confidence—their Beatleness—instantly set them apart, regardless of what one thought of the music. There would be no more comparisons with Elvis.

A three-way relationship quickly developed between the fans, the Beatles, and the media. Writing about them was not only fun for journalists, but it sold newspapers. Had they been jet-lagged, tired, or sarcastic to the point of seeming hostile, the vibe in the room might have been different and the instant rapport might not have happened. The press might have been less effusive, or even negative. As it happened, the press, for the most part, decided to love them.

The significance of this first US press conference cannot be over-stated. Today, exceeding expectations to create delight is recognized by business gurus as a key factor in successful product launches and customer relations—but all that came naturally to the Beatles.

The early press coverage gushed with enthusiasm—further fueling the Beatlemania they were writing about. The Beatles were interesting and amusing, and journalists loved writing about them. And though they were not yet taken seriously, their confident seduction of the press gave them authority.

The Beatles' irreverent attitude and loud but unspoken endorsement of freedom spoke to the cultural and political tumult gaining momentum in the US. And while much of that tumult was beyond the understand-ing of young fans, they'd been listening to "I Want To Hold Your Hand" and studying album covers for over a month, and that they understood very well:

It was January 1964. I was thirteen. I was getting a ride home from school on a chilly Midwestern night sitting in the backseat of my friend's brother's Mercury when I heard the fade out verse to "I Want To Hold Your Hand." I had never bought a single or an album in my life, but when I got home five minutes later, I was possessed. . . . I immediately began pestering my mother to take me to a local discount store where I snapped up *Introducing the Beatles* and *Meet the Beatles*. I took them home and played them endlessly, fascinated by the music, the melody, the energy, the voices, the whole gestalt. I stared at the album sleeves. I had never seen people like this. Male, b. '49

CHAPTER TWO

Something New

February 9, 1964–July 1964

I remember reading an article in the newspaper that said "Beatles to Invade America," and since I didn't know who the Beatles were it kind of scared me. I guess I was thinking they were some kind of terrorists or something. When I found out they were a music group I was very relieved; when I heard them, it changed my life forever.

Male, b. '53

WHEN I ASK FIRST-GENERATION FANS about their first awareness of the Beatles, the response is usually a detailed account of how the Beatles entered his or her life and how he or she became a fan. For kids who were already listening to the radio and buying records, the story begins in the weeks leading up to the *Sullivan* broadcast. "I Want To Hold Your Hand" was released the day after Christmas—too late for gift-giving but perfect timing for school vacation. A typical response was: "I first heard them in late December at an ice skating rink. There was a jukebox and they were playing 'I Want To Hold Your Hand' over and over. I knew what they looked like from newspapers and magazines" (Male b. '51). Another: "My neighbor bought the 45 and we studied the cover, trying to figure out who was who. We had never seen anything like it. I bought two of them and wrote the names on one cover. We wanted to learn everything about them" (Male, b. '51).

The song entered the *Billboard* Hot 100 chart in January at number forty-five and was number one by the first of February.[1] Younger kids also knew the song and were aware of the Beatles, thanks to a friend's older siblings, an older kid next door, a babysitter, or car rides with parents:

I was sitting on the floor with my friends playing with toy soldiers. My friends' older sisters, they were thirteen or fourteen, were listening to records in the next room and they put on "I Want To Hold Your Hand." I ran into the room to ask what it was. I saw the cover and immediately became a fan. I started hanging out with the older girls and listening to the records. Male, b. '54

My next-door neighbor was about five years older than me. He invited me over when I was nine years old to listen to a new 45 he had: "I Want To Hold Your Hand." We played it over and over and over again, watching that orange and yellow label spin while that sound grabbed us. Male, b. '55

We had a babysitter who kept us dancing around like little monkeys so we would be ready to sleep at naptime. That was where I was first exposed to the Beatles. By the time the Beatles were on *Ed Sullivan*, I knew a few of their hits from listening to our babysitter's records. Male, b. '59

I was in the car with my Dad when the guy on the radio said the Beatles were coming to the US. "Who are the Beatles?" I asked. Dad says, "Watch *Ed Sullivan* this Sunday." Boy, was I glad I did! Male, b. '55

Sunday Night

Watching *Ed Sullivan* was a Sunday night ritual in American households—it's what you did on Sunday night and there usually wasn't much excitement around it. But tonight's show was eagerly anticipated by at least one family member, perhaps two or three depending on how many kids were in the family and how old they were. And it wasn't just the kids:

> We were waiting for it. It was a big night in front of the TV. Mom bought either the single or *Meet the Beatles*. She said they were like four Elvis Preselys, but I wasn't sure what she meant. Female, b. '57

> My dad told my sister and I we needed to watch the *Ed Sullivan Show* on Sunday. He said all week people had talked about a new singing group that was to appear on the show. Female b. '54

> Mom heard them in the car on her way to work, asked if I had heard of them, and said they'd be on *Ed Sullivan*. I watched it with my Mom and couldn't believe my eyes. I had never seen anything like it before. Mom was singing along—she knew the lyrics from listening in the car! Male, b. '50

> I liked the Beatles, but my sister, two years older, seemed truly infected. It was she that gathered the family around the TV for the *Ed Sullivan Show*. Female, b. '55

Several fans remembered having to make special arrangements to watch because of a regular Sunday commitment to church youth group. Said one: "I was president of the Young People's Fellowship at church and we met on Sunday nights. We asked the minister if we could watch it in the rectory; he had a thirteen-year-old daughter who wanted to watch it, too" (Female, b. '46).

Some fans old enough to stay up late saw the "She Loves You" clip on the *Jack Paar Show* a month before, and some may have seen them briefly on the news back in November, but this would be the first time most young people and their parents would see the Beatles perform.

Ed Sullivan promised viewers they would "twice be entertained" by the Beatles during the hour broadcast.

Sullivan, a stiff cardboard cutout of a man with a face that said, "School tomorrow!" introduced them, and the camera cut to the audience—mostly girls and young women in jumpers and Peter Pan collars applauding and screaming with delight—modeling the behavior and pandemonium fans would see at live Beatle shows in the coming years. Next, a bird's-eye view of the simple yet dynamic set—a circle of arrows converging on the Beatles.

Of course viewers' attention would have been drawn to them regardless of the set design, but the arrows made it more emphatic, commanding the viewer, "Look at this!" There's prescient symbolism in this circle of arrows, playfully directing and maintaining the viewer's focus on them. The Beatles' groupness is intriguing and invites fans to enter; Paul's left-handed guitar created an opening. This was fans' first look at an image that would remain forever familiar and evocative at its core, even as it changed.

The camera slowly zooms in and America gets its first close look at the four of them, live on stage. They are beaming with the thrill of being there and looked like no human beings we had seen before. Their long hair was charming and also disturbing, in the best sense. of the word. Zooming in on the details of their hair and suits made their groupness even more apparent, but also allowed the viewer to see them as individuals. Their obvious affection for each other was clearly on display for the world to see, a new twist on male camaraderie.

A close-up of Ringo, a middle shot of Ringo, George, and Paul, and then a tight close-up of doe-eyed Paul singing the second verse of the set opener, "All My Loving." There are moments, such as when he sings "the lips I am missing," and "while I'm away" when Paul's face is almost contorted with delight and performance energy. [2] The camera zooms out, tightly framing George and John singing background vocals. George takes a furtive glance directly into the camera, and John breaks into a slight smirk.

There is a lot going on here. There's a lot to look at and it's hard to take it all in. George does his little two-step during the guitar break and then joins Paul at his mic to harmonize on the chorus. As the song winds down, George and John are again cheek-to-cheek at the mic, glancing at the audience. The song ends and the camera cuts to the audience—the effusive girls and bemused boys are an integral part of the show, and they know it. The next number, "Till There Was You," from the Broadway show *The Music Man*, counters the impression—created by the hype and hoopla—that the Beatles are just a kids' act.

More tight close-ups of Paul, in a vamp that goes from doe-eyed to coquettish and back again. A quick cut to two teen girls in the audience, licking their lips. Cut to Ringo scanning the audience, and the song closes with a medium group shot. Then a sudden thunder-roll into "She Loves You," with George and Paul sharing a mic, their heads just inches apart.

John and Paul both sing lead on "She Loves You" but the camera seems to focus on Paul, with George nearby. For the first time, viewers see the hair shake and "woo" that looked, sounded, and felt like Beatleness. Finally, the camera finds John, wide stance at the mic, alone, and seeming to dominate. He glances affectionately at the other two up front. The repeating chorus closes out the song, with sustained emphasis on the word "glad."

Viewers barely had a chance to process what they just saw when they're hit by Madison Avenue at its best—an assaultive Anacin ad, incessantly chanting "pain, headache pain, pain, depression, pain, tension, pain, anxiety, pain, fatigue, pain, pain." The emotional juxtaposition to the Beatles' performance was striking.

The second set opens with "I Saw Her Standing There," more large doses of The Cute One and glimpses of the elated audience. The arrows were gone, replaced by a new set that also conveys perspective and commands the eye toward them. Viewers notice the choreography created by the natural coordination of their idiosyncratic body movements. George's guitar break triggers an eruption of rock and roll joy never before seen on American television. Viewers could feel the fun:

It was just amazing to see them after hearing the record. I was knocked out. They were so different from Elvis and Bobby Rydell, and the others. It was their energy—they looked like they were having fun, and you wanted to have fun, too. I loved the suits and the hair. Male, b. '50

There was something about them that caught my imagination. They were fun, interesting, exciting. I was reacting to their image, the music, the whole thing. Male, b. '56

I was in grade school; not a teenager—so it wasn't about them being hot, it was about the fun; the overriding sense that they were having fun. And the freedom they expressed was palpable. Female, b. '55

For their final number, they performed "I Want To Hold Your Hand." John stands slightly in front and apart from the other two. He seems edgy and impatient. Despite what the lyrics say, it's hard to believe that John would be content to merely hold your hand. Paul, maybe; John, no way. George, floating between the two, was quickly labeled "mysterious" because fans saw only flickers of his personality. They didn't get to know George or Ringo as well because neither sang lead and they appeared in fewer close-ups than John and Paul.

Sandwiched between the two Beatles sets were hackneyed magical acts, rat pack impersonations, acrobats, vaudeville retreads, and Broadway medleys. Nothing the audience hadn't seen before and nothing particularly memorable. The commercials satisfied adults' desire for anything "new and improved" and the Beatles satisfied young record buyers' desire for new and improved—and different. A male fan (b. '52) recalled: "'I Want To Hold Your Hand' was so bouncy and cheerful. Not like the other acts on *Ed Sullivan*. They were very different." Another male fan, four years younger, recalled: "Everything about them was appealing, nonthreatening, and humble; the bow, the accents, everything."

For girls just starting to be interested in boys, holding hands with a boy was, as one fan put it, "a big deal." It was the very first step in a longer sequence of romantic involvement they could only vaguely imagine. The Beatles' insistent request was especially compelling to young teenage girls because they got the sense that the Beatles would hold your hand *in public*.

Young viewers loved the music and the fun, but the hair got most of the attention. Parents found their hair amusing, not realizing that, overnight, boys' hair would become a battleground in many American households. A male fan (b. '52) remembered: "My mother and grandmother were laughing hysterically. I went to investigate. They insisted I sit down and watch these four 'long-haired' guys sing. My grandmother was laughing so hard, she couldn't speak."

Monday Morning

Though the word "Beatlemania" may seem trite so many decades after the fact, the significance of the phenomenon it describes becomes clear if we think of it as the moment tens of millions of children and adolescents began a six-year odyssey toward their adulthoods, with the Beatles at their side, or, more accurately, in their ears, eyes, brains, minds, and spirit. It was the beginning of the lifelong connection fans still feel with the Beatles and with other fans. It was a "big bang" moment in which Beatle fans were born; the moment "Beatle fan" became a key ingredient of their unformed and malleable identities.

Fans still have vivid flashbulb memories of how they felt watching the Beatles on the *Ed Sullivan Show*, and the excitement in the days, weeks, and months that followed:

> I remember a weird feeling of excitement, like something totally new was happening; something wonderful. To this day when I see clips I get the same inexplicable feeling. The music, their appearance, the girls screaming. They looked like they were having a great time. Male, b. '55

The whole atmosphere, on the show and in our den, was unforgettable. They were so engaging and obviously having the time of their lives! How could you not love them? Female, b. '55

I was in the bathtub. In those days kids had baths once a week and ours was on Sunday night, to be followed by *Disney* if we didn't dawdle. My sister came rushing in and told me to hurry because the Beatles were going to be on *Ed Sullivan*. I watched them with wet hair, and had never seen anything like it before. Female b. '55

It's been said that American Beatlemania began at JFK airport on Friday, February 7, 1964. Radio stations like New York's "W-A-Beatles-C" tracking their flight and the presence of thousands of fans at the airport was certainly significant. But Beatlemania began in earnest on school busses, playgrounds, and lunch lines the day after the first *Sullivan* broadcast. A male fan (b. '50) recalls that Monday morning: "Everyone had the 45 with the picture cover on top of their pile of books, to prove you were a Beatle fan. It was considered cool. Mom picked me up from school that day and we went and got the 45." Another male fan, also fourteen at the time, remembered it this way: "Everyone was talking about it at school the next day, and the girls were swooning. I bought all the 45s I could right away."

Beatlemania was the social contagion resulting from millions of kids sharing their Beatle enthusiasm with their friends and siblings after seeing the group on television. Kids who missed the first broadcast suddenly felt shut out of the conversation. There was some amount of passive peer pressure to become a Beatle fan, or at least have an informed opinion—whether you were six or sixteen. Fifty years later, those who missed it remember it as an event they missed:

The next day everyone was talking about them at the bus stop, especially the girls. I didn't know what they were talking about. It's all anyone talked about. I thought maybe it was a comedy act. I made a point of watching it the next week. My family watched it together. Male, b. '55

I heard about the Beatles after they appeared on *Ed Sullivan*. My aunt told my mom they were good but had long hair like girls. It wasn't until a couple of weeks later that I heard "I Want To Hold Your Hand" on the school bus. The bus driver turned the song up loud and all the students clapped to the music. I remember instantly loving the song. It's hard to explain how the song affected me. I still didn't know what the Beatles looked like but that song was incredible! I remember soon seeing pictures and Beatle related items everywhere. Male, b. '54

Some kids were forbidden from seeing it altogether: "Dad was against rock and roll so I didn't see any of the *Sullivan* broadcasts. I felt very left out at school, and it became forbidden fruit" (Male, b. '53). This young fan, not yet four years old, was also affected: "My grandmother always told the story of having to put her hand over my mouth when I stood up in church and started singing 'She Loves You'" (Male, b. '61).

Young people became instant fans. The press, though wowed by the Beatles at the airport two days earlier, was less than complimentary. *New York Times* critic Jack Gould dismissed them as a fad, and described televised Beatlemania as a "mass placebo."[3] It seems Mr. Gould was underestimating the power of the placebo effect. What Gould read as the band's "bemused awareness," fans read as "cool": wit, charm, intelligence, and now-ness. The *Herald Tribune* likened them to a circus act, and *Newsweek* used the words "nightmare," "disaster," "merciless," "preposterous," and "catastrophe" in one short paragraph.[4]

These snarky, self-important critics didn't understand what they saw and were incapable of seeing or feeling it from a young person's perspective. Their kids—and wives—were probably smitten too. The press loved speculating on how long the Beatles would last and often asked, somewhat condescendingly, that the band join in the speculation.

It was helpful that the Beatles' names appeared on the screen for a few seconds during their second number in the first *Sullivan* broadcast, because it was important to know who was who. Fans couldn't talk about them if they couldn't accurately identify them, and they certainly couldn't pick a favorite. Many fans recall that Paul and Ringo were easy to identify because Paul was so cute and Ringo had that big nose; George and John were harder to distinguish in those first few days.

The following Sunday, the Beatles appeared on *Ed Sullivan* live from the Deauville Hotel in Miami. It was the first of two Beatlemania booster shots that month. Broadcasting from a humid ballroom with less than ideal lighting and sound, the Beatles looked sweaty and so did the audience. But the humidity didn't dampen anyone's enthusiasm. After Ed's patronizing introduction—"Four of the nicest youngsters we've ever had on our stage"—the band opens with a tight, bouncy performance of "She Loves You." Here were those cute guys once again singing cheek to cheek. This time their stylish suits had velvet collars.

The camera finds an enraptured girl who couldn't have been more than ten or eleven; her rapture nuanced with just a touch of "What is this?" Another girl, perhaps a year or two older, is physically moved with joy after the first "woo." After the final woo, the camera finds another girl, a year or two older again, maybe fifteen or sixteen. She's got a Leslie Gore flip, a Peter Pan collar, and a post-woo glow. A woman several seats away, old enough to be her mother, is equally delighted. There are many older adults in the audience; after all, it's Miami in February.

The next number is "This Boy," sung in brilliant three-part harmony. They stand even closer than before, a closeness made possible by Paul's left-handed bass. John delivers one of his superb signature vocals, with pure, raw authenticity, the likes of which no TV audience had ever heard. Fans were getting to know John. As the song winds down, a wistful-looking girl of maybe sixteen or seventeen is singing along. She has a perfect blond pageboy, slightly teased on top, but not so teased as to look "easy."

John, Paul, and George affectionately communicate with each other through grins and knowing smiles, while performing masterfully. At the same time, they communicated a new proposition about maleness. They showed a generation of viewers that a softer, more feminine male is attractive to women. They put forth the idea that warm affection between male friends is okay, and that men can work as a collaborative group. As the song concludes, two young girls in the front row, maybe eight and ten, wildly clap with their whole bodies.

Paul talks clumsily to the audience between songs; then John gets into it and they're doing shtick for a moment or two. Paul announces the next song, "All My Loving," and the audience erupts in high-pitched delight.

They open the second set with "I Saw Her Standing There," and despite obvious mic problems, they carried on, cutting loose at the break, just as they did the week before. The song ends with a shot of the audience—rows of old but very alert men and women as far as the eye can see. Some women in the front, in their early thirties perhaps, wearing proper sixties dress-up clothes, are beaming and applauding with white-gloved hands.

During the next song, "From Me to You," the camera focuses on a Sandra Dee–look-alike. Her smile is so wide, every one of her perfect teeth can be seen. The set concludes with "I Want To Hold Your Hand," which had been getting incessant airplay for weeks. The three Beatles down front are smiling at each other again; visible electricity flows in all directions.

The camera work is more balanced, unlike the week before, which seemed a little Paul-heavy. A girl of no more than ten watches a middle-aged woman clapping wildly, several rows back. The woman's face is pure elation and she's oblivious to the little girl—and the three other people—staring at her with happy bewilderment.

America has gotten to know the Beatles a little better, and we've certainly gotten to know these songs better. John, Paul, George, and Ringo are becoming familiar, that is, like family. The excitement generated by the second broadcast added to the growing frenzy and preoccupation. Beatle wigs, in great demand, were among the early merchandise, and tennis rackets became guitars:

I was planning to bring my Beatle wig in for show and tell, but it was someone else's turn earlier in the week and he brought in a Beatle wig. I was upset because he stole my thunder. Male, b. '57

I remember heading straight down to the basement after school, where I strapped on one of my dad's old tennis rackets, and voilà! I was John Lennon! Male, b. '55

Next Sunday would be the second Beatlemania booster shot and final dose of Beatles until who knew when. Sullivan is "so darn sorry" that it was the last of three shows, and offers another patronizing comment about the "youngsters from Liverpool, England." He talks about their conduct as "fine professional singers" and as a "group of fine youngsters" who will leave an imprint on everyone who's met them." Of course he's sad to see them go—they brought infectious "youngster" energy and talent to his otherwise stale and lifeless show.

The set design is a series of floor-to-ceiling ovals with a contrasting background that seems to resonate with their dark suits, tapered trousers, and George's lanky physique in the middle. The lighting brings subtle motion to the minimalist yet information-rich set. Their suits shout "Now." Again, it's a lot to take in.

They open with "Twist and Shout," another Lennon performance that springs from the gut. Exuberant girls in the front row are clapping and bouncing in their seats. John gets them going, like they knew he would. His vocal energy escalates, getting grittier, raising the noise level throughout the audience.

A young woman, about college age, in a black turtleneck, is unable to contain what appears to be Lennon-induced ecstasy. The "ahs" rise to an orgasmic climax, and George and Paul join in the release. The camera finds a young woman in a madras blouse, about seventeen or eighteen years old, who seems to have ridden along with the song. She's attempting to compose herself, smoothing her blond flip back into place. The energy from the stage has overwhelmed the studio audience and is part of the show for viewers at home.

The second song in the two-song set is "Please, Please Me." Cut to groups of teens and older girls, thrilling to the performance. There's a lot of John in episode three, and the contrast between his smart edginess and sweet, perky Paul is becoming more apparent. George is pleasant and busy, and he remains mysterious. The song ends with the bow fans have come to expect, a respectful touch that, as many recalled, appealed to their mothers.

With the exception of Cab Calloway—who the Beatles probably enjoyed meeting—the other acts on the show were once again unremarkable. Most pre-Beatle variety show entertainment would soon become obviously passé. One almost feels sorry for comedian Morty Gunty, facing an audience waiting to hear the Beatles perform "I Want To Hold Your Hand."

They burst into the familiar chart-topper, with smiles and fancy footwork on display. Now that fans have seen more of John, they're even more certain that he wouldn't stop at handholding. Sullivan comes out when the song is over and invites the audience to really let go—and they do. It's clear that Sullivan got a kick out of presenting an act that triggers this kind of reaction. Indeed, it quickly became the high point of his forty-year show business career.

Sullivan not only presented the Beatles to America, but he did everything he could to legitimize them and elevate their status, despite the cynicism of the entertainment establishment. He featured them three weeks in a row, invited them out for a handshake after each performance, and repeatedly complimented their behavior, albeit in an awkward way. The first week, he conveyed the good wishes of Elvis and his manager Colonel Tom Parker, thus midwifing the passing of the rock-and-roll torch; the second week, he conveyed the good wishes of "rabid fan" Richard Rogers, thus midwifing the passing of the songwriting torch.

But Ed's anointment only meant so much. People of all ages enjoyed the Beatles, but they were still seen as a kid-oriented pop act, a new breed perhaps, but a pop act nonetheless. The industry assumption, including that of Sullivan's own musical director, was that they wouldn't last.

Meanwhile the Beatles had thoroughly captured the hearts and minds of American children and teens. They became a constant presence, which one fan compared to adopting another sibling. They were there as your day began and with you under the covers as you fell asleep. A male fan, age seven at the time, recalls: "Every day the sixth graders would lead the entire school bus through every song on *Meet The Beatles*. 'I Want To Hold Your Hand' and 'I Saw Her Standing There' would whip the bus into a frenzy. When I hear anything from *Meet The Beatles*, I'm back on the school bus, even today." Another male fan, four years older, remembers: "I had a transistor radio and I knew there were a couple of stations that played rock and roll so I listened in bed after my parents thought I went to sleep. I got very adept at finding Beatle songs on the radio."

Many older fans, already music lovers, had just been given radios for Christmas:

> I got an aqua clock radio for Christmas. I kept it on at all times, very low so no one else could hear it. I could be two floors down in the kitchen doing the dishes with the water running and still be able to hear the opening chords of "I Want To Hold Your Hand." I would race upstairs to raise the volume—my family thought I was crazy. I think it was those chords. They are still imprinted on my brain. Female, b. '51

> That's the year I started listening to the radio and I knew "I Want To Hold Your Hand" sounded different. . . . That was right after Christmas, so I had my own radio. Of course there was Leslie Gore and the Beach Boys but the Beatles were different than anybody else. Female, b. '51

If you didn't have a radio of your own, hearing it on your parents' car radio was, according to one fan, "like finding a piece of candy." Even without a radio, fans could summon the feeling: "I remember we were running through the woods and someone started singing 'All My Loving.' We knew the words and melody and could sing the whole thing" (Male, b. '55).

The Beatles became a cultural frame of reference, a topic of conversation for people of all ages. Walter Cronkite and Johnny Carson and your aunts and uncles all talked about them, but no one loved them like young people. This was the first time pop singers had gotten this much attention. With the exception of the Kennedy funeral—which itself was an unprecedented media event less than three months before—there had never been wall-to-wall coverage of *anything* before the Beatles.

Young people, of any age, didn't particularly care what adults thought about the Beatles, but the cultural chatter about them made them seem even more important. The Beatles were a very big deal. And for all but the very youngest fans with no recollection of "before" and "after," they were the first big deal. Every fan sensed that he or she was part of something big. One female fan, age nine, recalled the Beatleness spreading through her neighborhood: "Two weeks after *Sullivan* everything was out of control. It was like a fever had swept through. We had so many kids in the neighborhood and we all loved them. There were large families, some with eight or ten kids; lots of kids singing and dancing to the Beatles" (Female, b. '54).

Fans knew this wasn't just happening in their family, or their neighborhood, or their school, or even the whole US. They knew they shared this experience with young people all over the world and that they were suddenly part of a global siblinghood of Beatle fans.

The culture of childhood changed. Overnight, kids went from listening to Disney records and the Chipmunks to "Please, Please Me" and "I Saw Her Standing There"; from Candyland to the Beatles' Flip Your Wig game. Records became the gift of choice for birthdays and holidays. And while many fans of all ages had music of some kind in their life before the Beatles, it was often someone else's music, and it wasn't part of the daily routine. As one fan, age eight at the time, recalled, "Beatle music was ours. It became central to our lives." Dolls, cowboys and Indians, sports, Lincoln Logs, jacks, pickup sticks, and stuffed animals were pushed to the periphery.

Boys as young as eight and nine suddenly became more conscious of their appearance because they liked the way the Beatles looked. Their role models switched from Hercules, astronauts, cowboys, and soldiers—traditional male figures, strong and brave, to the Beatles, a group of effeminate musicians.

Two, three, or four Beatle fans in the family, not counting parents, was quite common, because most families had at least two kids, and they were typically less than two or three years apart in age. A male fan (b. '54) recalls, "There were about twenty houses on our circle, and there were at least three or four elementary school-age kids in each house—all Beatle fans." Beatle music was heard incessantly because if you didn't put the record on, your brother did; or you were at your friend's house across the street or two floors down, and your friend's older sister put it on. Fifty years later, the Beatles remain an important touchstone for siblings who grew up Beatleing together.

The youngest fans felt grown up because they liked the same thing the big kids liked. Older kids tolerated younger kids who liked the Beatles, even kid brothers and sisters, and often let them tag along to be tutored in all things Beatle and all things cool.

Mixed-age groups assembled in basements and living rooms across America to listen to Beatle records, giving children and tweens an early glimpse into teenagerhood making them grow up a little faster, or at least shifting their attention in that direction. One female recalls fantasizing about being a teenager when she was eight years old, recalling, "It was a feeling I associate with the Beatles and *American Bandstand*."

Fans found ways of making the Beatles present at school, too—with a Beatles lunchbox, sweatshirt, wallet, or loose-leaf book. They pasted the band's pictures to the book covers made from brown paper bags—if they were willing to cut up prized magazines. Fans still recall teachers, sometimes nuns, who would let a classmate read a poem she'd written about her favorite Beatle.

Anglophilia

Many fans became newspaper readers, scouring the paper for items about the Beatles to cut out and put into scrapbooks, which many still have. They followed news about the Beatles from all over the world, but were especially interested in England—the planet the Beatles came from. Suddenly a faraway place called Liverpool took on mythic overtones. The Beatles spoke in strange variations of an accent fans had heard before, bringing cool new words, like "fab" and "gear."

Anything having to do with England or Great Britain was suddenly about the Beatles and commanded interest and admiration. Any mention of England in school was an opportunity to legitimately think about the Beatles. Many fans remained Anglophiles throughout their lives, helping to make Beatle tourism the thriving industry it is today. Said one, "My husband thinks my 'Anglophile tendencies' stem from the Beatles, and to this day I am intensely interested in all things British. I had my first trip to London and Liverpool fifteen years ago. I visited all the requisite Beatle sites and had the time of my life" (Female, b. '51).

The music industry was quick to capitalize on the Anglophilia that hit American youth, launching the British Invasion and flooding the pop music market with other English bands. Some of these bands had members who had attended British art schools and were extremely talented and innovative, and some were put together to cash in on a craze that might not last.

Many bands, in both of the above categories, debuted in America on the *Ed Sullivan Show*, starting with the Dave Clark Five less than a month after the Beatles' first appearance. They performed "Glad All Over," which reached number six on the pop singles chart in April, making it the first British Invasion hit by an artist other than the Beatles. Soon the airwaves were filled with hits by British Invasion bands, including Gerry and the Pacemakers, Billy J. Kramer and the Dakotas, Peter and Gordon, Chad and Jeremy, the Kinks, the Animals, and Herman's Hermits.

The Beatle surge continued through the Invasion. When the Dave Clark Five appeared on *Ed Sullivan*, the Beatles held three places on *Billboard*'s Top 5: "I Want To Hold Your Hand" at number one, "She Loves You" at number two, and "Please, Please Me" at number four. The Beatles held the top three positions for the rest of March, and started April with a record-breaking five songs in the Top 5 (the three mentioned above, plus "Twist and Shout" and "Can't Buy Me Love") and fourteen songs in the Top 100. Meanwhile, the Beatles themselves were back in England filming their first feature film, *A Hard Day's Night*.

Fans were immersed in Beatles music, photo magazines, and every conceivable kind of merchandise—school supplies, wallets, clothing, dolls, wallpaper—when confronted with *In His Own Write*, a book of poetry, stories, and drawings authored by "the writing Beatle," John Lennon. Influenced by and compared to works by James Joyce, James Thurber, and Lewis Carroll, the book features bizarre imagery, a menagerie of weird characters, wordplay, and nonlinear narratives. One fan, age nine at the time, recalls that his parents were afraid the book would disturb him but he found it "hilarious." Many fans enjoyed its "quirkiness" and can still recite portions of it by heart.

Older fans were more likely to engage with Lennon's book, one recalling that he found it extremely clever, but that it required a little bit of work. A female fan, age eighteen at the time, said it inspired her to start writing poetry. In general, fans found the book compelling but strange—foreshadowing a reaction many would have to the Beatles' output in the years ahead.

In the six months between the *Sullivan* broadcasts and the American release of the film A *Hard Day's Night*, the Beatles' various American record companies released eight singles and five albums—there was no shortage of Beatle music to explore. Most discussion of the Beatle catalogue today references the UK releases and dismisses the US releases as not the "real" thing. And while it's true that American fans got a somewhat distorted sense of the band's development, *Introducing . . . the Beatles*, *The Beatles' Second Album*, and *Something New*—all released during this period—were hugely important records for these fans. Along with *Meet the Beatles*, these were the records they listened to incessantly—in their rooms, in their friends' basements, and at the after-school center. When fans talk about the Beatles entering their bloodstream, these records were the delivery system.

These albums included hits as well as deep cuts not heard on the radio. *Introducing . . . the Beatles* and *The Beatles' Second Album* are brilliant collections of eclectic covers and early Lennon-McCartney gems. *Something New* introduced songs from *A Hard Day's Night* a month before the movie came out, fueling anticipation. Hearing "Komm, Gib Meir Deine Hand" was amusing and reminded fans of all ages, again, that they were part of an international fan community.

Girls and boys could buy records, enjoy the music, read the Beatle books that quickly appeared, discuss them incessantly, and turn the transistor radio dial back and forth in search of that distinctive sound that "felt different" from other music. However, many fan behaviors were widely seen as more appropriate for boys or for girls. Gender norms intersected with Beatle fandom in numerous ways.

Picking a Fave

Today, fans often bristle, understandably, when asked, "Who's your favorite Beatle?" But as kids, it was important—especially for girls and young boys—to pick a favorite, even if your choice was arbitrary, constantly changing, or really your second choice because your best friend claimed your true favorite first:

> It was important to pick a favorite. I picked George because I wanted to be different and I liked the little two-step he did when he played. He seemed cool and mysterious. Female, b. '61

> I was seven, and a Lennon lover from day one. A neighbor girl, ten years old, who was forever changing [her] favorite Beatle said, "You only like John because I do." My sister, age nine, got right in her face and told her, "Cheryl always liked John!" That was the only time I recall my sister standing up for me. Female, b. '56

> I came into school and my friend said I had to pick a Beatle to love by recess, and she showed me the cover of "I Want To Hold Your Hand." I wasn't that familiar with them at the time, so I looked at the picture and chose George, maybe because of his outstretched

arm. But I switched to John the next day. There was something in his eyes. He seemed like the smart one. Female, b. '53

The Beatles were a rich and complicated stimulus, and picking a favorite gave fans a focus or point of view in the countless hours of conversation about them. For boys and girls engaged in Beatle-themed dramatic play or fantasy, as many were up into their teens, your favorite Beatle became your persona in the game. Therefore, as a practical matter, you couldn't have the same favorite as your closest Beatle buddies. Also, by having a different favorite from your friends, you could chip in for a magazine and share the pictures.

Paul's angelic face, long, smooth hair, and effusive affability made him the most appealing to young boys and girls. He was also the most androgynous of the group. Ringo was cute in a different way, and his separateness on the stage made him seem vulnerable. Ringo seemed to need special care, like a "puppy dog."

One of the characteristics of adolescent thought is that boys and girls develop personal fables in which anything is possible.[5] This is why when adolescent girls picked a favorite Beatle, it was a lifetime commitment: "I remember the girls in my small group, we each had a different favorite Beatle. There could be no sharing, because we each were going to meet our favorite, fall in love, and marry them!" (Female, b.'51)

John was especially popular with the older girls and Moms, who thought he was "handsome" and "intelligent." He seemed "older" to many younger girls, who were deterred from making him their favorite because he was married and had a child—it wasn't right to fantasize about a married man. Picking John as your favorite was adventurous. A politically active seventeen-year-old, past the personal fable stage, "immediately fell in love with John": "He was different. He looked intelligent. He looked like someone who might sing 'We Shall Overcome,' or at least appreciate it. He looked very cool; interesting, alienated; almost a fifties tough look."

Picking a favorite provided the youngest fans with content for dramatic play and conversation, and gave pubescent girls a cherished personal fable and point of view for endless conversation at slumber parties.

Pubescent and teen boys were less inclined to pick a favorite—not necessarily because they were more serious about the music—as some male observers maintain—but because the Beatles' camaraderie and groupness was a bigger part of the appeal for them. As one male fan, age thirteen at the time, put it, "Each of those guys looked like they were hanging out with the three best friends you could possibly ever have." Another male fan described them as "Four very tight, good friends, in their own bubble; they created a safe place in the world for each other." Tween and teen boys found the Beatles' new presentation of male friendship very appealing. This presentation, and their hair, were two key elements of the alternative proposition for maleness that the Beatles presented.

Beatleing

It was important for fans of all ages—boys and girls—to display their fandom in some way, letting others know they too are "in the know." One way of doing this was to buy not only records but the Beatle paraphernalia that suddenly appeared. For many young fans, their first experience going to the store with friends, or saving allowance money, or earning money from lawn mowing or babysitting, was about buying Beatle stuff. Diverting lunch money was also common.

Fans remember knowing approximately when the next record was coming out, calculating how much they'd have to save each week, and budgeting. They rode their bikes to Grant's, Kresge's, Woolworth's, suburban corner stores, downtown stationery stores, and rural general stores—to buy Beatle stuff. The Beatles weren't merely the soundtrack to important events in fans' lives, they were the actual substance of the events, and triggered the rite of passage from children to consumers.

Beatle trading cards appealed to the youngest fans of both sexes, who were at the age when children enjoy collecting, counting, and sorting various objects—stamps, coins, plastic dinosaurs, etc. These cards, now collectors' items, made for endless hours of Beatleing: discussing favorite cards with friends and siblings; trading duplicates; putting them in the spokes of your bike; assembling the puzzle on the back; proudly showing off your collection, or finding a perfect new box for the collection as it grew. And the thin slab of powdery pink gum was the bonus.

For the youngest fans, playing house now meant someone would take the role of John, someone would take the role of Cynthia, and a teddy bear served as baby Julian. A female fan (b. '57) recalls, "We'd make up these elaborate stories about their lives and act them out, in our own little way."

These same boys and girls, the six- to twelve-year-olds, also pretended with tennis racket guitars. But many boys soon or eventually opted for the real thing and began playing guitar, imagining themselves as Beatles, or at least doing what Beatles do: feeling the fun of playing music with their friends, and perhaps attracting girls.

No Girls Allowed

Some boys in their teens were already playing guitar when the Beatles came along and never went through the tennis racket stage. It was much harder for girls of any age to emulate them as musicians because the Beatles were men, and girls didn't see any women playing electric guitars—they had no role models.

It's often said of Beatle fans, "Boys wanted to be them and girls wanted to be with them," and my interviews with fans who were post-puberty at the time are consistent with this observation. But there's more to it. Many young girl fans also wanted to be them and have that kind of fun, but once they reached a certain age, cultural messages and gender norms made it easier to fantasize about being *with* a Beatle than to think about *doing* what a Beatle does. However, it doesn't necessarily follow from that, and it would be a mistake to conclude, as some observers do, that girls weren't as interested in the music. Just because you don't want to or can't do what they do doesn't mean you appreciate it any less. A female fan, age thirteen at the time, said Beatle music made her "really listen" to the transistor radio on her pillow: "I was familiar with all kinds of music, Ray Charles, Stax; but there was something different about them; the beat, the chords, the harmonies. You heard it, you felt it, and you saw it; all your senses were alive. You were glued to the radio and couldn't wait for the next song."

Boys loved the music and wanted to re-create it. Cultural norms gave them permission to try and to create personal fables about "becoming Beatles." Girls loved the music too but, for the most part, were not socialized to see themselves as people who create it. Girls didn't know about female rock pioneers like Wanda Jackson, Lorrie Collins, Janis Martin, or Rosetta Tharpe. And girls didn't know there was a woman, Carol Kaye, playing bass on many of their favorite records. Girls' love for the music was expressed through close listening, singing along with it, dancing to it, connecting with their friends through it, and focusing on the lyrics—that's what the culture permitted.

In a world where boys played with erector sets, rockets, and toy guns and made science projects that involved wires and electricity, they could easily see themselves using an electric instrument, a tool, to create music—especially if it was suggested to them by men as appealing as the Beatles. Girls and women didn't use tools or instruments or mess around with cords, wires, and amps.

Girl fans saw band after band appear on the scene, British and American, with male musicians. Fans understood, consciously or subconsciously, that girls and women didn't play guitar in bands. That was still true four years later, as this female fan, born in '55, explains: "I started to play guitar in 1969 but quit because I never thought I'd be good at it, which I now regret. But I also stopped because for a young girl wanting to play electric guitar, there were no role models. I didn't want to be Joni Mitchell. I wanted to be John Lennon. Electric guitar seemed liberating; it's what I wanted to do but it didn't seem to be an option. For my brother, it was more of a birthright."

And girls definitely didn't play the drums. A female fan, age thirteen at the time, recalls taking band at school and being the only girl in the drum section: "Ringo was my favorite, so I wanted to play the drums; he made it look fun and easy. But the boys were so horrible to me; they made me miserable. I quit after a while; it didn't come naturally to me." It was more fun for this girl, and countless others, to fantasize with her friends about dates with the Beatles—where they'd go, what they'd wear, and how they'd do their hair—than to put up with what we would now call a "hostile environment" at band practice. Girls got the message.

Male fans were drawn to the camaraderie and tight bond they saw in the Beatles, and wanted to try to create that experience for themselves. Male friendships, at any age, are more likely than female friendships to be activity based—a reason for getting together rather than simply enjoying each other's company.[6] When girls gave up the tennis racket or plastic guitar at age eleven or twelve, they watched their brothers and guy friends practice in garages and basements. A male fan (b. '51) recalls: "Girls came to our rehearsals and brought their friends. There was a mystique about being in a band. Junior high and high school would have been completely different. Being in a band built my confidence."

Like the girl fan who wanted to play the drums, this male fan, age nine at the time, also thought the Beatles made playing an instrument look fun and easy. Like many young male fans, he learned to play an instrument and made music a focal point of his life. He wasn't discouraged and didn't tell himself it wasn't natural: "It's cliché, but I wanted to play music after seeing them. They made it look fun and easy. I entered a talent show in summer camp, thinking I could pick up a guitar and play, like a bicycle you could just get on and ride."

Certainly, there were girl fans who started playing an instrument after seeing the Beatles early on, but in nowhere near the numbers that boys did—and the history of rock music reflects this. If girls attempted to start bands, it was a short-lived effort. In the months and years following the *Sullivan* broadcasts, it was easier for girls to imagine themselves happily dancing in a cage than playing an electric guitar.

Boys could also emulate the Beatles by growing their hair, or attempting to. Some girls got Beatle haircuts as a way of identifying with them, but a Beatle haircut on a girl is not as noticeable and not as much of a statement—of Beatle fandom or rebellion—as long hair on a boy. Some girls wore a fisherman's cap like John's, but girls were more likely to wear the English schoolgirl look. It's interesting, too, that boys, with the Beatles' inspiration, rebelled against the cultural norm forbidding long hair on men, but girls didn't push against the norm that kept them from playing rock and roll until some years later.

The Beatles' hair presented boys with an invitation; a challenge—and they accepted. Growing your hair long—or fighting with your parents over it—was another way for boys to emulate the Beatles and feel aligned with them.

For pubescent boys, the Beatles presented what one male fan, b. '50, called a template: "The mania coincided with puberty. You were already in a state of flux and you were going to change no matter what. They provided a template or a model for that change. A complete package—dress, humor, style, play music—and girls will like you. My peer group started remodeling itself around them—dressed like them, played guitars like them, made witty comments like them."

The mania coincided with puberty for girls, too, and they were also in a state of flux, but their response was very different: "I was twelve and my hormones were raging. I had heard 'I Want To Hold Your Hand' on the radio and I had *Meet The Beatles*, but they all looked the same to me. When I saw Paul on *Ed Sullivan*, my heart started beating outside my body. I had had some crushes at school, but this was different. He was the most beautiful man I'd ever seen. I wanted him; I wasn't sure exactly what I wanted, but I wanted him." Another wrote: "I used to dream of being with Paul as his girlfriend, even though I had no clear idea of what that meant. I used to kiss the TV during the close-ups, thinking somehow it made me closer to him."

Young teen girls created personal fables about marrying a Beatle; young teen boys created personal fables about being in a successful Beatles-like band. Both long shots, of course. But a critical difference is that along the way, those boys learned how to play and perform music, wrote songs, found their creative voice, became more confident, and came to see themselves as artists. And many boys inspired by the Beatles did make music a centerpiece of their lives, bringing personal enjoyment and varying degrees of success.

A Presence in the Household

The Beatles became an integral part of family life and affected family dynamics in a variety of ways. Many fans said one or both parents were concerned that his or her extreme fascination and engagement with the Beatles was a serious obsession, as did this man (b. '52): "My parents felt that I spent too much time in Beatle-related activities. They did not like the music and couldn't understand how I could be so taken with them, after being raised in a classical music environment. We had many disagreements about them." Yet, the Beatles also provided parents with leverage to manage their kids' behavior. Good behavior and good grades were rewarded with records, concerts for a lucky few, or assorted merchandise. Conversely, parents used the threat of Beatle-deprivation to control children's behavior.

Early on, some parents liked the Beatles and some didn't; some were neutral and didn't pay much attention. Some fans, mainly women, had pleasant memories of fathers who liked the Beatles and would surprise them with records from time to time: "My dad brought home two 45 records: 'I Want To Hold Your Hand' and 'Do You Want to Know a Secret.' I don't remember him listening to them, but my sister and I played them constantly, on a little aqua kiddie record player" (Female, b. '56).

In general, mothers were more likely to be the pro-Beatle parent:

I was twelve when I watched the Beatles on *Ed Sullivan* for the first time with my parents. My father couldn't have cared less, but he put up with listening to Beatle music every night on my transistor radio while we had dinner. My mother loved them, especially John, and their music. Every time I came out of my room after playing a Beatle album she would comment on various things about the songs, usually something about John's singing. It was clear she enjoyed hearing them. She went with me to pick out a perfect set of Remco Beatles dolls, to buy *In His Own Write*, and many other early 'Beatle events' in my life. She allowed me to literally wallpaper my room with their pictures—to hell with the woodwork and wall paint. Female, b. '52

Several fans said their mothers bought them Beatle records, but they couldn't listen to them when their father was home. Another fan recalled: "Mom liked them but they conveyed an image Dad didn't like. I think he thought the hair was unmanly and rebellious. He would grouse about it. Mom enjoyed them but didn't let on to Dad" (Male, b. '56).

Dads were like some of the older boys who didn't see the appeal of the Beatles, or were reluctant to admit it if they did—maybe because they were jealous that their girlfriends, and some of their guy friends, were paying so much attention to these four men. Perhaps these fathers and older boys felt threatened by what the Beatles represented. Fans recall fathers threatening to turn off the TV if anyone screamed, and some, seeing their kids' over-the-top enthusiasm, joked about changing the channel—and some actually did.

My mother and I were watching the Beatles on TV. I can remember almost shaking with excitement before the Beatles came on. My father walked in and changed the channel to the news. My whole world just fell apart. My mother eventually persuaded my father to put it back on. I did get to see it but that awful moment is still with me today. Male, b. '55

My mom loved the Beatles, but my dad was not a big fan. When I was twelve, I broke my arm while listening to "I Want To Hold Your Hand" and my dad blamed the Beatles. I got a little too excited dancing around the room and fell. They had to take me to the hospital. It was a very bad break. My mom still loves them and calls me if she sees something about them on TV. Female, b. '52

One of my most painful memories is the night my father "caught" my sister and me fawning over our beloved magazine and picture collection, took the entire cache outside and burned it all before our eyes. After all these years, that can still bring tears to my eyes. Female, b. '51

A Regular Boy's Haircut

The Beatles' hair was widely perceived as outrageous—which could be good or bad, depending on who was doing the perceiving. It was the first thing anyone noticed. The press compared the look to Captain Kangaroo and Moe from the Three Stooges—two characters quite familiar and appealing to young Beatle fans. But the exuberance at school on February 10 was not about Moe or the Captain:

All the boys had their hair combed down and were trying to talk in British accents and wanted to learn to play guitar. Female, b. '51

They burst into my consciousness and I thought they were the coolest thing when I saw them on *Ed Sullivan*. Dad was driven to distraction by the long hair. All the guys combed their hair down the next day. Male, b. '56

The next day at school, seventh grade, all the greasers and hoods had combed their hair down and it was even longer than the Beatles' hair because they had high pompadours. Male, b. '51

A female fan, age eighteen at the time, recalls the reaction of her parents and male friends: "Mom and I were amused, hysterical. Dad didn't like the hair. And all the guys said they were queers or fairies" (Female, b. '45). Another fan recalls a father with a similar reaction: "After the Ed Sullivan shows when everyone was living, breathing, and talking Beatles, they became a passion for me. My father was extremely homophobic and at one point forbade me to listen to their records or watch them on any shows. That passed after a while when he got advice from other parents" (Male, b. '51).

Clearly, fathers did not like the Beatles' hair. Even those who found it amusing at first quickly began to dislike it when their sons started finagling longer intervals between haircuts. The Beatles inspired boys to rethink the whole haircut thing. A male fan, age nine at the time, recalls: "My dad used to bring me for a haircut, and he would say 'a regular boy's haircut.' And the barber would scrape the back of my neck. So when I saw the Beatles, I thought, 'I bet they don't have to go through that,' getting a regular boys' haircut." The Beatles were not regular boys, and their haircut was not regular for a boy. This powerful memory shows how the Beatles validated the disdain this boy already felt for the "regular" at age nine. They validated his not wanting to get his neck scraped and they empowered him to resist.

It was important to be identifiable as a Beatle fan—to tell the world you were part of this new thing; that you were a Beatle celebrant. Short hair on boys became unacceptable, not cool. Parents, father's especially, were disturbed by this. They didn't want their sons looking effeminate and thought they looked silly. Perhaps the hair triggered fears their sons were or could become homosexual—an unthinkable nightmare in 1964. Also, if your son walks around with long hair, it reflects badly on you as a parent—it means your son has become a "nonconformist." Parents found this unsettling because it proved, as Dylan said on his album released just a few weeks before, that your sons and your daughters are, indeed, beyond your command.

Parents in the 1960s had a hard time with gender norm violations. On one hand, they wanted to encourage their children's interests and wanted to see their children happy; yet, on the other hand, they were fearful of encouraging nonconformity. Most parents at that time didn't see how rigid gender roles limited their child's ability to grow into a well-rounded, self-actualized adult with a broad range of competencies. For many parents, any hint of behavior or interest that violated gender expectations was cause for concern. Some parents, though not all, were even uneasy about their sons buying fan magazines such as *16* and *Tiger Beat*, or hanging Beatle pictures on their bedroom walls.

Learning from the Lyrics

The Beatles' domination of the *Billboard* charts that April put fans into a Beatles echo chamber. Fans heard these songs *constantly*. Many observers dismiss these early songs as ear candy, silly love songs that are not particularly meaningful, relative to the Beatles' entire body of work. But in the spring of 1964, the relentless, incessant exposure to these *relatively* unsophisticated songs had an impact, especially on girl fans, who, in general, paid more attention to the lyrics.

Many of the youngest fans became regular listeners to Top 40 radio with the arrival of the Beatles, and quickly acquired transistor radios of their own. The seven-, eight-, nine-, or ten-year-old listening to Beatle songs in his or her room at night, or on the playground, was transported to a new world of two minute stories about grown-ups, set to music.

Those who call early Beatle lyrics trite or insignificant forget that a large proportion of Beatle fans were children. The particulars of each two-minute story are different, but every song exposed young fans to grown-up conversation and, naturally, they attempted to glean meaning from it.

The songs in the April echo chamber—"Can't Buy Me Love," "Twist and Shout," "She Loves You," "I Want To Hold Your Hand," and "Please Please Me"—were bouncy, high-energy explosions with compelling melodies and novel harmonies, appealing even to preschoolers—who suddenly had something in common with their older siblings. Four- and five-year-olds spun around and quickly learned to "sing along," even if only singing nonsense syllables that sounded right to them; actual words and meaning would emerge later.

In the elementary school years, children become aware that there's a complex palette of human emotion, and begin to understand the role of emotions in their own and others' behavior. These realizations enhance children's ability to empathize with others. Beatle lyrics examine the nuances of the social world children are discovering and trying to understand: What am I feeling, and should I express it? How do others see me? What do people expect of me? How do I connect with other people? Why do people act as they do? What should I do or not do to avoid feeling embarrassed or vulnerable?

The Beatles didn't tell fans what to think or feel, but the grown-up conversation in the songs resonated with children's need to understand how the social world works, and provided them with useful information as they thought about these big ideas for the first time.

One female fan, age seven at the time, recalls being actively engaged with the lyrics from the beginning: "I have a vivid memory of listening to *Meet the Beatles* with my brother, who was ten, and wondering who George would be telling not to bother him. So I asked my brother, who replied, "Probably his mother." The naiveté of the brother's response is humorous now, but these were two children trying to create or find meaning in the story that went with those infectious beats and rhythms.

Fans with similar memories of misheard or misunderstood lyrics share these stories with a touch of embarrassment. But these alert listeners brought whatever emotional awareness, intellect, and social experience they had to these songs—that's how people of all ages engage with art. If the result was childlike, it's because they were children.

Young fans were able to glean some meaning, however vague, from these early songs. And they heard urgency, but it wasn't the usual urgency of childhood. It wasn't the urgency of "Come on, you'll be late for school." It was abstract urgency—for fun, for connection, and for embarking on the adventure of life itself.

Fans were asked to consider the concept of pride, and when apologies are in order—all in the name of love and connection, the goals of the adventure. They heard the Beatles questioning the value of the diamond ring, a powerful symbol in girl culture.[7] They learned that men and women can make each other happy and sad with words and gestures, and that principles of fairness and reciprocity should rule these relationships.

These issues aren't simple and fans surely didn't understand it all. Young fans were oblivious to the sexual innuendos. But every two or three minute burst was an invitation for fun and further understanding of the grown-up world. All pop songs brought that invitation, but Beatle songs seemed to offer a greater payoff. These songs, with their delightful, challenging promise of enhanced understanding, became nurturing and vital necessities. They sounded different and, perhaps more importantly, *felt* different from anything that came before. They felt like Beatleness.

Teenage girls also heard the urgency, but for them, it had a romantic or vaguely sexual tinge. These girls heard the Beatles singing *to* them in a way younger girls didn't. Listening alone in her room after school, or to the transistor radio before falling asleep, each girl discovered that moving in a certain way could produce a tingling, blissful feeling. They didn't know what they were doing, but it felt good. And the Beatles were there.

This was 1964, and while teenage girls were given strict and often confusing rules about dating and sex—from parents, from "experts" like Pat Boone and Connie Francis, and from pop songs—no one talked about blissful feelings.[8] Many female fans told me that very little was explained to them about puberty and female sexuality, so they didn't understand the weird feelings they were having toward the Beatles.

A Fan Ritual

Much has been written about why girls screamed at Beatle shows, and many observers see the screaming as evidence of girls' lack of serious interest in the music. But as discussed above, girls and boys engaged with the music—and the whole Beatle experience—in different ways. Girls loved the sound and feel of the music and listened to the words. But they went to the concert to see the Beatles, to be part of the event, and to scream.

Anticipating a live Beatles' performance, female fans said they would discuss with their friends beforehand whether or not they would scream—not quite daring each other, but conspiring to do something uncharacteristically bold, expressive, and free—something they couldn't do anywhere else. Some girls planned to scream, and did. Some said they wouldn't but lost their inhibitions in the contagion of the crowd. In some ways, the screaming functioned like a laugh track, telling fans how to respond and giving them permission to emote.

Girls screamed at Beatle shows because it was expected and because it was allowed. It was the only public place where girls could feel that free and uninhibited. They screamed because they were thrilled to be there, in closer proximity to the Beatles, accepting the Beatles' invitation to leave madras, loafers, crew cuts, and white gloves behind. They screamed because they allowed themselves to feel that mysterious sensation they felt when they heard these songs on the transistor radio under the covers before falling asleep. They screamed because it made them part of the show.

Maybe the screams were a way of thanking the Beatles for the music and the mayhem; maybe they were screaming because no one was offering them an electric guitar or organized sports—outlets available to their brothers and male friends for self-expression and release of sexual energy.

Each girl had her reason for screaming, but when they put their voices together they made a unified and powerful statement. The clear message—the *loud* and clear message—was that girls like men who look and act like the Beatles.

If the screams were sublimating romantic and sexual desire, as many observers believed, there was a subversive element to the behavior and to the unconventional, controversial object of desire. The *Washington Post* critic who called the Beatles "conservative" and "asexual" didn't understand that their androgyny represented a new kind of sexuality that, in the words of Barbara Ehrenreich, "mocked the gender distinctions that bifurcated the American landscape into 'his' and 'hers.'"[9]

Cheered Up and Ready for Change

According to the "Kennedy Rebound Theory of Beatlemania," the Beatles boosted the national spirit after the assassination and made us more receptive to the happy tumult the Beatles ushered in. The *Saturday Evening Post* agreed saying, "[T]hey served for a time to divert us. We wish them well. We like them better than Cyprus, Panama or South Vietnam."[10]

Clearly, they were a national diversion and the national mood was lifted. That said, "Beatlemania" would have happened anyway. The significance of the timing, overlooked in fifty years of conjecture, is that they too represented a new frontier.

Like Kennedy, the Beatles were youthful, cool, competent citizens of the world with authentic charisma and a natural ability to speak off the cuff and charm a crowd. They seemed to represent the future in the same way Kennedy once had. But they added the impatience of youth to those qualities, and communicated that impatience, that "now" and that "freedom," to their young audience. Somehow the Beatles suggested it was time to move off the cusp, cross the threshold, and work through the contradictions of the Kennedy era. Fans old enough to remember see a connection:

Kennedy was a symbol of youth and change. He awakened new hope for change from our parents' world; more inclusive of young people, more fun. With the assassination, that beacon went away. Now we have LBJ, who was gruff and old. Then the Beatles came and we grabbed on to this shining light. Male, b. '50

JFK gave my generation hope; we were captivated by him and the energy around him. The Beatles had the same energy. JFK didn't have a crew cut; he had style and wit; he teased reporters at the press conference. Like the Beatles, he had youthful energy that made everything seem possible. Female, b. '46

In the meantime, the social contradictions of the Kennedy era continued. Throughout the spring and summer, President Johnson initiated several items on the Great Society agenda, the Civil Rights Act was signed into law, and NASA's Gemini and Ranger launches moved the nation a little closer to the goal of sending a man to the moon.

But three civil rights workers were killed in Mississippi and the US was getting more embroiled in Vietnam. Young people, especially on college campuses, were growing weary of the Cold War and other policies that seemed increasingly absurd, immoral, and unethical. They were starting to ask harder questions in louder voices—though no one was really listening.

The Beatles' style, exuberance, unique sound, and overall audacity seemed to speak to and for these disenfranchised and impatient youth, eager to move forward.

Those threatened by forward movement discredited and denied the forces of change. This was the "damn the messengers" strategy of the anti-Beatle dads, the jealous boyfriends, and the snarky journalists. They had a vague sense that the Beatles were a threat to the status quo, and they knew it had something to do with the hair.

A Singular Event

The Beatles sudden omnipresence throughout the spring and summer of 1964 was a strange, singular event in American pop culture. Referencing them—in political cartoons, sitcoms, comedy routines, magazine articles, novelty songs, comic books, and advertisements became essential to any communicator who wanted to appear current and now. But beyond the media, Beatleness had become part of the environment in neighborhoods across America: "One of my fondest memories of Beatlemania is when the big kids would include me in their epic hide and seek games. There were teams, and the boundaries were the entire neighborhood. We'd run through yards, jump fences, hide in trees, and pretend we didn't hear our parents calling when it was time to go home. Beatle music was always playing—from an open window, a car radio, or someone's transistor" (Male, b. '55).

The Beatles still ruled the charts in August '64, but fans were also listening to the Invasion bands, Motown, and the Beach Boys. Old standbys like the Four Seasons were somehow hanging on. Just when the energy of Beatlemania might have started to dissipate, *A Hard*

Day's Night was released in movie theaters across America—another booster shot of Beatlemania—guaranteeing the band would remain top-of-mind in a pop music environment that was starting to get more interesting—no small thanks to them.

Fans listened to the *A Hard Day's Night* album with cover in hand, looking into the eyes of the peekaboo images on the front, and animating the Beatles by making up captions to go with the expressions on the three-by-five grid of headshots on the back. Soon fans would actually see them come alive. They would get to watch them interact with each other on the big screen, get to know them better, and watch four distinct personalities emerge.

August also marked the beginning of the band's first US tour, during which fewer than a half million lucky fans would have an experience that made them the envy of those less fortunate— an experience that, five decades later, is recalled with awe as a moment of personal connection with history.

CHAPTER THREE

British Boys

August 1964–November 1965

I wasn't part of the "in crowd"; I had three or four good friends. But I was on equal footing with the popular kids because I saw A Hard Day's Night.

Female, b. '55

FANS WERE HAPPILY IMMERSED in the Beatles, and everything about them was becoming delightfully familiar. The relationship between the fans, the Beatles, and the media that began in February was becoming even more intense, and there was lots of buzz about *A Hard Day's Night*. Fans were about to renew their relationship with the group and fall even more deeply in love.

Feeling the joyful anticipation that only the Beatles could elicit, fans walked into the theater not knowing what to expect, but it was the Fab Four, so little else mattered. Some teen girls dressed up for the occasion: "We wore our Beatle sweatshirts even though it was a hot August day. A mob poured in to the theater. We were listening to the radio until it started. My friend passed out and her radio fell apart" (b. '51). Another recalled, "Mom made me a herringbone jumper, and I had a white shirt and a red tie like we had seen on the girls in the fan magazines" (b. '50).

Young moviegoers across the country—preschoolers, college students, and everyone in between—were called to attention by the opening chord of the title song, and their attention didn't waver for ninety-two minutes. The song's urgency, the determined pursuit of the Beatles by the fans on the screen, and director Richard Lester's inventive camera shots immediately set the pace and tone for the entire film. Fans could easily imagine themselves among the crowd of young people in the opening sequence.

For many young fans, the first few minutes of the film were a bit unsettling. Not expecting a black and white film, many were disappointed. Also, the Beatles' accents were surprisingly hard to understand. But eager ears and eyes adjusted quickly, and fans sat mesmerized, getting, as one male fan (b. '52) put it, "a glimpse into their happy world."

Most fans neither knew nor cared about Richard Lester's connection to the Beatles' favorite radio comedy program, the *Goon Show*, or that the film was an innovative synthesis of French New Wave, *cinéma vérité*, and madcap comedy. They didn't know or care that it cost only five hundred thousand dollars and was filmed in six weeks. No one knew or cared that what began as an effort to cash in on the latest teen craze would become a film of historic significance. It was, in the words of one female fan, age sixteen at the time, "the Beatles on the big screen in all their gorgeousness."

Fans of all ages saw more of the camaraderie and esprit de corps that so intrigued them on the Sullivan broadcasts, but they could also focus on them as individuals and hear the clever banter among the group and their entourage. Even seeing them move around was fascinating.

A Hard Day's Night offered what one fan described as "long-term exposure." Fans were able to see more aspects of the four distinct personalities and could look deeper into the aspects they'd already come to know and love. They'd see a wider range of body language and facial expressions. They could study how the Beatles walked, stood, leaned, sat, and picked up their instruments. Fans also got a closer look at their clothes, hair, and cool style.

The film allowed fans to be with the Beatles everywhere they went—"in a train and a room, and a car and a room, and a room and a room." And a bathtub. The accents were thick and the repartee was quick. The British working-class lingo was charming but confusing. One really had to pay attention. Much of the humor was over the heads of young fans, but they didn't have to catch it all to appreciate the fun the Beatles were having. Fans saw that these guys didn't have to go anywhere to have fun; they somehow brought the fun with them.

The film is deceptively simple: a fictionalized account of a day in the life of the Beatles and their managers as they arrive in London and prepare for a live television show. Viewers who looked for a linear plot found little other than the group's having to keep an eye on Paul's mischievous grandfather. The dynamic between their handlers, Shake and Norm, was a running joke throughout the film, as was the fact that Paul's grandfather was "very clean."

Some older viewers may have had some familiarity with art house cinema, but for most fans, *A Hard Day's Night* was their first experience with a movie that wasn't really "about" anything—how it made you feel was more important than what it was about. The other popular movie for kids at the moment was the much more traditional and child-oriented *Mary Poppins*. The Disney film appealed to the Anglophilia of young Beatle fans too—as though the Beatles themselves were somehow connected to the Victorian London depicted. "Supercalifragilisticexpialidocious" was fun to sing, but it wasn't as cool as "Can't Buy Me Love."

Many fans remember *A Hard Day's Night* as the first movie they wanted to see more than once and have fond memories of sitting through it multiple times. A female fan, age thirteen at the time, remembers that hot August afternoon: "We were over the moon to sit there and watch them for ninety minutes; to see them interact and how funny and adorable, and witty and fun they were. We watched it a few times." This male fan, six years younger, also saw it more than once. "My older brothers took my younger brother and me. In those days you could watch the movie again, so we did. We were mesmerized."

Seeing the film multiple times—"sitting there all day and trotting along with them"—made it easier to mimic the accents and remember bits of dialogue and other details. Fans recall the joy of watching the Beatles on the big screen in a cool, dark theater on a hot summer day— and how important it was to glean as much as possible from this rare opportunity for "long-term exposure" to the Beatles:

My aunt took me to see *A Hard Day's Night* every day over the summer. I learned all their mannerisms and accents. Male, b. '54

We went crazy at the movies—it was so entertaining, the music, how they looked, the accents, and we picked it apart, looked at their clothes; were they wearing ties or turtlenecks. Female, b. '51

One female fan (b. '48) says she saw the film fifty-seven times that summer. Another fan recalls how he and his brother figured out a way to see it every weekend: "We were dying to go, but none of the parents wanted to sit through it. So we enlisted our great-grandmother to go with us. So here's this ninety-year-old woman wearing support hose with a couple of boys in a hot theater in the South watching a matinee showing of a Beatle movie. We dragged her back every weekend. She had no idea what she was watching. She lived long enough to see *Help!* She was wonderful to do that for us. I will never forget her for that" (Male, b. '58).

Boys and younger girls were surprised that girls were screaming in the theater:

Girls were screaming and I thought, "Yeah, I want to be part of this. I want to make music and cause this reaction in people." Male, b. '51

My older sister was screaming with the older girls. I said to her, "It's just a movie." I thought the Beatles were funny and I wanted to listen. It had no sexual content for me. Female, b. '55

I went with my sister and her friends who were a few years older than me. I asked my sister why they were screaming, and she said, "Why aren't you?" Female, b. '55

As the above quotes suggest, fans responded to *A Hard Day's Night* in the same gendered ways they'd been responding to the Beatles for the previous six months. Boys of all ages projected themselves into the film as members of the Beatles or a similar kind of group—to attract girls, to make music, and for the camaraderie and pure fun.

The youngest female fans were drawn to the music and the fun that always surrounded the Beatles—they "made you happy, like eating your favorite chocolate" (Female, b. '55). A woman who was eleven at the time—not yet a teenager—recalls that after *A Hard Day's Night*, "We wanted to look like them even though we were girls. We all wore black turtlenecks." But girls only a little older wanted to be the girls on the screen. One female fan, thirteen at the time, recalled, "You imagined yourself in the nightclub with them."

Though the Beatles were often referred to as "lads," "youngsters," or "boys," fans didn't see them that way. When asked to think back and try to remember if they saw the Beatles as kids or as adults, fans found the question interesting and had to think about it for a bit. Some said they saw them as something in between, like "older teenagers" but not "full-fledged adults."

Many younger fans thought the Beatles were adults, but were quick to follow up with "not like my father" or "not like the adults I knew" or "not stuffy like my parents." One female fan (b. '55) described them as "a different kind of adult." A male fan, age fourteen at the time, said, "They were part of the teen spectrum; I was at one end and they were at the other. But I was on their wavelength; they were comrades."

I asked fans if the Beatles' jackets and ties made them seem more like adults. One male fan (b. '50) who saw them like "older brothers who you could imagine being like" said they were "like older kids wearing their school clothes, or what we'd wear to a dance."

The Beatles' ambiguous status was part of their appeal and their power. Fans saw them as "kids" and related to them as such; but they also saw them as "adults" with adult authority. This dual-perception added to the Beatles' power as role models, making the film a significant factor in the band's consolidation of cultural influence.

New Points of View

On the surface, *A Hard Day's Night* was a fun romp with the Fab Four. But there was much more going on—in the film and in fans' imaginations. Though fans responded in gender-specific and age-specific ways, all fans recalled how "cool" and "witty" and "endearing" the Beatles were; how they "brought nothing but pleasure and fun." A few minutes into the film there was a surreal moment when the Beatles are suddenly off the train and running along the train tracks—letting fans know that things are not necessarily as they seem, and to be prepared for shifting perspectives.

Just below the surface, the film invited viewers into a world where basic assumptions about age, gender, and class were being questioned. Fans were open to this invitation because they loved and trusted the Beatles. They captured young people's attention—emotionally, viscerally, and intellectually—in a way that no other media figures ever had before. Lester's engaging technique and the Beatles' music and screen presence drew viewers in, surrounding them with points of view—literally and metaphorically—that were new.

Fans may have walked out of the theater trying to mimic the accents, recalling the funny bits, and thinking about them as "male perfection," but the Beatles' attitude and the film's iconoclastic sensibility also left an impression, and perhaps a more important one. Explicit or implied commentary on the "establishment" permeates the film.

Fans saw the Beatles "talking back" to adults, but unlike the rebellious bad boys in *Blackboard Jungle*, *Rebel Without a Cause*, or *West Side Story*, the Beatles challenged adults with their intelligence, wit, and charm. As one male fan (b. '52) put it, "They made fun of the fussy adults in positive ways; they were funny and kind."

Throughout the film, the Beatles behave in a more adult–like manner than the adults and other authority figures around them. They settle disputes, respond rationally to the irrational, put forth reasoned and principled arguments, and reprimand misbehaving adults.

Dialogue and comedic routines throughout the film focus on their hair—the gender role violation that was disturbing fathers across America. In addition, the Beatles are seen combing their hair, having makeup applied, grooming themselves, bathing, and sitting under hair dryers—behaviors generally associated with women. In one scene, Paul's grandfather decides that they are "a bunch of sissies." They don't refute this, and accuse him of being jealous.

Film critic Roger Ebert, who was a huge fan of the film, observed, "The film was so influential in its androgynous imagery that untold thousands of young men walked into the theater with short haircuts, and their hair started growing during the movie and didn't get cut again until the 1970s."[1]

The film expresses the same irreverent attitude toward the boundaries and symbols of class expressed in Lennon's "rattle your jewelry" comment to the royal family in 1963. For example, a strategically placed napkin transforms a gambler's tuxedo into a waiter's uniform. When accused of trespassing after playfully romping about on a field in what seems to be a celebration of pure freedom, they metaphorically toss some mud at the property owner, succinctly deflating his pomposity as they apologize for hurting his field.

A male fan, only seven at the time, recalled, "They weren't angry, but they were antiestablishment. That was attractive to kids." Indeed, they became appealing role models—modeling a style and attitude that is rebellious as well as intelligent and clever. They "misbehave," but it always seems justified because they're wiser and seem more competent than the adults around them.

Social norms and assumptions are challenged in every scene, with humor, intelligence, and frenetic energy. The film's generally subversive vibe, combined with the Beatles' appeal and superhero-like ability to defeat or seduce everyone around them explains the film's enormous cultural impact.

What Do the Grown-ups Think?

Fifty years later, it's clear that *A Hard Day's Night* was a critical catalyst for the youth movement and the social and political change of the sixties. Young people were paying close attention.

Regardless of age, fans could engage with the film and glean an "antiestablishment" message. The "coolest guys on the planet" were speaking the same language as *Mad* and Dr. Seuss. A male fan (b. '50) said, "I thought it was cool how they dealt with authority, and they were having a good time." A fan six years younger said he was "mesmerized by *A Hard Day's Night* and loved their smooth comebacks; how they made jokes on everyone else."

Even the very youngest viewers who saw *A Hard Day's Night* as a purely visual and musical experience and were unable to follow much dialogue, were drawn in further and became bigger fans. They wanted to be in on the cool thing the big kids liked.

The full impact of the film cannot be appreciated without looking at how it was received by mainstream culture. Most film critics were expecting a jukebox musical that would serve merely to prolong the Beatles status as teen idols. That's not what they got.

Critics at the *New York Times*, the *Village Voice*, *Time*, and *Newsweek* ran out of superlatives trying to describe the film and how it made them feel. They commented on the Beatles' charm, wit, intelligence, and comedic skills; several evoked the Marx Brothers. The avant-garde cinematic techniques were also mentioned. Some even mentioned the music!

Significantly, every reviewer felt compelled to express his surprise at liking the film and talked about his "resistance." This defensive undertone in the reviews was mainstream culture—male opinion leaders at major newspapers—reluctantly acknowledging that, as one male fan

(b. '52) put it, "Something in the world was changing because of the Beatles."

Just like at the JFK airport press conference six months earlier, the Beatles exceeded expectations—delighting and surprising film critics and anyone who was paying attention. The effusive critical response to *A Hard Day's Night* was game-changing.

Newsweek declared them "daring and fresh" with a "sardonic edge." The reviewer grudgingly acknowledged the Beatles' endearing person-alities and then declared, "The legitimacy of the Beatles phenomenon is finally inescapable." *Time's* critic described the Beatles as "clear-eyed innocents imprisoned by fame . . . but never for a moment blinded to the really flagrant foolishness of the adult world around them."[2] *Life* magazine said the Beatles "don't give a damn for the prejudices of their elders."[3]

A Hard Day's Night was a turning point in how the culture thought about the Beatles, and it sealed for all time the three-way relationship between the Beatles, the media, and the fans that began six months earlier. Enthusiastic press coverage created a solid foundation for the continuation of Beatlemania and for the Beatles growing influence on young people and the wider culture.

With the exception of the *Village Voice's* Andrew Sarris, who called them "a sly bunch of anti-Establishment anarchists . . . too slick to tip their hand to the authorities," critics didn't connect the dots in terms of the film's potential impact on young people or on their relationship with the Beatles.[4] They didn't see the significance of their sons and daughters also thinking the Beatles were "daring and fresh," or that when the Beatles pointed out the "flagrant foolishness of the adult world," they were pointing it out to fans, too—the largest-ever generation of young people.

Critics accepted the Beatles' alternative proposition, even if they didn't realize they were being offered one or what the implications might be. It's as though the Beatles were communicating in a language that only young people could understand. The critics were so taken by surprise—by their own reaction and by the Beatles' many talents—it didn't occur to anyone to consider the film from the fans' perspective. The *New York Daily News* described the film as "clean, wholesome fun," not realizing it was the Trojan Horse of juke box musicals.

Six months earlier, fans began the daily practice of "scouring the papers" for articles about the Beatles, so when mainstream culture elevated the Beatles' status to something more than kid stuff, fans were aware of it and it elevated the Beatles in their eyes, too. It's not that young people cared what critics or adults in general thought about the Beatles, but they were talking about "our" Beatles in a new way, without the usual dismissiveness. The group's new status gave them more authority and more significance in the eyes of fans—who started paying even closer attention.

A Hard Day's Night completed the transition from the "Kennedy sixties" to the "Beatle sixties," and a clash of sensibilities was emerging. Young people could feel the tipping point as they watched the Beatles happily cavort through a world of inept adults and dysfunctional systems. Though their freedom is curtailed by screaming fans and television schedules, their wit, charm, and intelligence—their Beatleness—allowed them to proceed on their own terms, hurting no one and winning converts to a new sensibility. As one male fan (b. '52) put it, the film "suggested a different way of being."

I Can't Believe I'm Here!

Fans were watching *A Hard Day's Night* at the movies when the Beatles came back to America for their 1964 tour. Seeing the Beatles in concert conferred special status: you were the envy of all your friends and of your younger siblings, who were told they were too young to go. Fans told stories about saving up money, sending it off in an envelope, hoping the tickets would arrive, and feeling relief and elation when they had tickets in hand.

The Beatles coming to your town suddenly made your town seem special. Many girls felt they "just had to see them" and were determined to make it happen, by any means necessary. One fan, age fourteen at the time, recalls: "My friends and I bought tickets and didn't tell our parents because they said we were too young to go. We told our parents we won them, and so my Mom drove us. No one in Dallas had ever seen such traffic. When it was over, we called them to pick us up, and they'd just gotten home. We saw them pull up but we were having so much fun talking with the other girls, we hid in the crowd and didn't get into the car for forty-five minutes."

Some fans without tickets convinced parents to take them to the concert venue, to be part of the scene and to be closer to the Beatles. Some got lucky: "My friend's parents drove us to DC just to be there and were surprised that tickets were available. We ended up seeing the show. I was afraid my parents would be angry but they weren't. Mom was happy for me. I flew high from that concert for a long time" (Female, b. '50). The screaming is a big part of the memory of live Beatle shows: "You heard two notes and then the screaming started. And the flashbulbs. There weren't many guys there, mostly girls. I still have the stubs and program in my scrapbook. I feel very lucky to have seen them. People are impressed when I tell them" (Female, b. '51).

Anticipating the next Beatle record was a special feeling; but anticipating a live concert was something else again. Girls would count the days and talk with friends about what special outfits they'd wear. Many girls wore an English schoolgirl jumper, white blouse, and tie—like Pattie Boyd wore in *A Hard Day's Night*.

One female fan, age sixteen at the time, recalls the evening as "hot, sweaty, and a little anticlimactic after all the anticipation." Yet, decades later, anticlimactic or not, fans consider seeing the Beatles an "experience of a lifetime." In fact, several fans said the experience and its memory have become even more special with the passage of time. One female fan, age twelve at the time, still feels gratitude toward the stranger who cheerfully shared her binoculars.

The excitement of the Beatles coming to town wasn't limited to the show. There was also the excitement of going to their hotel and trying to get a close look, or to realize the dream of a face-to-face encounter. Even if you weren't successful, at least you tried. Most fans had never set foot into their city's upscale, landmark hotels, so it was an adventure into another world. They knew they'd meet other fans on the same adventure, with the same mission; sometimes they'd join forces. One older fan, age nineteen at the time, recalls the August night in '64 when she and her friend drove to the Vernon Manor Hotel in Cincinnati: "It was pouring rain. We found a place to park and ran into a group of boys, about thirteen, who had found an open door that led to a stairway. I think we must have known what floor the Beatles were on, maybe from the radio station. When we got to that floor we opened the door to the hallway and there were guards everywhere. We were all escorted out of the hotel. We knew we had gotten pretty close to them. It was very exciting."

Seriously attempting a live encounter with a Beatle or four at their hotel required research and planning. Some scoped it out in advance to determine how to get in and find uniforms that would give them access to the guest floors.

These escapades, with their determined, Lucy and Ethel spirit, have been described by Larry Kane, Judith Kristen, and others, but their significance as, literally, escapades, has been overlooked.[5] Fans wanted to meet the Beatles—that was the primary purpose. But they also wanted the thrill of the challenge: Could they outsmart security? Break the law? It felt daring and bold, but it was also relatively safe. And it was empowering, regardless of the outcome. Like screaming at live shows, these attempts to breach security were opportunities to misbehave in public, in the safe surround of other fans. The Beatles' presence in fans' lives often brought moments of escapade—moments in which fans felt alive and free in new ways.

Invasion

The summer and fall of 1964 were filled with musical amazement for young Beatle fans. Many were just discovering pop music and Top 40 radio. Five decades later they thank the Beatles for initiating their interest and opening their ears.

The recording industry on both sides of the Atlantic was eager to cash in on young America's love for the Beatles and wasted no time signing guitar-driven, beat-heavy bands. It's like they were saying, "Okay, you like them, how about this?" A male fan, age eight at the time, recalls the British Invasion as "a whole new world; there were so many great records to buy."

For the next two years, the flood of new music from Britain and the US was nothing less than a pop music renaissance. It was an extraordinary moment to have one's musical consciousness come alive. The transistor radio continued to be a crucial companion—a lifeline to the music and to all things cool:

My transistor radio was the best gift I ever got in my life. It made you feel powerful because you didn't have to ask your parents anymore if you could change the station. Male, b. '55

Before I heard the Beatles, music didn't mean that much to me. Hearing the Beatles at age eight made me realize even at that young age that music meant something and could be important. Many's the day I remember playing in the dirt with my Matchbox cars with a cheap transistor radio playing the local Top 40 station, jammed with Beatles, Stones, Beach Boys, etc. Male, b. '56

Older fans who were already following pop music and buying records were equally delighted—but in a slightly different way. They were able to appreciate that the Beatles and the acts following on their heels were different from what came before. They were familiar with little stories put to music and could hear how the Beatles raised the bar. Over time, fans came to expect more substantive lyrics, more complicated harmonies, jangly guitars, and bouncing, driving beats.

Young fans were suddenly engaging with the sounds and stories of pop music, teen-oriented TV and radio programming, and the Beatles—that was a lot to process at once. Because the music brought kids of different ages together, there was a sort of trickledown effect, with everyone learning from the oldest kids in the group—the de facto opinion leaders—who would alert younger kids to what was "good" or "cool."

The immediate post-Beatles British Invasion continued throughout 1964 and 1965. The Dave Clark Five followed "Glad All Over" with "Bits and Pieces," and "Can't You See That She's Mine?" In three years, the Dave Clark Five had fifteen top-twenty hits and appeared on the *Ed Sullivan Show* eighteen times. Beatle fans paid considerable attention to the Dave Clark Five. A female fan, age eight at the time, remembers: "My friend Michelle and I were sitting on the bench in a little park, looking at a *16* magazine and trying to learn the names of all the guys in the Dave Clark Five. We couldn't get enough of these English bands. When another one came along you wanted to know about them." A male fan, also age eight at the time, remembers the Dave Clark Five being responsible for him and his friends wearing "dickies."

For a brief moment, this quintet with the "Tottenham Sound" seemed like they might be serious contenders to the Beatle throne, and unlike some of the other first wave invasion bands, they didn't try to sound like the Beatles. They had a distinctive sound, more R&B than the Beatles, with a booming drum. Their songs were infectious and upbeat with strong vocals, and featured saxophone and organ. And it didn't hurt that keyboard player Mike Smith had McCartneyesque good looks.

Peter and Gordon's debut single "World Without Love" hit number one in June 1964 and made a big splash. Not only was it a Lennon-McCartney composition, but Peter Asher was the brother of Paul's girlfriend, Jane. The duo didn't break the top ten again until "I Go to Pieces" in February 1965 and only once again after that.

Another duo from across the pond, Chad and Jeremy, had a number seven hit with "A Summer Song," which held that position for over two months. Clearly trying to raise their profile, the not quite one-hit wonders appeared on the *Patty Duke Show* and the *Dick Van Dyke Show* in early 1965. Rolling Stones' bassist Bill Wyman cited them as an example of "mediocre" bands who "meant nothing in England but were a great success in America" because they had "English accents . . . and boots."[6]

Gerry and the Pacemakers, managed by Brian Epstein and from Liverpool, also captured the attention of Beatle fans. They were presented as purveyors of the same "Mersey Sound" fans were taught to associate with the Beatles. The Pacemakers had several top ten hits throughout the summer and fall, including "Don't Let the Sun Catch You Crying," "How Do You Do It?," the bouncy and suggestive "I Like It," and their final hit, "Ferry Cross the Mersey," a commercial homage to Liverpool and a blatant try for a Beatle halo effect.

Billy J. Kramer and the Dakotas, another Liverpool band managed by Epstein, recorded several Lennon-McCartney numbers. Like the other British Invasion acts—those with staying power and those without—Kramer appeared on the *Ed Sullivan Show* and on the new pop music showcases, NBC's *Shindig!* and ABC's *Hullabaloo*.

It would soon become clear that a Liverpool sound and Epstein's touch would not be enough to sustain the attention of Beatle fans.

The Stones Roll In

In June, the relatively unknown Rolling Stones performed "I Just Wanna Make Love to You" and "Not Fade Away" on ABC's *Hollywood Palace*—another variety show that, like *Sullivan*, was aggressively trying to cash in on the pop music explosion by featuring acts "for the youngsters." Fans heard "Tell Me" and "It's All Over Now" on the radio throughout the summer and knew the Stones were another British act, but many didn't really start paying attention until they appeared on *Sullivan* in October.

Stones manager Andrew Oldham marketed his band as the anti-Beatles: scruffier, a bit more menacing, and famously not content to merely hold your hand. But Oldham's campaign wasn't necessary—fans had ears and eyes and would have come to the same conclusion. The blues-oriented, proto-punk Stones had, like the Beatles, enormous stage presence but with a different, darker energy, consistent with their sound. All new bands were compared to the Beatles, but the Stones were held up to special scrutiny. A female fan (b. '55) remembers arguing with her babysitter about the two bands, and her babysitter insisting the Stones were "cooler."

Like the Beatles, the Stones would go through many phases over the years, but first impressions are very powerful, and despite superficial similarities, these bands were always fundamentally different. A male fan (b. '52) said he enjoys connecting with other Beatle fans because they're "good people." I asked if he would make the same assumption about Rolling Stones fans, and he said no, but couldn't explain why.

The Animals, another early British Invasion band with a tougher, more bluesy sound than the Beatles, had a hit with their cover of "House of the Rising Sun," which held the number one position for three weeks. Their electric version of the traditional folk song is considered by some to be the first "folk rock" record.

The Kinks had their first top ten hit in late '64 with "You Really Got Me," followed by "All Day and All of the Night" and "Tired of Waiting." One male fan (b. '55) remembers: "Bands like the Dave Clark Five became irrelevant when I heard the Kinks; there was no longer a need for five nondescript guys; we liked the Kinks' original sound and we liked how they looked."

Beatle fans of all ages were immersing themselves in the new music, but as one female fan (b. '54) put it, "We liked the Stones and the Animals and the Kinks but the Beatles were the main course." Another fan remembers: "I was a freshman at Syracuse University in September 1964. My roommates and I were huge Beatle fans. Our dorm room was named 'Lennongrad' and was decorated with posters. Mostly of the Beatles, but I remember also having the Kinks. We kept a poster of the Rolling Stones in the closet because they were too ugly to keep in full view. Someone put up a five-foot-tall poster of the Beatles on the stairway, and it was customary to pat it when walking by (this was long before *Laverne and Shirley*)."

The Beatles appeared on *Shindig!* in October and sang a cover of "Kansas City"—which showed up as filler on the much loved but "not real" *Beatles VI* the following June. They also sang "I'm a Loser," which would appear on the equally loved and equally not real *Beatles '65*, just in time for Christmas. The Dylan-inspired "I'm a Loser" made an impression:

I loved "I'm a Loser"; I liked the attitude, and it had a folky quality. It was their first introspective song. It was revealing. The words were different, and required more work. Male, b. '49

I watched it with a cousin who pretended to despise the Beatles but who loved "I'm a Loser." I thought, wow that's kind of different. Male, b. '54

Beatle fans were also listening to American music on Top 40 radio, most notably the Supremes, whose "Where Did Our Love Go" knocked "A Hard Day's Night" out of the number one position in August. The Supremes continued to dominate the charts for the next few years—the only female performers to consistently do so. The Supremes were also regulars on *Sullivan*, with their glamorous gowns and elegant choreography. Diana Ross lit up the stage in the same subtle way that Paul McCartney did—with eyes, eyebrows, and head tilts.

Listening to pop songs as little stories set to music, young fans heard the Supremes and other black singers telling the same kind of stories the Beatles told. The melodies, instrumentation, harmonies, and beats were different—the music had a different sound—but at the level of human experience, the stories were the same.

As the year was drawing to a close, fans started hearing another new group on the radio, with an unmistakable British accent. The song was "I'm into Something Good," and the group was Herman's Hermits, a blatant—and successful—attempt to cash in on young record buyers' Anglophilia. The Zombies, another British band, also had a hit in late '64 with "She's Not There," and the Rolling Stones had their first top ten hit in December, with "Time Is On My Side"—one of the numbers performed on their *Sullivan* debut.

Fans of all ages were engaged with Top 40 radio like never before. But the Beatles were the centerpiece—and it wasn't just the music. The Beatles gave fans a topic of conversation they never grew tired of, adding a new dimension to their friendships and connections with others. And they sparked playfulness and imagination in even the youngest fans: "We had a Christmas party, and we took out badminton rackets and started shaking our heads and jumping around. One of the girls felt there should be a drummer, so she went behind us and did that. Everyone wanted to be the Beatles. We thought about them a lot" (Male, b.'56).

Holiday gift giving became easy for parents of Beatle fans. Fans who didn't have a transistor radio got one; those who already had radios and a record player got records: "I got *A Hard Day's Night* and *Beatles '65* for Christmas in 1964. I played them over and over—alone and with friends. With friends, we'd have a slumber party, trade magazines, and write little poems and stories about them; alone, I'd fantasize about Paul, that he was singing directly to me" (Female, b.'51).

Beatles '65 was released just in time for Christmas. Most fans didn't know it wasn't a "real" Beatle album. They listened to it, engaged with it, and loved it. The album added Beatleness to their daily lives and relationships:

My grandfather loved "I'll Follow the Sun." He used to ask me to play it. Male, b. '50

My older sister had *Beatles '65*. She got home from school much later than I did. I would go into her room and put it on. I especially remember "I'm a Loser" and "I'll Follow the Sun." I would listen until she got home. Female, b. '55

Beatles '65 was the first album I bought with my own money. I remember when I put it on and heard "This happened once before, when I came to your door." It sounded amazing. It melted me. Female, b.'56

I asked my mother what "whim" meant after hearing the word in "Baby's in Black." Female, b. '56

In with the New: 1965

Fans remained constantly exposed to the Beatles throughout the fall and winter of 1964 and into the new year. "Eight Days a Week" b/w "I Don't Want to Spoil the Party" was released in mid-February; it hit number one two weeks later and held the position for nine weeks. Fans remember being wowed by the A-side's distinctive fade-in intro, and they remember parents and DJs talking about the "drink or two" lyric on the B-side.

A month later, *The Early Beatles* was released, an album with songs previously released on Vee-Jay Records. A month after that came another single, "Ticket to Ride" b/w "Yes It Is." Fans noticed the more sophisticated themes:

These were no longer just love and breakup songs; they were emotionally sophisticated; more adult but still catchy. I remember singing it in the car with my cousin. My aunt wanted us to sing it again and again. Female, b. '55

There were complaints from parents about the line: "living with me." I listened to the words. It didn't sound bad to me, but it made me more aware. Male, b. '50

In addition to the more "grown-up" lyrics, "Ticket to Ride" and "Eight Days a Week" also had a different sound. One male fan, age ten at the time, remembers, "I loved the tonal quality, the chimey, trebly, guitar sound on 'Ticket to Ride' and 'Eight Days a Week.' I didn't care about the lyrics."

Fans also noticed the printed words "From the United Artists Release *Eight Arms to Hold You*" on the familiar orange-and-yellow swirl label. Another Beatle movie was on the way!

"Eight Days a Week" is an upbeat, clever expression of love and happiness. The handclaps add to the authenticity of the feeling, like audible jumps for joy. It's a happy little story. "Ticket to Ride," in contrast, opens with the words, "I think I'm gonna be sad," over a one-chord drone. It continues in a weary plod, shuffles a bit in the middle and then starts the weary plod again.

The parents, adults, and other "establishment" types who didn't like the "living with me" line—presumably because they thought it implied and therefore advocated sex without marriage—didn't hear the song through fans' ears. They didn't notice the useful and validating information—useful for men, validating for women. In this story, a woman is unhappy in a relationship because she doesn't feel free. Perhaps the weariness of the vocal is that of a man trying to adapt to a changing world, a world where women want to be free. Maybe he's grappling with his willingness or ability to change.

There was an uncharacteristically long three-month gap between the singles "Ticket to Ride" and "Help!," during which *Beatles VI* was released. The album hit number one a month later, and held the position for six weeks. It was another one of those early Capitol collections that entered and altered the hearts and minds of American fans: "I remember I bought *Beatle VI* in stereo and played it on the big Magnavox console in the living room. I played it for my parents, who were into music. I asked them if this wasn't the best thing they ever heard" (Female, b. '56).

A constant flow of new Beatle music, played in heavy rotation on the radio, created a spring '65 echo chamber, though it was not quite as intense as that of '64. And unlike '64, the songs that preceded and followed the Beatles on the radio also had newer sounds and were more interesting.

In *British Invasion*, Barry Miles points out that more than a quarter of the songs on the *Billboard* Hot 100 were British as 1965 began. But even more dramatic is that 48 percent of the number one songs that year were by British artists—a third of them Beatle songs. The year before, in the Beatles' breakthrough year, British artists represented only 39 percent of number one songs, but a third were Beatle songs. The Beatles maintained their high-profile presence on American radio, even as their fellow countrymen flooded the airwaves.[7]

Beatle fans were listening to other bands too, and buying their records. Twenty percent of the number one songs in 1965 were Motown artists. The Supremes, especially, continued to give the Beatles serious competition at the top of the charts, as "Eight Days a Week" lost the number one position to "Stop in the Name of Love."

Yet the sequence of songs occupying the number one spot in spring '65 also shows increasing diversity in the music entering the consciousness of young radio listeners. After knocking the Beatles out of the number one spot for the second time, the Supremes surrendered the position to the trivial British band Freddie and the Dreamers' "I'm Telling You Now." Another British band, the Mindbenders, followed with "The Game of Love"—a song definitely not about holding hands—that held the spot for three weeks.

Record buyers kept it very British but much more innocent when they made Herman's Hermits' "Mrs. Brown You've Got a Lovely Daughter" number one for three weeks. From this second hit forward, all future Hermit hits would feature the same exaggerated British accent. "Ticket to Ride" displaced Mrs. Brown and her "luvly daughter" on May 22, but the Beatles were displaced a week later by the Beach Boys' "Help Me Rhonda," starting a stretch of American artists in the number one spot, including the Supremes, the Four Tops, and the Byrds' breakthrough cover of Dylan's "Mr. Tambourine Man"— heralding the arrival of folk rock and bringing Dylan's imagery and ideas to a young mass audience.

The stretch of American artists in the number one position was broken by the very British and very audacious "(I Can't Get No) Satisfaction," which held the position for four weeks, despite bans in several cities. Thirteen months after the Rolling Stones' debut on American television and two months after their second *Sullivan* appearance, young American record buyers were finally paying serious attention to the group. At the time, *Newsweek* called the Stones a "leering quintet" and said "Satisfaction" was full of "tasteless themes." And while Otis Redding and others have said they couldn't make out the words, this young woman, and many others, heard the words just fine: "I remember when 'Satisfaction' came out. When the girl told him, 'Baby, better come back maybe next week 'cause you see I'm on a losing streak,' we wondered if this was about the woman having her period. It was pretty shocking" (Female b. '45).

According to Mick Jagger, "it was the song that . . . changed us from just another band into a huge, monster band. . . . It has a very catchy title. It has a very catchy guitar riff. It has a great guitar sound, which was original at that time. And it captures a spirit of the times . . . which was alienation."[8]

Four weeks of "Satisfaction" at number one was quite an earful for young radio listeners. The social commentary and titillating lyrics were ousted from the number one spot by the most trite and the most British of all the Invasion hits, Herman's Hermits' "I'm Henry the VIII, I Am," a British music hall song dating from 1911, which front man Peter Noone learned from his Irish grandfather. The very American Sonny and Cher displaced Herman and Henry after a week, and their breakthrough "I Got You Babe" held the position for three weeks—making it the first number one record in two months to feature a female voice.

Top 40 radio was becoming more diverse and more challenging for young listeners. Even the last three Beatle singles were weightier and required more work. But Dylan's "Like a Rolling Stone" was heavier still. At a little over six minutes, the confrontational folk-rock opus was startling for a number two hit and presented young listeners with what music critic and Dylan expert Andy Gill described as "a vicious tirade of recrimination."[9] Radio listeners previously unaware of or disinterested in Dylan were intrigued by the song's powerful statement, though the substance of the statement remained unclear.

Seven Songs

The *Help!* soundtrack was released in mid-August, two weeks after the movie opened. The record included twelve songs, only seven of which were Beatle songs—and two of those were previously available as 45s. Fans were paying for an album but getting only five new songs. One fan recalls: "I thought my *Help!* album was lacking after my pen pal in the UK told me what was on her album. I felt a little cheated, and I became aware that they were marketing to us. My friend and I wrote letters to the fan club about it" (Female, b. '56).

Fans may have been disappointed by the number of new Beatle songs on the *Help!* soundtrack, but they saved their pennies to buy it and made it the number one album in the country for nine weeks: "I finally had enough money to purchase my very first Beatle album, the soundtrack from *Help!* My parents took me to the store to buy it. I get up to the register and when the cashier rang me up I was three cents short. Thank goodness my father showed up, dipped into his pocket and produced the pennies!" (Female, b. '54).

It's not clear how much attention fans paid to the five cuts from Ken Thorne's *Help!* film score, but it would likely have been their first encounter with sitar music. Several well-known Beatle songs are done in the Indian raga style, foreshadowing not only "Norwegian Wood" but also "Within You Without You."

New Sentiments

Elaine Tyler May, now a history professor at the University of Minnesota, was in high school in 1964 and remembers how female fans heard Beatle songs. "Every girl wanted to be treated the way their songs indicated they would treat them. There was a sweetness and gentleness in their view of women and romance."[10] Girls listened to the music, too, but May's observation is consistent with what I heard in the fan interviews. In general, girls seem to have paid more attention to the lyrics than boys did—perhaps getting a fuller experience.

Female fans were, to some extent, socialized by these lyrics, forming ideas and expectations about the kind of men they want to be with, how they want to be treated, and how they might expect to be treated. The Beatles showed male and female fans how intelligent, sensitive, and articulate men think about women. Several songs on *Help!* are poignant in this regard.

"You're Going to Lose That Girl" has a distinctly Beatle sound, yet sounds like nothing that came before. The harmonies, the melody, and the poetry are all new—and so is the sentiment. The song's little story is similar to "She Loves You"—a male friend giving advice to another friend. But this time, female fans heard the Beatles delivering an ultimatum on their behalf. The music in the story, the energy of the layered production, the spine-tingling weaving and counterpoint in the vocals, and the unusual percussion are a world away from the music accompanying the "She Loves You" story.

The male and female roles in "The Night Before" reverse the usual scenario in pop music. It's basically a man asking, "Will You Still Love Me Tomorrow?" Like several McCartney lyrics, it comments on love's fleeting nature catching one by surprise. The guitar riff on the break sounds like these two people conversing, and the background vocals repeating "the night before" are almost taunting.

"Another Girl" is an "I'm breaking up with you because I met someone else" song. It speaks to male fickleness. He's honest and direct with Girl Number 1, perhaps excessively so, as he sings the praises of Girl Number 2, who, with her many talents, will be his friend through thick and thin. Referring to women as "friends" is almost a Lennon-McCartney trademark. A male fan, age twelve at the time, recalls, "I took solace in that 'I found someone better' attitude. I wanted to sing it to a girl who wouldn't give me the time of day."

And It's in Color!

Fans didn't know the Beatles were high on pot during most of the filming of *Help!,* or that it was filmed in the Bahamas so they could explore tax shelters—it was another Beatle movie and it was in color!

A female fan, age eleven at the time, remembers when her mother took her to see *Help!* A year and a half after the first gush of Beatlemania, the Beatles continue to be a force in fans' childhoods and are still affecting family dynamics: "I had been a bad girl in school and had to write two hundred times, 'I will not talk at school,' but I had no notebook paper so we went to the store. *Help!* was playing at the drive-in near the store. We pulled out of the parking lot and into the drive-in theater so I could see *Help!* Mom said, 'Don't tell your father I'm keeping you out late on a school night!' I remember *Blue Hawaii* playing first, then *Help!* So while Elvis was on the screen, I was writing my homework on the dashboard of the car."

Inevitably, fans compared *Help!* to *A Hard Day's Night*—at the time and when talking about them in the present. Fans loved the color, the "travelogue" quality, and the music, though overall they liked *A Hard Day's Night* better.

But even if some fans weren't thrilled with *Help!*, they were all struck, yet again, by the Beatles' obvious affection for each other and the strong bond between them. The Beatles were also not thrilled with *Help!* and derisively referred to it as another "buddy movie"—but that was a large part of its appeal.

Male and female fans enjoyed watching the Beatles interact with each other; they liked looking at their friendship on the big screen and seeing the creative and protective energy that connected them. Fans imagined having close friends or siblings with whom they could mind meld in the same way:

The camaraderie struck me again—the interaction and love between them; their brotherly affection for each other was beautiful. My mom pitted my sister and me against each other. But they seemed like siblings with no rivalry, only pure love for each other. Female, b. '49

They had a camaraderie like my older brother and his friends from the naval academy. Male, b. '52

I loved the feeling of them as a family. I thought that was how they lived. Female b. '53

The Beatles' absurd living situation in the film—four separate doors leading to one space—played with and ultimately confirmed the viewer's sense of the Beatles as "buddies" or brothers. Their efforts to protect Ringo and their general "us against the world" approach added to this impression. The greater vulnerability expressed in the songs contributed to it as well. Buddy movie, perhaps; but there was something new about the way these men interacted with each other and with the rest of the world—with humor, affection, colorful clothes, and long hair. They were a new breed of buddy—at least on the screen.

John acknowledged in the seventies that the song *Help!* was autobiographical; that he was in his "fat Elvis period," overwhelmed with fame and not sure who he was or what he wanted. Paul, Ringo, George, and others in John's inner circle said they were unaware at the time that the song was, literally, a cry for help. Fans, however, were a little more tuned in:

> I remember thinking it wasn't a boy-meets-girl song and hearing what sounded like an honest cry for help. I assumed whoever was singing was the writer, and I wondered what John could be so upset about. He seemed to have a fabulous life. It made me like him more because he wasn't perfect. Female, b. '55

> At my elementary school there was a big parking lot with boulders around it. Someone had a car radio on blasting "Help!" and we were listening, jumping from boulder to boulder, wondering why John Lennon would feel down. It made me realize that the adult world was more complicated. Female, b. '61

The title song is one of seven they "perform" during ninety minutes of pop-infused silliness. Fans recall being "blown away" by the music:

> I remember liking the comedy, but what impressed me most was the songs. "You've Got to Hide Your Love Away," "You're

Gonna Lose That Girl," "Help!," and the others were so naturally melodious, and the lyrics were interesting. Male, b. '59

Help! was a quantum leap from *A Hard Day's Night*—in the close-ups you could see their technique and learn how to play the songs. Male, b. '51

Fans of all ages liked the tongue-in-cheek humor and remember finding some lines in the film hilarious. Phrases like "I can say no more" and "Go to the window" found their way into conversation. And "fiendish thingies" suddenly entered fans' lives. John's pit bed and Paul using a woman's body as a guitar were fondly remembered.

Older fans recall the film as "well-made but kind of corny" (Male, b. '51), with a "dopey" story and "bad comedy" (Male, b. '48). Fans used words like "gimmicky" and "contrived." One said it was "less exciting because it was fabricated to put them on the screen." Similarly, another said the Beatles didn't look as comfortable on the screen as in *A Hard Day's Night*.

Help! was a comic book that read itself to fans while they watched and listened to the Beatles. It presented a colorful gadget-filled world, both supermodern and surreal. A world where it makes sense to wake someone up by calling them on a telephone from across a large room and playing an alarm clock into the phone. Wind-up toy teeth cut the indoor grass. The Beatles' clothes are torn off and they're knocked off their feet by an aggressive bathroom hand dryer—one of several instances of gadgetry run amok. The intelligent silliness and stylish physical humor were engaging for viewers of any age.

Like *A Hard Day's Night*, it moves nonstop and the viewer doesn't know what to expect as the Beatles frolic through absurd situations saturated with color and frivolity. Both films required close attention. And both films allowed fans to get a close look at the Beatles' facial expressions, hair, and clothes. Several fans remember noticing that they were dressing more individually; fewer ties, more turtlenecks, John's bright red shirt. And this was the first time fans saw them in "play clothes"—faded jeans and T-shirts.

The question of whether fans perceived the Beatles as "kids" or "adults" came up again in a conversation about *Help!* with a male fan who first saw it at age nine: "I was surprised to see them drink beer in the movie. It violated my sense of them, because only grown men drink beer. It bothered me a little. I didn't want them to be grown up."

Both Beatle films opened fans' eyes to new points of view, literally and metaphorically. Comparisons with *A Hard Day's Night* are inevitable, and *Help!* is easily dismissed when not considered on its own terms. *Help!* gave most fans their first experience with the pop-art aesthetic and early mod style. It showcased cutting-edge British music, fashion, and art, and parodied the very British and gadget-filled James Bond films.

The seven songs in the film were a new kind of Beatle song, presented in visually compelling ways—the "Ticket to Ride" sequence with the four changing faces viewed through a rotating ski pole, their black coats against the blue-white snow, Paul viewed in close-up along the neck of his bass. Any number of moments throughout the film invited young viewers to feast on sounds and images that were completely new and completely fun.

The language used by the reviewer at *Time* suggests the film is more psychedelic than pop or surreal: "the color camera dances in and out of focus, zooms up and away, tilts with the music, splashes light like liquid, and cuts so fast from this to that that the effect is almost subliminal."[11] It's not clear what effect he is talking about, but, while sitting there happy and alert, taking in all the color and music and wackiness, fans saw the contrast between the Beatles and the inept authorities, just as they did in *A Hard Day's Night*.

Even when being stalked by cultists and mad scientists, the Beatles are more powerful and more in control than anyone around them. They are funny and clever, clown-like even, as they address the problem at hand with more intelligence than the people helping them.

John and Paul standing on either side of the seated Scotland Yard chief, in their Carnaby Street attire, snooping around and commenting on the items on his desk, asking about the unsolved Great Train Robbery, is a powerful moment in the film. Young people might not have understood all the banter, but they could see the intergenerational tension between the "famous Beatles" and the "famous Scotland Yard"—the same tension they were starting to hear in the pop music they were paying so much attention to.

Bosley Crowther of the *New York Times* said the film was "ninety crowded minutes of good clean insanity" in which "preposterousness is rampant." To avoid "being injured by mobs of young females and floods of mail," Crowther said he chose his words carefully when calling the Beatles' humor "insane."[12] He shows, with gratuitous condescension toward female fans, the same superficiality and lack of insight he showed in his review of *A Hard Day's Night*. He didn't see that the film's irreverence and the Beatles' attitude are what the film was ultimately about. But fans did: "I saw *Help!* a bunch of times. It was fun; I loved how cool they looked. They were rebellious, different from everyone else. John and George, especially, were irreverent; smart-ass" (Male, b. '51).

The Toppermost

Prior to the Beatles, no entertainer's management team had to plan and execute tours of Beatle magnitude—with security requirements and layers of logistics previously undertaken only by governments.

The fifty-five thousand fans drawn to New York's Shea Stadium on August 15, 1965, was the largest audience ever assembled for a concert. The event was a turning point for the American entertainment industry and for the collective power of rock and roll. Fans in attendance "had never seen anything like it" and knew they were "part of history": "When I recall my childhood, it's one of the first things I think of. It was a privilege to be there. People were elated; the excitement was overwhelming. Women were in tears; girls were taking their clothes off. And after, the streets were electrified: the honking, the mobs, the singing. I didn't realize how much they meant to so many people until I saw it" (Female, b. '55).

Walking from train stations and parking lots, sharing bus rides and binoculars, fans met other fans, and lifelong friendships began—foreshadowing the connections and friendships that would start at The Fest for Beatle Fans, an annual event that would commence nine years later.

Back to School with The Beatles

Fans of all ages could hear the Beatles evolving by fall of 1965, but younger fans still enjoyed playing Beatles make-believe. After a summer of Beatle immersion, including a new movie, this male fan, back in school and a third-grader at the time, recalls: "We had some toy guitars, so we took some construction paper and made electric guitars and taped them to the toy guitars; someone banged on something for a drum and we mimed the Beatles for a class party, singing 'Help!' and 'I'm Down.' The kids really liked it."

On September 12, 1965, nineteen months after the Beatles entered American consciousness, they were back on the *Ed Sullivan Show*.[13] By this point, the Beatles were major potheads. They still wore suits and they still bowed after their performance, but they were a little shaggier. They seemed older, wiser, and a little world-weary—though their more mature appearance didn't stop the star-struck Sullivan from making the same patronizing comments he'd made a year and a half before.

Their first set consisted of three songs: "I Feel Fine," the single released ten months earlier; "I'm Down," the B-side of the "Help!" single released in July, and "Act Naturally," the B-side of Paul's tour de force, "Yesterday," which would be debuted in the second set.

Just as their look was subtly evolving, so was the music. "I Feel Fine" opened with feedback—a sound that was not previously understood as music. "I'm Down" was an original raucous rocker, clearly inspired by the songs they used to cover. Again, fans saw the pure fun the Beatles were having on stage.

There were fewer audience shots than during their February '64 *Sullivan* appearance. But more importantly, the songs have a distinctly, yet subtly different feel than the ones they first performed on that stage. The second set opened with "Ticket to Ride," featured in the film *Help!* but released six months earlier. George then introduces a song "featuring just Paul," and viewers hear "Yesterday" for the first time. The song is beautiful but sad; Paul is beautiful but sweaty. With some silliness and shtick, John introduces the final song, "Help!"—an upbeat rocker expressing emotional pain and vulnerability.

The Beatles' final set is followed by another memorable Anacin commercial that dramatizes the tension under the happy veneer of suburban life: A husband barks, "Helen, I just came in, don't rush me," in response to his wife's reminder about a PTA meeting. There was a similar Anacin ad on TV at the time, in which an adult daughter lashes out at her mother, shouting, "Mother, please, I'd rather do it myself." These were still the early days of pharmaceutical advertising, indoctrinating a generation into the idea that there's a pill to cure every discomfort of modern living—a theme that would be addressed in two top ten hits over the next two years.

Nineteen months into their relationship with the Beatles, American fans continued to find them captivating, though the foursome didn't seem quite as buoyant as they did during their first *Sullivan* appearances. They continued to delight fans, but in ways that were a bit more subtle and complicated. The moptops had morphed into something else.

The simplicity of "Yesterday" and the gravitas created by the lighting and the intraband introduction was new, too. The sparse instrumentation—solo acoustic guitar—was not like rock and roll. The lyrics were sad and complicated, with a wisdom and sensibility that seemed far beyond the years of the young man who wrote them. Fans too young to understand or even think about the adult themes in "Yesterday" could hear and feel the song's beautiful weight. It made the Beatles seem more authoritative. The song served the same function "Till There Was You" served on the band's American debut. Parents liked it and happily made the Beatles part of the family:

I remember Paul McCartney singing "Yesterday" on the *Ed Sullivan Show*. I watched it at a family birthday party with lots of aunts, uncles, and cousins and I remember my uncle commenting, "Boy, this kid is so talented!" Male, b. '56

My mother and my aunt picked me up from school. As we pulled up in front of our house, my mother jumped out of the car and ran into the house. I didn't know what was going on. My aunt said that my mother had to go to the bathroom really bad! Then my aunt was stalling for time, talking about what color nylons I had on, trying to keep me from going into the house. When I finally got inside I heard "Yesterday" playing on the record player. My mom had bought it that day and was playing it for me. I just screamed and hugged her. Female, b. '54

"Yesterday" was released the day after the *Sullivan* broadcasts. Good planning. Three weeks later, it was the number one record in the country, and it held that position for four weeks before being ousted by "Get Off of My Cloud," which held the position for two weeks. The contrast between the two songs is stunning, capturing the contrast between the Stones' and the Beatles' sounds and images at the moment, and showing the extremes of music and message that were going into young people's ears and minds.

Looking closely at the flow and timing of Beatle product, and how the product was coordinated with tours, films, and TV appearances, one is awed by the engineering. No band had ever been as talented or as big, in so expansive a media environment, with so large a potential market. Capitol and EMI were in uncharted territory, reacting to the Beatles success as it unfolded—still seeing them as cash cows, not artists.

The Beatles' annoyance at being asked "How long do you think this will last?" was quite justified, and while they may or may not have given the question much thought, Capitol and EMI surely did. Their goal was to sell as much product as possible, and they didn't know how long the demand would last. Unfortunately, they viewed the product as chunks of widgets, and deftly figured out how to package the widgets to meet that goal. Considering the unprecedented scale they were working on, their marketing and promotion people deserve to be admired for their quick thinking. Their exploitation of American fans was nothing short of brilliant, but they distorted fans' understanding of the Beatles development as artists.

As illustrated by the fan quoted above with her "deficient" *Help!* album, fans were starting to become aware—through a pen pal, a record store selling imports, or a gift from a traveling relative—that there were different Beatle albums for the American market, a practice that ended with *Sgt. Pepper*. The albums first-generation fans knew and loved were lost with the switch to digital music until Capitol released *The Capitol Albums* in 2004 and the *US Albums* in 2014—enticing fans to buy them again, and again.

Animated Moptops

The fall '65 TV season reflected what was happening in the world and in film. As the Cold War hummed along in the background, not quite drowned out by the sound of music, the spy comedy *Get Smart* debuted. The gadgets, absurd humor, and Agent 99's mod outfits shared a sensibility with *Help!*, both drawing heavily on Bond films. *The Man From UNCLE*, a more conventional approach to espionage, was beginning its second season, and Scottish-born David McCallum, the show's Russian-born Illya Kuryakin, had become a *16* magazine heartthrob. Meanwhile, on the Flintstones' season opener, famous manager Eppy Brianstone turned a singing Pebbles and Bam Bam into an overnight sensation.

The Beatles were exploring drugs, evolving artistically, and changing in ways that would make them less accessible to their youngest fans, yet this was the moment they were transformed into cartoon characters and became Saturday morning entertainment for children.

Each episode of the *Beatle Cartoons* featured two story segments and a sing-along segment for which viewers were encouraged, by the forever moptop Beatle characters, to follow the words on the screen and sing along—just like the "follow the bouncing ball" cartoons fans watched when they were younger.

The youngest fans, preschoolers when the Beatles came, enjoyed the cartoons and "watched them for as long as they were on"; some older fans found the voices so wrong as to be "annoying"—but many watched them anyway. By the time *Yellow Submarine* came along three years later, fans were accustomed to the Beatles as cartoon characters.

The youngest fans I interviewed, born in 1961, don't remember a pre-Beatle world, but their earliest Beatle memories are the cartoons. The series was very popular, turning millions of toddlers and preschoolers into lifelong fans.

The show's creators, the network, the sponsors, and of course the Beatles all made money on the series which, while not without some artistic merit—after all, it did include Beatle songs—was cynically exploitative of its young viewers.

Most Excellent

When fans scoured newspapers for items about the Beatles in October 1965, they found a picture of the four Beatles in a row, dressed in dark suits, their hair longer than fans had ever seen it. They were holding up the medals they'd just received at their investiture into The Most Excellent Order of the British Empire. Their international success and the British Invasion that followed had made "a substantial contribution to the balance of trade," or as George put it, "After all we did for Great Britain, selling all that corduroy and making it swing, they gave us that bloody old leather medal with wooden string through it."[14]

Many World War II veterans returned their medals in protest, evoking the opening scene in *A Hard Day's Night,* when the elderly commuter tells them he "fought the war for your sort" and Ringo counters with "I bet you're sorry you won."

The protest against the Beatles MBEs, like the dialogue on the train, speaks to the growing conflict between youth and the older generation, a conflict embedded in the now iconic image of the Beatles with their medals. The photo also captures the unique and enormous power the Beatles had at that moment. Lennon might have gone momentarily insane looking up at the Shea crowd, but he also, as he told Sid Bernstein, "saw the top of the mountain."[15]

The MBE photo presents contradiction and instability. It freezes a fleeting moment of incipient change. The freedom symbolized by the hair makes their suits seem all the more confining; now it's the suits that look silly, not the hair.

For the Youngsters

The new season of *Shindig!* and *Hullabaloo* provided young music fans with a never-ending parade of British and American pop bands performing familiar hits, introducing their next hit, or both. These shows were the first "must-see TV." Young music fans wanted to be able to talk with their friends about the songs, the bands, the dancers, and the fashion.

The Who made their American debut on *Shindig!* in October, performing "I Can't Explain," with the Union Jack prominently displayed behind them. Though often associated with the early Invasion, The Who didn't have their first hit, "Happy Jack," until June '67—the same week the Beatles released *Sgt. Pepper*.

The Kinks also appeared on *Shindig!* in October, and performed "Who'll Be the Next in Line" and "See My Friends," wearing ruffled shirts, extremely tight pants, and very long hair. Though neither song became a hit, the Kinks were developing a strong base of fans who liked the band's heavy guitar sound and androgynous mod style. As one male fan (b. '55) said, "The Kinks had an edge we couldn't articulate at the time." The Eastern-influenced, proto-psychedelic "See My Friends" presented viewers with a taste of things to come.

That same month, *Hullabaloo* guest host Jerry Lewis introduced Barry McGuire, who performed his nihilistic newsreel "Eve of Destruction," which was number one in the country at the time, despite being banned by many radio stations across the country.[16] [17]

Lewis told the young audience the "song has a lot of important things to say about the way we grown-ups are running the world" and was an example of how "a song can be popular and also have an important message." McGuire sang with anger and anguish, clad in colorless, caveman casual, against a dystopian backdrop.

The Byrds, often referred to at the time as "the American Beatles," made several appearances on these programs, performing Dylan songs and earning their recognition as the originators of folk rock. During their fall '65 *Hullabaloo* performance of "The Times They Are A-Changin,'" Jim McGuinn, with unruly, truly moptop hair and suit jacket, looked over the rims of his tinted, rectangle granny glasses right into American living rooms and told parents, "Your sons and your daughters are beyond your command." His facial expression said, "Deal with it." The image evoked the same conflict and instability as the Beatles posing with their MBEs.

McGuinn later said, "I feel like there's some sort of guerilla warfare, psychological warfare going on, and I feel like a guerilla. I feel good."[18] Many parents didn't realize that it was impossible to allow the Kinks, the Byrds, and Barry McGuire into their living rooms and not expect their children to be affected by it.

Hullabaloo and *Shindig!* were on the air because ABC and NBC knew they could make money selling music fans' eyeballs and eardrums to advertisers. But they didn't realize the extent to which the artists and performers presented on these shows were sparking viewers' imaginations, presenting them with new ideas and new questions.

Increasingly, popular music was offering young people new ways of thinking about the world and their place in it. These TV shows were yet another regular source of messages empowering young people to throw off what they were coming to see as excessive and unnecessary restrictions in their lives. It would get easier to leave the house in a short skirt or stretch out the weeks between haircuts, and students around the country would risk arrest as they called for free speech on campuses nationwide.

As 1965 drew to a close, young people saw race riots on TV, along with their favorite music. Their brothers and other young men they knew were among the over two hundred thousand soldiers fighting and dying in Vietnam. The war was escalating, despite early reports indicating that the US was losing.[19] The first of many demonstrations against the war took place in Washington, DC. Many of the young men at the demonstration had long hair.

Fans heard the Beatles and other pop music becoming more diverse and more complicated, giving fans more to think about, more to enjoy, more to play, and more to talk about. Of course, people other than fans were talking about the Beatles, too.

Reverend David Noebel, founder of Summit Ministries, published a pamphlet titled *Communism, Hypnotism, and the Beatles: An Analysis of the Communist Use of Music,* in which he said the Beatles are "a Communist plot to jam the nervous systems of young people," and that America needed to make sure "four mop-headed Anti-Christ beatniks don't destroy our children's emotional and mental stability and ultimately our nation."[20] Though paranoid and ignorant, Noebel recognized something profound.

As the year of the pop music renaissance drew to a close, the Beatles were about to release a new album. By now, fans had come to expect the unexpected:

It was fun to see what the next album was going to be like. You didn't know what to expect but you knew you'd like it. It was the Beatles. Male, b. '53

CHAPTER FOUR

The Embodiment of Cool

December 1965–January 1967

If people didn't like the Beatles, you didn't want to be around them.

Female, b. '47

AFTER A YEAR OF NEW BANDS, new sounds, and more substantive lyrics, the Beatles upped the ante with *Rubber Soul*, a mind-boggling year-end treat.

Despite Capitol's distortion of the Beatles' musical progression, fans could hear and see them evolving in various ways. A female fan, age ten at the time, remembered, "Just when you thought you knew them and had a sense of them, it would be something new." But the leap from *Help!* to *Rubber Soul* seemed quantum in every way. Their look and sound had an unexpected level of sophistication, and the lyrics spoke of man-meets-woman rather than boy-meets-girl. Many of these changes were foreshadowed in *Help!*, but *Rubber Soul* brought them into full flower. Even the youngest fans were engrossed and open: "My perception of them was changing; I was changing too, realizing the complexity of people, and that the Beatles weren't always happy-go-lucky. It was strange, but you listened" (Female, b. '56).

Before even getting to the music, fans were intrigued by the "weird," "cool" cover, which said "The Beatles" on the back only. Legend has it that the image was the serendipitous result of the cardboard projection surface slipping out of place while the Beatles were viewing photographer Robert Freeman's proofs. But the band's enthusiastic embrace of the distorted image may also owe something to the fish-eye lens photograph on the Byrds' debut album, *Mr. Tambourine Man*, released the previous June.

The album's title—a clever variation on an old blues man referring to the Rolling Stones as "plastic soul"—appeared in "bubble letter" typeface designed to look like liquid rubber. The design had an immediate influence on poster art of the period and continued to influence typographic design for decades.

The Beatles' look, from the very beginning, communicated something new and important and continued to be an essential element of the whole Beatle package for male and female fans of all ages. They vividly remember the first time they saw this new iteration of the Beatles:

I was at my cousin's lake house. It was late at night and we were sitting around the bonfire. We were listening to it over and over, looking at the cover. It was very different. Male, b. '53

I got *Rubber Soul* for my eleventh birthday. The cover blew my mind, the image and the graphics; I sensed that it was different, something about that dripping image. Female, b. '55

One female fan, age sixteen at the time, said, "The cover struck me as very sensual; they looked grown up and sexy." Another female fan, age nine at the time, remembers looking at it and trying to decide "who was the most handsome" and which one she'd want to go out with when she was "a little older."

The Beatles' hair, especially, remained a focus and still seemed significant in a way that was hard to put into words. Male fans, especially, took notice of the hair:

I was at a party and *Rubber Soul* was playing over and over and over. It was the first time I heard it or saw the cover. I noticed their hair was longer and they weren't dressed identically. Male, b. '50

I remember staring at the cover and looking at their hair. I thought they were the coolest guys in the world. They seemed so sure of themselves. Male, b. '56

A few fans remember being startled and reacting negatively to the Beatles new appearance and to the image as a whole: "I didn't care for the cover. I found it scary, difficult, unpleasant. They looked menacing, like they were looking down on a victim. They looked like wooly mammoths, brown and leathery" (Female, b. '54).

Even fans who found the cover off-putting could not resist what they heard when the needle hit the record. At only thirty minutes, the experience was brief but stunning. It was so satisfying, they wanted to repeat it again and again. One female fan (b. '48) recalls, "I memorized it in a weekend." Another, eight years younger, said, "I played *Rubber Soul* in my room, over and over and over until I knew it."

Listening Closely

Rubber Soul, with its complicated variations on familiar themes, new ideas, ambiguous meaning, and "instruments we'd never heard before," kept fans listening closely even after incessant play. Indeed, "close listening" began with *Rubber Soul*. It also differed from other Beatle albums in that it was recorded with minimal reverb, making it sound more intimate and less "noisy," as though they were right there with you, singing into your ear. Vocals that seemed more present combined with newly sophisticated lyrics meant that fans of all ages "started paying more attention to the lyrics with *Rubber Soul*."

Listening to a record "over and over" was part of the Beatle fan experience from the beginning, as was listening to the lyrics. Adolescent female fans had come to appreciate lyrics with pronouns carefully chosen to facilitate fantasizing about being with a Beatle. The more substantive lyrics on *Rubber Soul* were seen as a further progression from personal songs such as "I'm a Loser" and "Help!," and although the Beatles were still love objects for teenage girls, it was becoming more of a stretch to pretend they were singing to you. Now, repeated listening was not merely a matter of enjoying the songs or fantasizing. These songs required some "work."

Although the Beatles had been in the lives of American fans for less than two years, they consistently brought fans enormous pleasure, many saying "they opened my ears to music." Fans expected the Beatles to continue providing them with engaging musical experiences, and so when confronted with challenging lyrics, even the youngest listeners were happy to do "the work" because "it was the Beatles and we accepted it." As one female fan (b. '55) said, "I didn't fully grasp it, but anything they did was ok with me."

The lyrics continued to reveal, to both male and female listeners, how intelligent, sensitive men think about women, but the relationships, characters, and situations were becoming more complicated. These songs coaxed them out of their comfort zones, deepening their emotional and intellectual engagement with the Beatles, and they also gave fans of all ages more to talk about:

> Their lyrics seemed more about their personal experience. We used to talk about the songs, wondering what they were saying. Female, b. '45

> I stared at the album cover, absorbed in the music, not thinking about anything else. I tried to figure out what the songs were about. My brother played it over and over and over. I never got tired of it. It wasn't like that with other artists. Female, b. '54

Fans found the album "thrilling," whether listening alone or with friends. As one male fan (b. '53) put it, "Alone, you could play it over and over or repeat particular songs and no one would complain, and with friends, you'd get their input and discuss the songs."

Listening to "Think for Yourself," a male fan, age fifteen at the time, recalls, "It sounded like George was telling someone off and I wanted to understand it." Six years younger and listening to the same song, a female fan remembers looking up "opaque" and "rectify" in the dictionary so she could "understand the song."

Younger fans remember hearing the expression "I'm Looking Through You" and wondering what it meant. Perhaps it was "a British phrase." A male fan, age fourteen at the time, remembers liking how the song "wasn't angry but was very direct; telling you what's going on." A female fan, age nine at the time, remembers being drawn into the lyrics of "Girl": "'Fame,' 'leisure,' what does this mean? It got me thinking about relationships in a new way. It put me in an emotional frame I wasn't ready for. I didn't need to be thinking about this yet. It matured me" (Female, b. '56). A male fan, also nine at the time, wondered about the line, "A man must break his back to earn his day of leisure," and sensed that "the Beatles were telling you things you would understand eventually."

The early songs provided the youngest fans with glimpses into the world of dating and romance long before they would experience it. And although fans were maturing too, the rapid development of the Beatles lyrics widened that gap. But even fans old enough to relate to the boy-meets-girl lyrics and the introspection on *Beatles '65* and *Help!* were challenged by *Rubber Soul.* "Norwegian Wood" was especially vexing for fans of all ages:

I played it a lot, but I didn't understand it. What is he talking about sleeping in the bathtub? It was odd and interesting. Female, b. '49

I wondered why someone wouldn't have any chairs in their house, but the idea of someone sleeping in the bathtub was funny. Male, b. '55

I know I didn't understand it. All I knew was that there was some mysterious, captivating woman and that they didn't live happily ever after. Male, b. '56

Older fans reacted to the song's fairly explicit discussion of casual sex in different ways:

"Norwegian Wood" seemed risqué at the time, a guy staying over and it's time for bed. Even though he slept in the bath, it really did seem a little shocking. Female, b. '45

Whatever else it was about, "Norwegian Wood" was about sexual freedom; it exuded sexual freedom. Female, b. '46

As in the early days of Beatlemania, fans looked for legitimate reasons to bring the Beatles to school. The "cool" and "different" sitar on "Norwegian Wood" and the French lyrics on "Michelle" provided such opportunities:

In fourth grade, I had to do a social studies presentation on the culture of India, so I brought *Rubber Soul* to school and played "Norwegian Wood" for the class. Female, b. '56

I brought the words of "Michelle" to French class and asked the teacher to help me translate them. Female, b. '51

Several fans, all female, remember noticing a disconnect between the threatening lyrics of "Run for Your Life" and the positive sentiment of "The Word," making the album seem even more puzzling. Thinking about Lennon singing both songs, one female fan (b. '56) recalled, "I didn't know people could be this complicated. It was hard to reconcile." A large proportion of fans listening to the song were, in fact, "little girls." Love songs with grown-up themes stimulated the imagination, but "Run for Your Life" was a little too grown-up, too threatening.

Fans didn't know or care that the offending, homicidal line was taken from an early Elvis Presley song, "Baby, Let's Play House."[1] They were quite tuned in to all the lyrics on *Rubber Soul*, and many found this song off-putting. Years later, Lennon said it was his least favorite Beatle song and regretted writing it.[2] If anyone at the Beatle machine was concerned about millions of fans listening, in perpetuity, to John Lennon sing about murdering the object of his affections, completing the LP in time for Christmas was a higher priority.

Fans recall listening to "In My Life," and finding it "very sad" and "contemplative." Unlike some songs on the album, it was easy for young fans to understand but sounded "grown-up" nonetheless. A female fan, age eleven at the time, vividly recalls "sitting in a rocking chair in the living room, looking at the album cover, and thinking about the words to "In My Life," a song that legitimized and encouraged reflection and introspection for fans at any age.

Say The Word and Be Like Me

Fans were used to hearing the Beatles sing about love, but "The Word" was a love song of a different kind. A year and a half before the "Summer of Love" and their 1967 anthem "All You Need Is Love," the Beatles were advocating love as a universal principle, and, quite explicitly, positioning themselves as the spiritual leaders of the emerging youth movement and counterculture, announcing they are "here to show everybody the light." On behalf of the Beatles, John invites fans to "say the word" and "be like me."

Love as a universal principle is part of the Judeo-Christian heritage—there is nothing subversive or countercultural about it. In fact, some fans thought the song was about Christianity. Fans heard and considered this familiar message, now proffered by their beloved Beatles who were, as one fan put it, "starting to illuminate every part of our life" (Female, b. '55). The Beatles' power—both culturally and in the eyes and ears of fans—reached yet another new height with the release of *Rubber Soul*, and so the song's message and authority were significant.

More than just a "favorite group," fans were, increasingly, finding great personal value in what the Beatles had to say, and discovering great beauty in how they said it. Still, younger listeners knew they were "a few years behind really understanding and appreciating what the Beatles did."

With *Rubber Soul*, the Beatles came to occupy a role in fans' lives and a place in their psyches that was different from any previous fan-performer relationship. Years later, Lennon said the Beatles were merely "in the crow's nest" looking ahead at what was coming. But when writing "The Word"—on a multicolored lyric sheet and high on pot—they seem to have had a moment of megalomania that wasn't all that delusional. Fans of all ages "looked up to them and wanted to be as cool as them"; they were "the embodiment of cool."

Rubber Soul was a lot to absorb, and some fans "were not there yet." A male, sixteen at the time, remembers playing the album for friends who didn't like it, preferring the relative simplicity of earlier songs: "They were looking for 'Eight Days a Week.'" Another fan, a child of eight at the time, remembers keeping the album "at arm's length" because she didn't understand it. That said, the album went to number one in January '66 and held that position for six weeks. With its warm brown cover, acoustic, folky sound, intriguing lyrics, and intimate vocals, the American *Rubber Soul* is often mentioned as fans' favorite album.

Rubber Soul was also a hit with the press. Less than two years after summarily dismissing the Beatles, *Newsweek* called them the "Bards of Pop" and praised the album, saying the Beatles' "blend of gospel, country, baroque counterpoint and even French popular ballads" created "a style that was wholly their own," with songs "as brilliantly original as any written today."[3]

Working It Out

"We Can Work It Out" b/w "Day Tripper"—the first of several Beatles double A-sides—was released the same day as *Rubber Soul*. The number one song in the country at the time was the Byrds' "Turn, Turn, Turn," which held that position for three weeks thanks to record buyers' continued enthusiasm for the still-new hybrid genre of folk rock and a growing appetite for songs with themes other than romantic love. But some young music fans still enjoyed The Dave Clark Five and made "Over and Over" number one for a week at Christmas.

Simon and Garfunkel's "Sounds of Silence"—more folk rock— took the number one position away from the Dave Clark Five as the new year began, but "We Can Work It Out" rose to number one a week later and held the position for three weeks. It's interesting to note that just two years earlier, there was a brief moment when the band who gave the world "Over and Over" and the band who gave the world "We Can Work It Out" had comparable appeal.

After not seeing the Beatles since their September '65 *Sullivan* appearance, fans watched them on NBC's *Hullabaloo* in early January, on film, performing "We Can Work It Out" and "Day Tripper." Though these black and white films were not especially imaginative and soon seemed rather primitive, they can rightly be called the first promotional films or "videos."

One of the youngest fans I interviewed was not quite four when "We Can Work It Out" was on the radio, and distinctly remembers hearing "life is very short and there's no time . . ." every morning at the same time, and has "continuous Beatle memories from there." A song that was number one for three weeks can have a huge impact on a young person's life if it hits at a critical moment.

"We Can Work It Out" was the last of six number one singles in a row on the American charts, setting a record at the time. And it was the Beatles' eleventh number one in less than two years. Strange that they were nominated for eleven Grammy's and didn't win a single one. Stranger still to consider who did: Roger Miller's "King of the Road" was awarded best contemporary vocal performance over Paul McCartney's performance of "Yesterday," and the Statler Brothers' "Flowers on the Wall" won best contemporary performance by a group, vocal or instrumental, over the Beatles' "Help!" Grammy's egregious snub of the Beatles reveals how threatened the American music industry was by the Beatles' raising the bar and taking music—and record buyers—in new directions.

While "We Can Work It Out" is ostensibly about a romantic relationship, it can also, like "The Word," be heard as a statement of universal principles. The song's even-handedness fades with close listening, but it espouses compromise and the importance of communication for resolving conflict. What many fans would later refer to as a "Beatle philosophy" was first heard in these songs. Unusual instrumentation, such as the harmonium, prepared fans' ears for what would come later.

One of the Beatles most beloved songs, "We Can Work It Out" is a true collaboration, expressing John and Paul's different essences and essential differences. Many observers have commented on John and Paul's complementary natures, but they don't explain why this yin-yang is a critical piece of the Beatles' appeal, of "the magic," if you will.

The human brain is wired to appreciate music, and so it likely serves some evolutionary advantage, mood enhancement perhaps, or social cohesion. The integration of John and Paul's opposing essences can be heard in the lyrics, the color palette of their voices, and in the feel of the music itself, all evoking and reflecting a wider range of human emotion. Brains light up at the richness and complexity. It's neurologically pleasing.[4] It's Beatleness.

"We Can Work It Out" was heavily acoustic and featured a prominent, prototypical sixties pop tambourine. Its flip side, "Day Tripper," had a spiraling riff, a steep crescendo, and lyrics that kept fans guessing. A male fan, age ten at the time, remembered, "She took me half the way there? I had no idea what that meant." Teenage fans knew the line was sexual, but no one was quite sure what a day tripper was.

Young fans who didn't understand the words or idioms in the lyrics often heard nonsense syllables, but some tried to create meaning. A female fan, age nine at the time and unfamiliar with the phrase "one-night stand," heard the words as "She only plays where Mike stands" and wondered who Mike was.

Whether they grasped the meaning or not, fans "played the grooves off" this 45; it was a potent double-dose of what many consider the "quintessential Beatle sound."

Top 40 Diversity

Beatle fans listening to the radio in early 1966 were hearing many new bands with new sounds and were getting used to songs about things other than the standard pop song theme. Twenty years earlier, 90 percent of the songs on the hit parade were about love and romance. Ten years after that, nothing had changed. But by 1966, only 70 percent of songs were about love and romance, and the other 30 percent covered a range of topics.[5]

The Mamas and the Papas, with their sunny, intricate harmonies, had hits with "California Dreaming" and "Monday, Monday." Simon and Garfunkel followed "Sounds of Silence" with "Homeward Bound" and "I Am a Rock." Dylan had his third top ten hit with "Rainy Day Women," telling radio listeners "Everybody must get stoned." The Beach Boys had a number three hit with the West Indian folk tune "Sloop John B." Johnny Rivers tapped into ongoing James Bond and Man From UNCLE love and had a hit with "Secret Agent Man."

The Rolling Stones revealed a softer side with their chamber-pop hit "As Tears Go By"—perhaps a response to "Yesterday." Their follow-up hit, "19th Nervous Breakdown," also eschewed conventional themes but reverted to their usual berating assault. Often overlooked in the ongoing, male-dominated "Stones v. Beatles" conversation is the stark contrast in how the bands portrayed women, and gender dynamics in general, to impressionable young listeners who project themselves into these little stories.

Beatle lyrics explored the basic pop theme with greater complexity and nuance, paving the way for others to do the same. But their follow-up to "We Can Work It Out," "Nowhere Man," was their first 45 to explore different themes altogether. When fans heard the song on the radio in March '66, they didn't know that the song came to Lennon when he gave up after hours of trying to write something "meaningful and good" or that it was an autobiographical contemplation on living in the suburbs, fame, creativity, and lack of direction.[6] And most fans were not aware that beatniks had been referring to unhip people as "nowhere" for years.[7] They heard melodic Beatlemusic, with new guitar sounds and three-part harmonies. No reason to engage with heavy lyrics if you don't want to when there was all that.

But fans age ten and up do recall "trying to find meaning in the lyrics" when presented with the Nowhere Man—a character not to admire or emulate, yet still sympathetic, "like you and me." He has no opinions, is closed-minded, has no direction in life, and is not engaged in the world. The song is preachy like the "The Word," though it addresses a different set of issues.

"Nowhere Man" asked fans to look at the world around them. When they looked, they saw the escalation of a war that was dividing the country and larger and more frequent demonstrations against it. They saw National Guard troops being called out to quell race riots. They saw students demanding freedom of speech, freedom of dress, and freedom from traditional paths to "nowhere."

Adolescents are, by definition, in a state of flux and uncertainty. At the same time, their newly acquired capacity for abstract thought and moral reasoning allows them to see the world in all its complexity. They have to figure out who they are, what they value, and what their place in the world will be. American philosopher Kenneth Burke called literature "equipment for living," because it offers wisdom and common sense that people use to guide their lives. The same can be said about young people's relationship with pop music.[8] Regardless of Lennon's intended meaning and his derision of fans who look for meaning in his songs, "Nowhere Man," like many Beatle songs, was deluxe equipment for living:

> In high school I brought in lyrics to "Nowhere Man" for a modern communication course. The song just spoke to me; it's hard to explain. Like Brian Wilson's "I Just Wasn't Made for These

Times." The teen years are confusing, and this spoke to me. Male, b. '49

"Nowhere Man" touched us as teens, with our depressive thinking. The Nowhere Man is missing out; you need to listen to everything, pay attention. Male, b. '48

Top 40 songs were presenting more diverse subject matter, and folk rock brought poetry and social commentary. Traditional romantic themes were being expressed in more nuanced and explicit ways. All this new music was encouraging young people to ask questions and to use their moral reasoning skills. Beatle fans were going through the normal turmoil of growing up just as the music, and the rules, were starting to change. The "equipment for living" was becoming even more of a necessity. And it was disturbing in the way art should be.

"Nowhere Man" was still on the charts in April 1966 when *Time* appeared on the newsstands with an all black cover with the words "Is God Dead?" in large red text.[9] The gist of the cover story was that science had eliminated the need for religion to explain the natural world, making God seem unnecessary and irrelevant to people's lives. At that moment, it seemed the entire culture was singing and reading and talking about new ways of seeing the world and new ways of being.

The following week *Time*'s cover story explored "Swinging London."[10] In the two years since the Beatles became global megastars and fans became Anglophiles, London became a modern cultural center, with young artists, designers, photographers, pop stars, and entrepreneurs creating a new aesthetic—sexy, androgynous, colorful, retro, and fun—that spread to the fashion houses of Paris and to the neighborhoods of suburban America: "It set you apart to dress that way. It made you part of a fun club with a certain way of thinking; you felt free from the stodginess of the time. You could get a few guys together, form a band, play at the VFW, and wear mod clothes" (Male, b. '50).

Dylan's *Blonde on Blonde*, his third electric and final pre-accident album, was released in May '66. This double album is often viewed as Dylan's response to *Rubber Soul*, released six months earlier.[11] The two-year conversation between the Beatles and Dylan had unleashed unprecedented creative energy, fueling changes in consciousness along with changes in music. And after *Blonde on Blonde*, young men with even the most hard-to-manage hair felt freer to let it grow.

The Byrds gave their fans Dylan's words with Beatlesque music; the Beatles added some Dylan attitude and introspection to Beatlemusic. As Dylan said in 1966, "You can make all sorts of protest songs and put them on a Folkways record, but who hears them?"[12] It would have been hard to imagine, even six months earlier, that a stark, literary-infused confession of alienation and misanthropy like Simon and Garfunkel's "I Am a Rock" could be a number three hit. English teachers across the country were starting to build lessons around the words of Paul Simon and Bob Dylan.

Comparing her feelings about the Beatles and Dylan, a female fan (b. '51) recalled, "We were also listening to Dylan, but the Beatles were more of a big, fun, visceral thing, and we wanted to dance and listen to the harmonies. Dylan was a more cerebral experience."

The Mothers of Invention's experimental, double album *Freak Out* came out a week after *Blonde on Blonde*, and while it was not necessarily on the radar screen of younger Beatle fans, many older siblings and neighborhood teens were taken with the outrageous album—and introduced others to its over-the-top humor and iconoclastic take on conformity, censorship, hypocrisy, and sexual inhibition. *Mad* magazine on steroids, with sound.

Talking about the album and his band several months later, Frank Zappa said, "I am trying to use the weapons of a disoriented and unhappy society against itself. The Mothers of Invention are designed to come in the back door and kill you while you're sleeping."[13]

Zappa, not a drug user, can be credited with popularizing the term "freak out," which for him didn't mean a bad LSD trip or even an anxiety attack but rather a "process whereby an individual casts off outmoded and restricting standards of thinking, address and social etiquette in order to express creatively his relationship to his immediate environment and the social structure as a whole."[14] Notably, he refers to the music of the day as "rock," not "rock and roll." The Beatles were big admirers of Zappa, and, as with Dylan and the Beach Boys, they had a dialogue through their records.

A Psychedelic Single

In May '66 the Beatles released "Paperback Writer" b/w "Rain," their second single in a row about something other than romantic love—a theme they would not return to on a 45 until a B-side three years later. Like "Help!," "I'm a Loser," and "Nowhere Man," "Paperback Writer" had a vocal intro that called the listener to attention, as if to say, "Listen up, you're about to hear something important!" It made their communication with fans more emphatic.

The Beatles once again created short films to promote the single, but this time the production was more elaborate and self-conscious, showing a more developed understanding of what could be done with this new art form. When the films aired on the *Ed Sullivan Show,* fans saw the Beatles with slightly longer hair, cool sunglasses, and bemused demeanor. Again, these were songs unlike anything fans could have imagined:

> The first time I heard "Rain" and "Paperback Writer" I was sitting with my neighbors at their picnic table in their backyard. I remember the incredible harmonies. We played it back to back, over and over. Male, b. '54

> I remember getting "Paperback Writer" at the card store. There was a cantankerous old guy behind the counter, but he was nice to us kids when we went in to buy records. It was the soundtrack to the summer, along with The Lovin' Spoonful and Herman's Hermits. "Rain" was a little strange; we preferred "Paperback Writer." We didn't understand the lyrics and didn't care—we just went around singing it. Male, b. '55

Another male fan, age ten at the time, also "didn't know what 'Paperback Writer' was about and didn't care: It was phonetic syllables to sing with music." In contrast, a female fan, also age ten, said, "it was the first song where I really tried to figure out the words. It made me think about the craft of writing. It made me think that you could have a career as a writer and that cool people write."

Fans meandered in and out of the lyrics, sometimes hearing them as meaningless syllables, other times thinking about what the words might mean. But even fans who "couldn't care less about the lyrics" were still affected by the words. Quality song lyrics, even the most "simple," have a linguistic complexity that adds contour and interest to the very sound of the words—separate and apart from their meaning at any level. The sound of the words is a factor in the Beatles' international appeal and why preverbal children are so responsive to them. With three distinct voices weaving in and out in shifting combinations, their songs are compelling even though the words aren't clear.

After "joy," "cool" is the word that comes up most often in talking with fans about the Beatles. I asked the fan above if she could explain what "cool" might have meant to her at the time: "hip, cutting-edge, proudly on the fringe of society; very admirable." That's how many ten-year-old fans saw the Beatles. There were few things in their lives more enthralling.

Fans were intrigued by "Rain," too, but for different reasons. Once again, they were reveling in another Beatle song that was, literally, blowing their minds—overloading their brain circuitry: "I loved the drone and the lilting voice, and all the layers; it was more melodic and complicated. It had instrumentation you didn't hear in bands like Herman's Hermits" (Female, b. '56).

Fans encountered three minutes of Indian-influenced vocals and never-heard-before production effects. The Beatles were talking to them from a new soundscape, offering observations on something as utterly commonplace as how people react to the weather. The song invited fans to reflect on reality, and to see differently.

If we define a psychedelic song as one that attempts to capture or induce a state of altered consciousness as one might experience with hallucinogenic drugs, then "Rain" certainly qualifies. The record's dreamy, floating quality was created using varispeed and other new studio techniques. After an insistent, almost nagging vocal, fans hear Lennon's familiar voice singing otherworldly gibberish that still sounded vaguely like English—further playing with reality. Said one: "I had a tape recorder, so I knew it was backwards. I loved how gimmicky it was. They dared to be different once again. With them, it's like those sounds belong there, but other people couldn't do it" (Male, b. '48).

The lyrics also contribute to the psychedelic effect. On the surface, the words are simple, with an almost childlike, nursery rhyme quality; easy to learn and fun to sing. But even the youngest long-term fans—now between ages eight and eleven—with Beatle-attuned ears and sensibilities, could feel the weight and pull of other meanings.

Like "Nowhere Man," "Rain" makes a case against people who think and behave conventionally, and invites, almost pleads with the listener to consider alternatives. The song builds on the Beatles' claim, first made in "The Word," that they have special knowledge to share. Here, the focus isn't on love but on something even more basic. Through the metaphor of weather, they present fans with a complex, three-part proposition. First, they're endorsing a critical relationship with reality. Secondly, they're introducing the concept of "state of mind," and thirdly, they're telling fans they have power over it.

The song goes a little further than "Nowhere Man" in setting up an "us v. them," with fans and the Beatles on one side, and conventional thinkers or "straight society" on the other. Fans are asked to think about thinking and the connection between thought and reality. That said, many fans simply heard an "amazing" new Beatle song with cool new sounds and effects.

Several fans recall playing "Rain" for friends who found it "too strange." Fans rarely said they "didn't like" a new Beatle record they found inaccessible. Instead of rejecting it outright they said, "I wasn't ready for it." Fans trusted them.

A Trunk Full of Tunes

Beatle fans were still marveling at *Rubber Soul* when Capitol released *Yesterday and Today* in June '66, another album assembled for the US market. Fans heard only five new songs on this skimpy eleven-song collection: "If I Needed Someone" and "Drive My Car" from the *Rubber Soul* sessions eight months earlier, and three songs recorded two months earlier for what would be the "real" *Revolver*—"I'm Only Sleeping," "Dr. Robert," and "And Your Bird Can Sing." Many already owned the remaining six songs on three 45s released over the previous six months.

Like *Help!*, the appropriately titled *Yesterday and Today* asked fans to buy a new album but didn't deliver an album's worth of Beatle material new to their ears. A male fan (b. '53) recalls, "I didn't mind that I already had all the 45s. It was easier to have them all right there on the album." Like the other American albums with the same ignoble purpose, *Yesterday and Today* deepened fans' engagement with the Beatles and shortened the wait between albums.

Though the "new" material spans a six-month period of rapid artistic development, the five songs seemed cohesive in that they all had challenging lyrics and musical sophistication that extended the promise of *Rubber Soul*.

This collection of songs, beloved by fans at the time, was lost for decades after the transition to digital music, and was primarily remembered for the controversy over the original "butcher cover," which depicted the Beatles wearing butcher smocks and posing with raw meat and dismembered baby dolls. Given the exploitative nature of the album and a photograph that invited interpretation, the cover was said to be a statement about Capitol "butchering" their albums. However, no such meaning was intended. The Beatles were happy to not face yet another boring photo shoot and played along with photographer Bob Whitaker's odd request. John and Paul both liked the idea of a shocking photo, and John especially liked that it would change their image a bit.

It's been said that the band's dour, dressed-down look on the "trunk cover" expresses their reluctant acceptance of the new cover photo.

Certainly, their clothing is less coordinated than usual, but they are probably dressed in their "real" clothes: John in one of his favorite jackets, Paul looking a bit collegiate, Ringo a little fancified, and George looking bohemian in an oversized fisherman sweater.

By this time, fans were not only expecting the unexpected from the Beatles, they accepted that the unexpected might have meaning that wasn't readily apparent. Some fans didn't learn about *Yesterday and Today*'s original cover until years later, but several who remember the episode and understood the butcher cover as a criticism of Capitol records "defended them and their sense of humor." The interpretation was consistent with fans' growing perception of the Beatles as artists and, increasingly, as people who question the status quo through art.

Having first heard backward recording on "Rain" only a month before, fans heard more of John's fascination with the technique on "I'm Only Sleeping." Like "Rain," recorded less than two weeks earlier, the song is sonically and lyrically psychedelic, and positions John again as an observer of both the world outside his window and his own consciousness.

After so many recent songs that left fans clueless, this one made sense. The experience of being woken up but wanting to be left alone to sleep and dream is universal, and especially familiar to teenagers. Despite the song's strangeness, fans could relate to it. They were encouraged, again, to reflect on "states of mind" and to understand mundane experiences in new ways. They were happily engrossed, but also wondering what could possibly come next.

Sex, Drugs, and Pop

As songs on Top 40 radio started addressing more diverse themes, drug references—real or imagined—also started to appear. By the summer of 1966, some radio stations refused to play the Byrds' "Eight Miles High," Dylan's "Rainy Day Women," The Association's "Along Comes Mary," and the Stones' "Mother's Little Helper." During this same period, Paul Revere and the Raiders had a hit with their anti-drug "Kicks."[15]

Drugs were becoming part of the cultural conversation. A July 1966 article in the *New York Times* entitled "Offerings at the Psychedelicatessen" provided readers with an overview of the effects, laws, relevant jargon, and general goings-on within the drug culture.[16] Referring to marijuana as "Lady Hemp," the article notes, "Though she is a long way from acquiring respectability, a lot more people in America today are looking at her with a lot more tolerance than they used to."[17]

The 70 percent of songs on Top 40 radio that still addressed traditional themes were not only expressing more of love's complexity; they were also becoming more sexually explicit—reflecting and furthering permissive attitudes. At the same time, they depicted more egalitarian relationships, expressed more optimism about the outcome of the relationship, and rarely expressed an expectation of commitment or exclusivity.[18] In other words, the "sexual revolution" could be heard on Top 40 radio.

The "living together" implication in "Ticket to Ride" that upset parents the year before, and the "one-night stands" of "Day Tripper" earlier in the year seem quaint compared to Tommy James's "Hanky Panky" and Neil Diamond's "Cherry, Cherry"—for which those two Beatle songs and "Satisfaction" paved the way. But pop music was not completely abandoning traditional relationships. The Beach Boys' "Wouldn't It Be Nice" fantasizes about living together and the joy of spending the night together, but marriage is the unquestioned assumption. Similarly, the Hollies' jangly "Bus Stop" also mentions marriage several times.

They're Gonna Crucify Me

A little over a month after the "butcher cover" affair and less than a month before the start of their 1966 tour, the Beatles found themselves at the center of controversy when John's casual observation about the declining popularity of the church—made during an interview with the

London Evening Standard the previous March—was taken out of context and reprinted in *Datebook,* an American fan magazine.

Conservative news outlets and radio stations across the Bible Belt seized on the opportunity to, as several fans put it, "knock Lennon and the Beatles down a peg." Brian Epstein flew to the US to try to contain the controversy, but the matter wouldn't be settled until Lennon himself apologized.

A very young female fan (b. '61) recalled people talking about the comment: "I thought, 'Wow, someone famous thinks they're more popular than God.' That was fascinating to a child."

One church-going female fan (b. '45) recalls her minister talking about it: "He said the Beatles were a bad influence." As she saw it, "They were just free spirits who made you feel free and more like yourself."

Another fan (b. '49) remembers visiting family in Arkansas that summer who called Lennon "lowlife scum," but she thought what he said "made sense": "If you asked young people, would you rather go to church or a musical event, what would they say? Come on. There's no question." Another fan had a similar reaction: "Some of my girl friends didn't like it, but what he said was true. Would you stand in line for two days to take Communion? Of course not; but you'd stand in line for three days to see them" (Female, b. '48).

Though the reactionary record burnings may have been more about publicity for the radio stations than genuine outrage at what Lennon said, reaction to the comment speaks to its truth. And there was that "Is God Dead?" *Time* cover only a few months before.

The excessive umbrage over Lennon's self-evident comment, like the Grammy snub, revealed the extent to which mainstream culture felt threatened by the Beatles, even as it got giddy over them, embraced them, and unwittingly gave them the very authority it resented and feared.

In the midst of the Jesus comment controversy, "Yellow Submarine" b/w "Eleanor Rigby" was released. *Revolver,* which included both songs, was released the same day.

This new single was the fourth in eight months to capture a unique moment of artistic development. "We Can Work It Out" b/w "Day Tripper" offered boy-meets-girl pop songs with unprecedented musical and lyrical sophistication; "Nowhere Man" was a bittersweet, melodic exercise in self-loathing that fans heard as a reminder to pay attention; "Paperback Writer" and "Rain" were both significant departures from the acoustic songs the Beatles had recently been doing and introduced fans to new sounds that were, yet again, a harbinger of things to come. Lyrically, each song is intriguing in its own way, asking fans to engage with people and ideas they'd never considered.

The fourth single in this series and the final single of 1966, "Yellow Submarine" b/w "Eleanor Rigby," was a strange pairing. One song is the Beatles having fun in the studio, creating a children's song; the other is a somber, exquisitely orchestrated study in loneliness, with imagery that children found frightening. "Yellow Submarine" went to number two; "Eleanor Rigby" went to number eleven. A male fan (b.'50) remembers, "I wasn't crazy about that single, but I didn't want to put down anything they did or be negative about them."

Abracadabra!

Fans were wearing out the grooves on *Yesterday and Today* and *Rubber Soul* when *Revolver* entered their lives in August '66. A new Beatle album was always eagerly anticipated, but, now that fans could see them changing with each new release, their anticipation was enhanced by curiosity. They were awaiting a new experience, not merely a new record. Some fans would read an approximate release date in a teen magazine or newspaper and call record stores, or take a bike ride after school to see if it was in yet.

After the surprise of *Rubber Soul* and the string of 45s that followed, fans had high expectations, and couldn't wait to see and hear the next album. *Revolver* didn't disappoint on either count: "I loved looking at the cover. I looked at all the little pictures in the collage to see if there were even amounts of each of them. There wasn't anything I didn't like on the album, though I didn't understand it" (Female, b. '54).

When listening alone, fans would typically examine an album cover, flipping it over and back, reading every word on it, and studying the pictures. Klaus Voormann's drawing and collage presented fans with cutting edge visual art appropriate to the music inside, repeatedly occupying them for thirty-five minutes at a time, totaling hundreds of hours. Recalled one: "Every time I looked at it, I saw something new, even though it was just a black-and-white drawing with those eyes and little pictures in there. You could stare at it for hours" (Female, b. '51).

Several fans remember liking that there were older pictures of the Beatles in the collage; it provided continuity, and they "appreciated that the Beatles were recognizing their past." This was not the last time earlier images or sounds of the Beatles would appear in the midst of a new iteration.

Nine- to fourteen-year-old male fans especially "loved the back photo with John's paisley shirt, and the granny sunglasses" because they looked so "cool and mysterious." Fans often described Beatle music as different, but with the psychedelic *Revolver*, they started to use the word "mysterious."

Musically, *Revolver* was overall less immediately accessible to many fans, but older fans were more likely to appreciate it right away. As one female fan (b. '48) put it, "There was a different awareness in America that was reflected in *Revolver*. A lot of questioning authority, and they endorsed it. I didn't know anyone who didn't like it. It was a departure, less rock 'n' roll, more artistic."

Some older fans had to "explain their development" to friends, who at first liked only the songs that were immediately accessible. But even those who needed some time "knew it was cool" and "interesting," and they "liked that the Beatles were taking risks." Some found it "difficult," but they "listened to it a lot and got to know it." As one male fan (b. '56) said, "Anything they did was acceptable because it was them. I never rejected anything they did."

Fans were quickly grabbed by the count in and coughing at the opening of "Taxman," a song whose subject matter, many recall thinking, was a strange thing for the Beatles to be singing about; it was "very grown-up." The clever tit-for-tat lyrics were amusing and interesting even if you didn't understand the first thing about taxes. Several remember wondering who Mr. Wilson and Mr. Heath were—and were suddenly learning about UK politics. And "what's this about pennies on the eyelids?" Some did research on that, too.[19]

Fans were used to songs about unrequited love, by the Beatles and other artists, but "For No One" was something else. The purity of the vocal, the mundane details of the story, the sadly colored French horn, and the heart-wrenching melody created a new emotional experience for fans of all ages. One male fan, age fifteen at the time, thought it was "the saddest song you'll ever hear" and was "moved" by its "beauty and clarity." A female fan, eleven at the time, said the song "made the Beatles seem vulnerable and not above me."

Vulnerability in male singers was not new. But hearing this sad, beautiful song in the now familiar voice of the person who wrote it, sans effects, with "grown-up" instrumentation, made it more moving and authentic. Adolescents with broken hearts could wallow in the song, as adolescents do, knowing "the Beatles understand." A male fan, age sixteen at the time, said, "It's like they crawled into my head and knew what I was thinking and feeling."

A male fan, a child of seven at the time, "listened to 'For No One' and wondered how a love relationship could deteriorate the way Paul described." The placement of "For No One" after the upbeat, happy-in-love "Good Day Sunshine" creates a contrast that makes the song seem even sadder. A female fan, age eleven at the time, recalls the song had an "adult feeling" and was "very melancholy; not fun like their earlier love songs." The song was another glimpse into the adult world: "What I got from 'For No One' was that love was complicated; it could be dark and confusing, but it was part of being human" (Female, b. '55).

This same meaning could have been gleaned from many pop songs—and was. But in addition to being better songwriters than their peers, the Lennon-McCartney partnership had two intelligent, sensitive, and verbal artists with opposing personality types, resulting in a unique creative synergy. If we accept that meaning is cocreated by the artist and the audience, Beatle lyrics give listeners more to work with, and so the meaning and emotional impact are richer.

In "Good Day Sunshine," the album's bright spot and safe place, fans hear a simple story about two people in love going for a walk on a sunny day, and are even privy to what the couple are saying and thinking. The honky-tonk piano keeps their walk moving along. Oddly, the singer's feet are getting burned as he walks, suggesting he's not wearing any shoes.

McCartney's primary inspiration for "Good Day Sunshine" was "Daydream" by The Lovin' Spoonful—a band many Beatle fans liked for their catchy melodies, harmonies, and clever, sensitive lyrics. Their current hit, "Summer in the City," was in the middle of a three-week stretch at number one when *Revolver* and "Yellow Submarine" b/w "Eleanor Rigby" were released.

Fans noticed there were "three George songs" on *Revolver*—all different, but all with at least a touch of that essential Harrison grouse. "I Want to Tell You" expresses the earnest but compulsive musings of an insecure lover—one of those "sophisticated" boy-meets-girl songs. The psychedelic, Indian-infused, vocal fade-out "I've got time" brought fans to the brink of a cosmic rabbit hole, but the heralding brass of "Got to Get You Into My Life" pulls them back from the abyss of waiting forever.

"I Want to Tell You" introduced the idea of a distinction between oneself and one's mind as fans tried to figure out "It's only me, it's not my mind . . . " Years later, Harrison said he sang the lyrics incorrectly and intended to say, "It isn't me, it is my mind that is confusing things." His point, a passing observation, was that "the mind is the thing that hops about telling us to do this and do that" and "what we need to do is lose (forget) the mind."[20]

"She Said She Said" also challenged fans, with its talk of death and the conundrum of feeling like you've "never been born." For two and a half minutes they heard John recounting an impassioned conversation about something that seemed very important but totally incomprehensible. And the echoing guitar riff is a full participant in the conversation. Fans were bewildered: "It sounded deep and mysterious. I liked it but it was a little over my head. It sounded so different and didn't make any sense to me. I thought maybe someone more sophisticated than me, in New York or California would understand it. I guess I thought eventually I would understand it. You couldn't look it up in the dictionary." (Female, b. '51).

Eventually fans learned that the song was inspired by a conversation between John Lennon and Peter Fonda at a party in Los Angeles, during John's first voluntary acid trip.

More and more, fans were trying to make either concrete, linear sense or poetic, figurative sense out of lyrics that were increasingly more opaque, yet increasingly more compelling. The desire to create or find meaning is natural—especially for adolescents listening to pop music. But it was becoming more difficult to find meaning because, in many instances, the lyrics came from an altered state of consciousness. Meaning also becomes elusive when the songwriter's expedient need for lyrics collides with a sometimes greater focus on how the words sound than on what they actually say.

These songs were not simply beyond fans' real-world experience; they were also beyond the "real"-world experience of the person who wrote them. The music that "held the song together" when fans didn't understand the lyrics was born of painstaking, relentless innovation, driven by the goal of sharing an LSD experience with the straight world—including young fans. Appreciating these new Beatles seemed to require an expanded consciousness—or at least some open-mindedness. It would be another year or so before most fans would know with certainty about the Beatles' drug use, but older fans, some of whom had tried marijuana or LSD, knew that *Revolver* was an "acid-soaked" record.

"Eleanor Rigby" was among the more accessible songs on the album, though fans remember "trying to figure that one out, too." Several fans, age nine to eleven at the time, said the song made them feel sad; some found it scary. The "face in a jar by the door" made an impression the first time fans heard it. They didn't know what it meant, but many thought it sounded "cool."

A female fan, age ten at the time, thought "maybe it was one of those English expressions they used." Another fan, age eleven at the time recalled, "I appreciated the music, but I thought this was for bigger kids; maybe as I get older I'll understand it." And then there was the female fan, age five at the time, who said, "My memory of 'Eleanor Rigby' has skips in four places!"

Calling *Revolver* the Beatles' "finest, darkest work," the *New York Times* reviewer singled out "Eleanor Rigby": "They're asking where all the lonely people come from and where they all belong as if they really want to know. Their capacity for fun has been evident since the beginning; their capacity for pity is something new and is a major reason for calling them artists."[21] The song may have disturbed fans, or asked them to think about difficult, big ideas, but it also exposed them to an artistic sensibility.

Older fans were more likely to appreciate the full-blown psychedelia of "Tomorrow Never Knows," and the album as a whole:

> *Revolver* blew my mind more than *Rubber Soul*—the sounds, the backwards stuff, the weirdness of "Tomorrow Never Knows." The dissonance was wonderful. I loved the sound and the mood it created. Male, b. '51

> "Tomorrow Never Knows" was fun, with all those cool noises. It was an ethereal experience. I liked it. It was the Beatles, it was their familiar harmonies, but it introduced outlandish, experimental stuff. Male, b. '48

Other fans were much less enthusiastic. One male fan (b. '53) was "baffled" by the song, recalling, "It wasn't for me. It had an undertone that made me feel uneasy." Another male fan (b. '55) said, "I like music to be pleasing to my ear, and I didn't find 'Tomorrow Never Knows' pleasing to my ear." Another fan, age thirteen at the time, found "Tomorrow Never Knows" "musically off-putting," and its placement as the final song on the album made him uneasy: "It was the last thing they were leaving me with. It was scary wondering if I was going to like the next thing they did. I was hoping they don't completely go this way."

A female fan, age thirteen at the time, remembers, "I got worried when they started changing, that they lost their minds. We tried to find a song on *Revolver* that we liked, and we didn't."

One male fan summed it up this way: "They were evolving too fast for a kid of eleven. *Meet the Beatles* was for everyone; not so with *Revolver.*"

The Beatle Break

After *Revolver*, many young Beatle fans diverted their attention a bit. They took a "Beatle break." Interestingly, many fans had forgotten about this, and only remembered it as they shared their experience and told their story.

Fans were still listening to earlier Beatle music and were intrigued with the warm sound and grown-up lyrics of *Rubber Soul*, but *Revolver* was more than many fans were ready for. Young people often listen to music for mood enhancement, and some felt that the Beatles were no longer providing that consistently. As one female fan, age eight at the time, recalled, "I wasn't getting as much comfort from them at that point." Some themes and imagery were unpleasant. Even the upbeat and childlike "Yellow Submarine" was strange for a Beatle song. And you certainly couldn't dance to it.

Thanks to the Beatles, music was now a necessity for young fans. Herman's Hermits still had a few hits here and there, and of course there was Motown. But much of what the youngest fans heard on the radio was beginning to seem a little over their heads. Many remember listening to Dylan with an older sibling or cousin and not liking his voice; Dylan was "depressing" and "for older kids."

Young Beatle fans were not getting much satisfaction from the Stones, either. One female fan, age ten at the time, remembers, "The Stones didn't sound as good to my ears. They didn't have those nice harmonies, and the lyrics were less fun." Another female fan, a year older, remembered, "The Rolling Stones seemed to be for older kids, and they were too chaotic."

Even reliable hit makers like the Beach Boys, one of the few pre-Beatle acts still on the scene, were becoming less accessible. Their critically acclaimed 1966 album, *Pet Sounds*, yielded only two top ten hits. There were a lot of new sounds on the radio, but many young Beatle fans longed for their beloved moptops who were no more.

To satisfy this yearning, producers Bert Schneider and Robert Rafelson put out a casting call for a certain type of young hipster—no musical ability required—and created the Monkees and their Monday night, prime-time TV show. Born of the synergy created in LA when the music industry shifted from New York to the TV capital, *The Monkees* provided young Beatle fans with a fresh, new set of four charismatic young men who move through a world of uptight adults while singing infectious pop songs. The producers, along with Screen Gems and ABC, knew they had a formula that couldn't miss. But for Rafelson, it was also important to listen to what "today's generation" is saying and "not just tune them out because they have long hair."[22]

After close study of both Beatle films, Schneider and Rafelson came up with a product that was "post-moptop surrealism for pre-teens."[23] *New York Times* TV writer Jack Gould called *The Monkees* "a far-out bit" that was the bright spot of the new TV season. Likening the Monkees to the "Marx brothers in adolescence," he praised the show's "considerable wit and inventiveness, in line, photography, action, and attitude," that "broke the mold in situation comedy."[24]

The Monkees captured key elements of the early Beatle appeal, both in their show and on record. They also breathed new life into the careers of Brill Building songwriters whose fortunes changed after the Beatles made it just about mandatory for singers to write and perform their own material. Beginning with "Last Train to Clarksville," the Monkees had a string of hit 45s and LPs. In time, they too started writing their own songs, seized control of the operation, became a real band, and outlived the TV show.

Like *A Hard Day's Night* and *Help!*, *The Monkees* created a world in which witty, good-hearted youth do battle with the humorless, clumsy social order around them. A lot of demographic research went into the show, and it set its sights squarely on the ten- to fifteen-year-olds. As Micky Dolenz put it, "The Beatles had left a sort of vacuum when they evolved," and "up-and-coming teenyboppers didn't have anything to listen to that they could appreciate, understand, or relate to—until the Monkees."[25]

Some fans who took a Beatle break or put them on a back burner felt "disloyal," but as one female fan, age eleven at the time, put it, "I started listening to the Monkees and Davy Jones; they were more innocent, not that deep." A male fan remembered it this way: "The Beatles changed from a pop group to this remarkable thing, but not for a twelve-year-old. I wasn't ready for it. I went back to the early stuff, and also Herman's Hermits and the Monkees. Herman's Hermits in '66 sounded like the Beatles in '64."

The Monkees' music had the lightness and carefree spirit of the early Beatles, yet, at the same time, their songs, written by the best songwriters of postwar pop, reflected the sophistication the Beatles brought to the whole genre—with lines like "take a giant step outside your mind." On their first two albums, "The Monkees" were actually The Wrecking Crew, a versatile, LA-based studio ensemble that played on hundreds of top hits throughout the fifties and sixties, and into the seventies, for artists as diverse as the Beach Boys, the Righteous Brothers, the 5th Dimension, and the Tijuana Brass.

The Monkees' silliness, sight gags, cartoon graphics, gadgetry, mod clothing, and surreal situations felt like a cross between *Help!* and *Get Smart*. The quick editing created a sense of breathless hurry, and you didn't want to look away for a second. If the stodgy TV critic at the *New York Times* thought it was the hit of the new TV season, the young demographic was enthralled.

Though *The Monkees* was created for ten- to fifteen-year-olds, the show included subtle references to the emerging drug culture, from the very first episode. The show exhibited a counterculture sensibility, including the biblical "Money Is The Root of All Evil" motto hanging on the wall, and the band members' casual use of the word "man" at the end of sentences. The show's disrupted linearity, surreal subplots, speeding and slowing of movement, and jump cuts served up psychedelia for young viewers.

According to their promotional material, the Monkees wanted "to make every day Saturday night, to climb impossible mountains, to take a trolley car to the moon, and to deflate stuffed shirts." Viewers were invited to "follow the Monkees as they plunge into the funniest revolt against our conforming button-down society that has yet to come to television."[26]

In an interview shortly after the show went on the air, Peter Tork said, "There is a social revolution going on and the young ones are into it." He continued, "Dogmatism is leaving the scene. Youth is examining all the old-time premises that used to be taken totally for granted—sexual mores, artistic mores." Describing his draft status as "they thought I was crazy," Tork said, "I think you should stand for what you believe in, and I stand for love and peace."

Beatle fans remembered "debates" about the Beatles and the Monkees with friends and older siblings. There were many similarities and many differences, some more important than others. And ultimately, the Monkees were "just trying to be friendly" and were "too busy singing to put anybody down." But the most significant similarity is that the Monkees, like the Beatles, were exposing their young fans to countercultural ideas. Sometimes called the "Pre-Fab Four," the Monkees offered the cultural consciousness of the ever-new Beatles, but with the joie de vivre of the original Fab Four.

The Mania Continues

Despite the plethora of other new music and the Beatles' latest iteration, fans who didn't take a break still kept the Beatles front and center.

A female fan, age twenty-one at the time, remembers: "They were still our focus; we were still dreaming about them. We felt we could get along with them. They were not macho; not football types. It would be easy to talk to them. I'd want to hang out with them."

A female fan ten years younger remembers, "hanging out in the neighborhood" with her transistor radio, singing "Yellow Submarine" in the street and "acting out being them, with the accents, and poses."

Fans who saw the Beatles on their '66 tour were no less thrilled by the experience than fans who saw them at the peak of Beatlemania: "Seeing them was the height of my life. I was dressed up, with heels and stockings; in those days you dressed up for things, that's how you went places. When it was over we just sat there, we didn't know how to feel. You had to collect yourself. They were gone, the stage was bare, and you felt let down; but you were glad you saw them" (Female, b. '51).

I asked fans if there was still screaming at the shows—and why:

There was still screaming and some people fainted. You scream because you're excited to be there. You get caught up in it, like guys at a football game. Female, b. '49

Why scream? It's like at a kennel, a group mentality—you just jumped in and screamed. It wasn't sexual—I read that's what people think—but it was just being in the crowd, the excitement. We thought they were sexy, but all that means is that we liked how they look, sang, stood, and moved. Female b. '51

I'd been a fan for over two years—I couldn't believe I was in the same space as them—with ten thousand other people. I never dreamed it would happen. Female, b. '52

As in the past, press conferences were part of the 1966 tour. In light of the Jesus comment controversy, these once lighthearted, banter-filled love fests with the press had become a little more serious. One of the ironies of that incident is that it transformed the Beatles, especially Lennon, into people—pop stars—whose opinions mattered. Brian Epstein was able to make John see the greater good in apologizing for "the Jesus comment," and with his mates at his side, Lennon apologized, but his disgust with preserving the image was mounting.

The Beatles had done a fairly good job following Epstein's advice to not answer questions about American politics, but they could resist no longer. They came out against the Vietnam War at a press conference hours before their final New York concert.

One could argue that this was the moment "Beatlemania" ended. Or perhaps it ended when they walked off the stage in Candlestick Park a week or so later. However, if we define Beatlemania as the collective expression of each first-generation fan's relationship with the Beatles, it hasn't ended yet.

Here Come the Hippies

In the final months of 1966, LSD became illegal in the US, John Lennon met Yoko Ono at the Indica Gallery in London, and the Beach Boys released their brilliant, psychedelic symphony, "Good Vibrations." Meanwhile, the city of Los Angeles cracked down on teenage music fans for taking up too much space on Sunset Boulevard. While the Los Angeles–based entertainment industry promulgated countercultural ideas to young people nationwide through music, television, and film, these so-called hippie riots reflected the conflict between "young people speaking their mind" and an establishment oblivious to the impact of the media's empowering messages.

In December, the United States began bombing the capital of North Vietnam as antiwar protests continued to spread throughout the country. When protestors at Berkeley tried to evict Navy recruiters from campus, it led to police intervention, a mass demonstration, and a mass singing of "Yellow Submarine." One of the organizers produced a leaflet with a submarine and psychedelic graphics, which said, in part, "we adopt for today this unexpected symbol of our trust in our future, and of our longing for a place fit for us all to live in. Please post, especially where prohibited. We love you." Two months earlier, a six-foot Yellow Submarine filled with "messages of love, desperation, peace, and hope to all people in the world" was launched into the Hudson River by the New York City–based Workshop in Non-Violence—another adoption of the evocative symbol of harmony and goodwill. The Workshop also designed a pin that included a yellow submarine and a peace symbol on a black background, worn the following year by George and Ringo at the press party for *Sgt. Pepper*.

Lennon, enjoying his own Beatle break while filming Richard Lester's *How I Won the War* and sporting a short haircut for his role as Private Gripweed, was on the cover of *Look* magazine in mid-December, for a story called "John Lennon: A Shorn Beatle Tries It on His Own." Interestingly, the two other cover stories that week were on Sigmund Freud and the Pope—illustrious company, but the photo was of the guy who would sell the most magazines.

Lennon talked about the various avenues of creative expression he'd like to explore in the future. He also talked about how the Beatles had to "falsify a bit" in order to make it, and said now that they had "a bit of power" they could say, "This is what we're like." The interview is noteworthy in that he acknowledges the Beatles functioned as a Trojan Horse at the start of a culture war that would persist into the next millennium.

Lennon also mused on the power of pop music to unite young people all over the world, and, in the guise of humor, on his own power to dissuade this generation from fighting wars. He also said this: "But there's more talk about it than is actually happening. You know, swinging this, and all that. Everybody can go around in England with long hair a bit, and boys can wear flowered trousers and flowered shirts and things like that, but there's still the same old nonsense going on. It's just that we're all dressed up a bit different."[27]

Portions of the above quote are often taken out of context to illustrate John's cynicism about the sixties, but it was only 1966—there was much "sixties" left to happen. And John underestimated the significance of men in flowered shirts. But putting this quote into the fuller context of a rambling, informal conversation with an awe-struck journalist, what comes across is Lennon's effort to understand the implications of his global fame, about which he is clearly and strongly ambivalent. Enjoying his time on the film set, he says, "I haven't seen so much fresh air together for about four years." A metaphor, too, perhaps, for not having had time or space to step back and reflect.

When the Beatles established the goal of being "bigger than Elvis," they could not have imagined how cumbersome, in every way, that level of fame would be. The horrendous logistics took them off the road and, even off duty, they realized they'd given up any semblance of a normal life. They didn't realize that adding genuine artistry and intelligence to the equation meant that "bigger than Elvis" would bring the burden of authority—especially with a supersized, tuned-in fan base that included a vast number of young people who were not only losing faith in the people and institutions in charge but were also feeling empowered to say so.

The Jesus comment kerfuffle caught John by surprise. It was an aha moment that revealed one of the many downsides of "bigger than Elvis." Less than a year later, in a widely read, general interest magazine, he doubled down on the remark: "I said we were more popular than Jesus, which is a fact." John's candor shows that he should be taken at his word when he declares the days of "falsifying" are over. In addition, he repeatedly, in several contexts, talks about his belief in "goodness." The *Look* story, read by fans and non-fans further elevated Lennon as an important figure on the world stage.

Young fans on Beatle break kept The Monkees' "I'm a Believer" in the number one spot for an unbelievable seven weeks as the calendar flipped to 1967. However, they also enjoyed *Beatles at Shea*, a documentary on the already historic concert, which was broadcast on ABC in early January.

The first Human Be-In took place in San Francisco's Golden Gate Park, also in January, positioning the city as the epicenter of the counterculture and foreshadowing the Summer of Love.

Later that month, the headline "Paul McCartney Predicts Breakup of Beatles Soon" appeared in the *New York Times*. According to the article, McCartney is sporting "an Oriental mustache," and said the Beatles are "ready to go our own ways."[28]

One month later, a new double A-side was released.

CHAPTER FIVE

I'd Love to Turn You On

February 1967–December 1967

What could possibly top Rubber Soul *and* Revolver, *that steady progression, with deeper lyrics and fullness. Like a balloon that you thought was full but could keep blowing up.*

Female, b. '48

THE "COOL PHOTO" ON THE BACK OF *Revolver* was over six months old, and the last time fans "got to see them move around" was in the *Rain* and *Paperback Writer* films in May, three months before that. *Beatles at Shea* was a treat, but the footage was a year and a half old. The Beatles' "look" was always a key element of their presentation and communication, so fans were especially looking forward to hearing them and seeing what they looked like *now*.

On February 25, 1967, promotional films for "Penny Lane" and "Strawberry Fields Forever" debuted, in color, on ABC's *Hollywood Palace*. This variety show, along with *Ed Sullivan* and the *Smothers Brothers Comedy Hour*, was a likely place for young music fans to see their favorite bands. They would check the TV listings each week to "see if anybody good" was going to be on, and tell their friends.

Most fans had never seen films like these before, and they hadn't seen the Beatles look or sound like they now did—in full psychedelic splendor. They were familiar yet unfamiliar. Whether or not they liked the new look and sound, most fans appreciated that the Beatles were "constantly changing," and that "kept them interesting." "I loved their look, the backwards footage, the unusual sound and images in the video. I was intrigued. I knew I was looking at a piece of art" (Male b. '53).

The most striking thing about their appearance was of course their facial hair, which many fans, especially younger ones, did not like. One female fan, age eight at the time, felt "they weren't lovable anymore." Another female fan, age nine at the time, recalled: "The mood was different. Who were these Beatles? What happened to my brothers? It was mysterious and intriguing but more than I wanted. I think I went through a brief mourning."

Several female fans, in the eleven-to-fourteen range at the time, described their look as "unattractive." An older female fan (b. '46), involved in the student movement, saw the band's new look and facial hair as "a statement that they were part of and sympathetic to the movement and hippie culture." Like the younger fans, she saw it as "a move away from their original cuteness," but she wasn't upset by it. To the contrary, politically involved young people now saw the Beatles as powerful, supportive allies.

It was in these films that we first saw John in what would become his signature National Health "granny" glasses, which were also part of his Private Gripweed look in *How I Won the War*. John's hair was actually shorter and more conventional than in the *Rain* and *Paperback Writer* films. Paul's hair was about the same, and Ringo's and George's were both longer.

Their groupness was still very much there—maybe even more pronounced due to the mysteriously ritualized movement in their strange dreamworld—yet they were expressing more individuality. Their clothes, loosely color-coordinated but not identical, were thought to be a bit more "colorful and flamboyant" than what fans had previously seen.

It would be four months before the Beatles' drug use was confirmed, but several fans across the age range "knew those songs were druggy," and that "made it hard to relate to them." Preteens were more likely to express "disappointment" by the drug use, feeling that it was "wrong." Older fans were less judgmental, though many said that at the time they found drugs personally "scary."

Young fans recall their strong reactions to these short films, especially *Strawberry Fields Forever*: "I liked both songs, but I ran out of the room terrified from "Strawberry Fields Forever." The whole thing was dissonant and strange and it scared me. It gave me the creeps; the loopy sound, the drums getting louder, it was cacophonous" (Male, b. '61).

Those who heard "Strawberry Fields Forever" on the radio, without the film's "nothing is real" imagery, also found it disturbing:

I was scared when I heard "Strawberry Fields Forever" on the car radio. My mom had to explain to me why I didn't need to be scared of it. Male, b. '58

I was sick for a week that February and I heard "Strawberry Fields Forever" a lot on the radio. I got a weird feeling when it came on. I didn't know what to make of it. Male, b. '55

I thought "Strawberry Fields Forever" sounded like a funeral song, especially the opening keyboard chords. Then it just got spookier as it went along. I also thought Lennon sounded sad, which made me sad. I just couldn't listen to it and not get the creeps. Male, b. '56

Though the song is familiar to us now, it's easy to imagine how "Strawberry Fields Forever" could have scared a sensitive child or baffled a preteen—Lennon's vocal and the use of innovative production techniques create an otherworldly quality; the layered instrumentation, including a ghostly mellotron, created dense intensity. It was hard to pin down what this peculiar song was about, though many sensed it was trying to tell them something important.

For the younger fans who found this new incarnation of their Beatles overwhelming, the song marked the beginning of their Beatle break. A male fan (b. '56) recalls, "Within days, all the Beatles pictures were ripped off the walls and replaced by pinups of my new clean-shaven heroes, the Monkees."

Staying on the Bus

Like many recent Beatle offerings, "Strawberry Fields Forever" was weighty yet floaty, and asked fans to consider their relationship with reality. The song expressed an odd mix of insecurity, motivation, and resignation, along with self-awareness and utter confusion. Despite a hopeful undercurrent, it seemed sad. It wasn't easy and it wasn't fun. You couldn't dance to it. For some young fans, scarier even than the song itself was the prospect of getting to know these new Beatles. Fans remember DJs commenting on the song too:

> Dan Ingram at WABC said, "That's not a song, that's an experience." Male, b. '49

> The DJ on our local Cleveland station said, "That's the worst piece of garbage I ever heard." Male, b. '51

Teenagers were generally more open to these new songs and understood that some thought and repeated listening were required. Some young fans understood that too and were ready for the challenge: "I embraced it as it came, it was surreal and ethereal. Some of my friends dropped out of the Beatle experience. They preferred the happy things like 'She Loves You' but I was ready to continue the journey" (Female b. '56). A male fan (b. '49) remembers finding "Strawberry Fields Forever" "complex and a little hard to get a handle on." But it was "such a great single, it made the wait for the next album more torturous."

Fans who missed the videos on *Hollywood Palace* had another opportunity a few weeks later when the videos aired on ABC's *American*

Bandstand in March. When host Dick Clark asked teenagers what they thought of the films, most commented on the Beatles' facial hair, saying things like "It ruins their image" and "They look like somebody's grandfather."

A week after the *Bandstand* broadcast, "Penny Lane" was number one; "Strawberry Fields Forever" peaked at number eight in April. These two songs, each memorializing the author's Liverpool childhood, provide one of the purest examples of John and Paul's essential difference.

By this point, fans felt like they were indeed on a journey with the Beatles—an adventure, a trip. The destination wasn't important. Saying "they were ready to continue the journey" or that they "went along for the ride" expressed their belief, based on their experience of the Beatles thus far, that they were learning and growing from them and valued the new sounds, images, and ideas the band was presenting. They were challenged and enriched and wanted to stay tuned. It was doing something to them, and whatever it was, they liked it.

When I asked one young fan why her friends "dropped out of the Beatle experience," she didn't know. Fans often said the Beatles were becoming "weird," meaning strange, otherworldly, surreal. Some were neutral about the Beatles' evolution, some embraced it, and others took a break.

Those who were neutral or embraced the "weirdness" were, perhaps, a bit more open-minded and curious by nature—they found "weird" appealing, or were willing to give it a chance.

Two weeks after the release of "Penny Lane" and "Strawberry Fields," an article in the *Washington Post*, "LSD Is Taking a Trip Uptown," described how "psychedelia" was moving from "East Village lofts into the pop culture mainstream" by fashion designers, advertising agencies, and others who "mold the tastes of New York and by extension the nation."[1]

Something Happening Here

Top 40 radio continued to reflect diverse themes, and new bands continued to emerge, many from California. "Happy Together" by LA's Turtles knocked "Penny Lane" from the number one position in late

March. Holding the position for three weeks, it was displaced by the aptly titled "Something Stupid," sung by the unlikely duo of Nancy and Frank Sinatra. That the song remained number one for four weeks shows that Top 40 radio remained eclectic and that the old guard was hanging on.

In contrast, the ultra "now" Mamas and the Papas' "Dedicated to the One I Love" was a number two hit for two weeks in March, followed in June with their "Creeque Alley," a hit that name-drops the also very "now" Lovin' Spoonful, the Byrds' Roger McGuinn, and Barry McGuire in its autobiographical lyrics.

The Monkees had a hit with "A Little Bit Me, a Little Bit You," a song thematically similar to "We Can Work It Out" in its advocacy of communication and compromise in the face of conflict. Like much about the Monkees, the song was Beatles lite, delivering the worldview without the latter's artistry and depth—perfect for those on their break from the more difficult Beatles.

Buffalo Springfield, another important LA band, had a number seven hit in April with "For What It's Worth," a response to unwarranted law enforcement action during the "hippie riots" on Sunset Boulevard the previous November. The song, which ranks number sixty-three on *Rolling Stone*'s list of "The 500 Greatest Songs of All Time," captures the tension created by the establishment confronting "young people speaking their minds" and quickly became a well-known protest song.

While "For What It's Worth" was on the charts, many people, young and old, were indeed speaking their minds. Antiwar demonstrations were held in New York City and San Francisco, drawing larger and more diverse crowds than ever before. Protestors in New York heard speeches by Martin Luther King Jr. and Dr. Benjamin Spock, author of *Baby and Child Care*, a book outsold only by the Bible in the twentieth century.

Spock's book, first published in 1946, was a significant departure from earlier childrearing books in that he advised postwar parents— the parents of future Beatle fans—to be more flexible, affectionate, and child-centered. Supporters of the war and critics of the counterculture said Spock's advice had given rise to a "Spock-marked generation of hippies," believed to be undermining the very fabric of society. The outspoken pediatrician-pacifist knew the criticism was for his politics, not his childrearing philosophy.[2]

According to Norman Vincent Peale, conservative minister, syndicated columnist, and author of *The Power of Positive Thinking*, American youth raised on Spock's principles expected instant gratification and lacked discipline. Spock corrected Peale's misunderstanding of his approach, and also came out as a champion of the youth movement: "I certainly don't consider youths generally undisciplined. I think, in general, they're much more thoughtful and constructive than older generations. They're also, in general, more humanitarian."[3]

Hippies had been getting a lot of media attention in the months since January's Be-In. A male fan (b. '50) recalls, "We started hearing about hippies during that void between 'Strawberry Fields Forever' and *Sgt. Pepper.*"

When teenagers invaded San Francisco's North Beach, the beatniks who'd been living there fled to the somewhat rundown, working-class, racially mixed Haight-Ashbury neighborhood. College students and other young people started migrating to the area from around the city, the country, and beyond—and were dubbed "hippies."

By April, the city was already preparing for an onslaught of young people at the end of the school year—three months *before* Scott McKenzie's "San Francisco (Be Sure to Wear Flowers in Your Hair)" hit number four in the US and became a global hit.

Almost half the US population was under age twenty-five, and though they lived in small towns, suburbs, and big cities, their shared experiences created a strong generational identity. They shared bewilderment at concepts such as "mutual assured destruction" and "overkill," and experienced the edgy fear of watching American cities burn from the frustration of a stalled civil rights movement. They shared the pain of friends and family dying in a war that no one of any age seemed to understand. They shared the disillusionment after the Kennedy assassination only three years before. And they also shared the communal thrill of watching the Beatles on the *Ed Sullivan Show* only seventy-nine days after that national trauma.

Not all Beatle fans were hippies, but hippies were Beatle fans. They wanted to live the freedom the Beatles had planted in their imaginations and to question and quest as their music encouraged. The Beatles told them to pay attention, and they did. The Beatles told them about the power of The Word, and they took it to heart.

These young people, raised on Drs. Seuss and Spock, and *Mad*, were also listening to Dylan, the Byrds, the Mothers of Invention, and the Jefferson Airplane. They read Beat poets and were intrigued by a renegade Harvard professor who advised them to eschew the usual paths to success—just as the Beatles and other artists had done. According to actor Peter Coyote, a founding member of Haight-Ashbury's Diggers, "It was such an exciting, heady time to find out that under the official reality there was this seething turmoil of young people, learning new music, new thoughts, new ideas, new literature, new poetry, new ways of being."[4]

Could it be that this little neighborhood by the dock of the Bay was the epicenter for a new society? According to author Theodore Roszak, the hippies wanted to create "a world where people live gently on the planet without the sense that they have to exploit nature or make war upon nature in order to find basic security. A simpler way of life, less urban, less consumption-oriented, much more concerned about spiritual values, about companionship, friendship, community, sharing ideas, values, insights. A world in which that was considered more important than the gross domestic product."[5]

The Summer of Love was nigh, and the migration would soon be in full swing. Young people were in motion—and looking forward to the new Beatle album.

Amid all the talk of the hippies and the generation gap, CBS News broadcast *Inside Pop: The Rock Revolution*, hosted by the esteemed musical director of the New York Philharmonic and a composer with a household name, Leonard Bernstein. Oddly lit in half silhouette, the music enthusiast set out to bridge the generation gap by explaining the artistry and cultural significance of the best pop music, which he described as "odd, defiant, and free," with "something very important to tell us."[6]

A huge Beatle fan and proud of it, Bernstein explicated several of their songs and basically told America, "It's okay to like them; they're really good." He stopped short of calling them geniuses, although in later writing he effusively referred to John and Paul as "saints" and praised the band for, among other things, their "Fuck you coolness."[7]

The second half of the broadcast explored how pop music speaks to young people in their own language, reflecting their concerns about "the crisis of values in modern life." The highlight of the broadcast may have been the exchange between Graham Nash and Peter Noone in which the former tries to spark the political consciousness of the latter.

A Magic Presentation

It had been ten months since *Revolver* and the Beatles were, as one male fan (b. '56) put it, "Part of the fabric of your life, the backdrop." An older male fan (b. '48) put it this way: "You brushed your teeth, you went to the bathroom, you went to school, you listened to the Beatles."

The anticipation of *Sgt. Pepper* was unlike the anticipation for any previous Beatle album—or for any album, ever. *New York Times* critic Robert Christgau thought the record "was awaited in much the same spirit as installments of Dickens must have been" in the previous century.[8] Fans wondered what the band could possibly do that would top *Rubber Soul*, *Revolver*, and their most recent double A-side single.

Explaining his vision for the new album, McCartney said, "We realized for the first time that someday someone would actually be holding a thing they'd call 'the Beatles new LP,' and that normally it would be just a collection of songs or a nice picture on the cover, nothing more. So the idea was to do a complete thing that you could make what you liked of: a little magic presentation—a packet of things inside the record sleeve."[9] The idea, McCartney said, was "to put everything, the whole world into this package."[10] Everyone involved soon realized the practical limitations of Paul's vision, but its spirit was somehow preserved, and was appreciated by fans across a wide age range:

> I remember studying the *Sgt. Pepper* cover and thinking it was weird; trying to figure it out, wondering what it meant and who all the people were. They made a big impact on me very early on. Female, b. '61

> It was a concentrated stimulus. The lyrics, the blending songs, the people on the cover, the insert. I was aware of it as an artifact, as a product. It reeked of symbolism, real or not. It was intriguing to me. Female, b. '54

> The cover was part of the experience, the experience was more and more total. It created an environment. Who were all these people? People argued and discussed it. Female, b. '47

Fans recall "a lot of hype" surrounding the album, which raised even higher the already high expectations—of fans, music critics, other artists, indeed, the world. Some recall "not being as blown away" as they expected to be, and some, especially rock and roll enthusiasts, found it "overproduced." Some younger fans found it "confusing." A male fan, age thirteen at the time, recalls: "I didn't get it at all. Why write songs like this? I liked 'A Little Help from My Friends,' and 'Lucy in the Sky with Diamonds.' I didn't like side two at all. 'Within You Without You' didn't appeal to me. It was over my head, and I wasn't the least bit curious about it."

As with previous records, fans came to appreciate it with repeated listening. There was always some amount of peer pressure to like the next Beatle record, but the hyperhype around *Sgt. Pepper* made the peer pressure even greater. If you were ten or eleven, or fifteen and

These girls, age thirteen in 1964, performed "She Loves You" during
intermission at a dance recital in rural Tennessee. A ten-year-old male friend
played the part of Ed Sullivan, and a carefully rendered NBC peacock
completes the set. *Courtesy of Raven Parris*

MEET THE BEATLES

Fans of all ages wanted to be able to identity the four Beatles right away. This drawing was made by a six-year-old after watching the *Ed Sullivan Show* on February 9, 1964. *Courtesy of Richard Riis*

(Left) It's April 1964, the Beatles dominate Top 40 radio, and this fan, age thirteen, celebrates her birthday with her Beatles Club. *Courtesy of Lori Freckelton*

(Bottom) Fans in cut-off pedal pushers hold a sign expressing their love for the Beatles as they wait to see *A Hard Day's Night*. Notice fallout shelter sign in upper right. *Courtesy of Boston Public Library*

Elated fans in jumpers, skirts and blouses, kerchiefs, and mohair sweaters about to see the Beatles perform at the Boston Garden, September 12, 1964. *Courtesy of Boston Public Library*

These young fans were also waiting on line at the Boston Garden to buy tickets for the Beatle concert in September. Could they look any happier? *Courtesy of Boston Public Library*

Fans outside Boston's Madison Hotel—but it could be any hotel where the Beatles stayed—waving and hoping to catch a glimpse.
Courtesy of Boston Public Library

Conventional wisdom about the Beatle fan experience is that "Boys wanted to be them and girls wanted to be with them," but conventional wisdom is not always correct. *Courtesy of Estelle Babey and Marcia Hauenstein*

Young fans in Beatles Halloween costumes, 1964. The Beatles were quickly woven into the rituals of childhood. *Courtesy of Tom Frangione*

Siblings and cousins, ages four to ten, in Beatle wigs and birthday hats. Beatle music, images, and merchandise were a constant, fun presence in households across America. *Courtesy of Michael Versaci*

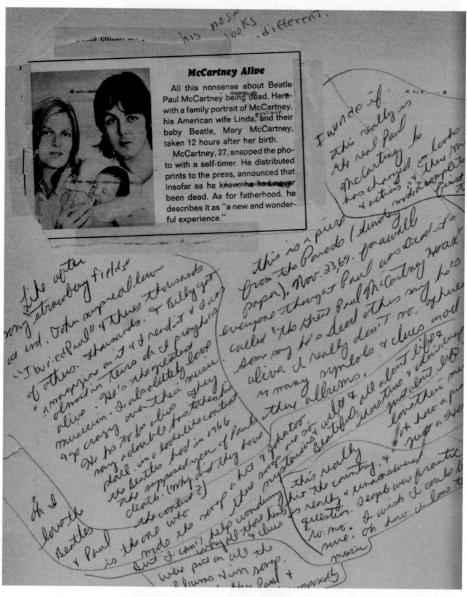

Fans of all ages got caught up in the Paul Is Dead frenzy in the fall of 1969. A female fan, age fourteen at the time, contemplated the rumor in her diary.

Courtesy of the Trudell Family

Though out of focus, photos like this are important keepsakes for fans who saw the Beatles perform live. This was shot with a plastic box camera, through binoculars, at Chicago's Comisky Park in August 1965. *Courtesy of Lori Freckelton*

This fan, age fourteen, plays a left-handed guitar and sports a polka-dot shirt and Beatle haircut as Paul watches over him. Though bent and torn, the photo still exudes Beatleness. *Courtesy of Pat Mancuso*

This fan, age thirteen, proudly poses with the latest Beatle album in December 1968. "Getting Beatle albums for Christmas was always a great treat." *Courtesy of Paul Comerford*

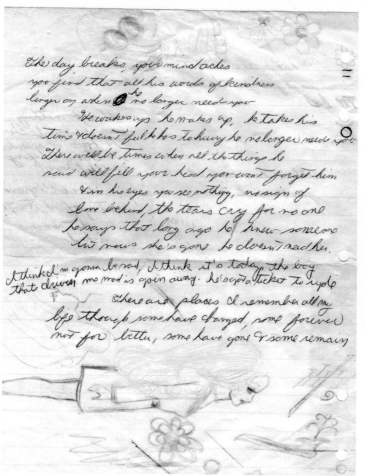

The day breaks, your mind aches
you find that all his words of kindness
linger on when he no longer needs you
He wakes up, he makes up, he takes his
time & doesn't feel he has to hurry he no longer needs you
There will be times when all the things he
said will fill your head you won't forget him
& in his eyes you see nothing, no sign of
love behind, the tears cry for no one.
he says that long ago he knew someone
but now she's gone he doesn't need her.
I think I'm gonna be sad, I think it's today, the boy
that drives me mad is going away. he's got a ticket to ride
There are places I remember all my
life though some have changed, some forever
not for better, some have gone & some remain

(Left) Equipment for living: Fans used Beatle lyrics to process and understand the ups and downs of young love. *Courtesy of the Trudell Family*

(Bottom) Asked what she was thinking about, this fan, age ten in the photo, said, "I wish I could remember. Probably marrying George Harrison." *Courtesy of Debra Norton*

you weren't excited about the record or "didn't know what to make of it," there were lots of big kids, cooler than you, asking, "How can you not like *Sgt. Pepper*?" And there were many opportunities for repeated listening, since the record was impossible to avoid. In fact, its instant ubiquity was celebrated the following year in the Johnny Rivers hit "Summer Rain" which mentioned it twice and incorporated Pepper-like production flourishes. But right away, young fans could see and hear that *Sgt. Pepper* was an important record, and that it required some work:

> You were confronted with something you had to consider. There was a lot to take in. I was aware of it as a piece of pop culture, as something being presented to me. Female, b. '54

> The cover felt more threatening than the music; no one was smiling and it suggested something vaguely negative and strange. I knew I'd be challenged by it in some way. Female, b. '56

> It was like approaching something forbidden that I wasn't prepared for; something leading me into forbidden territory. But it was the Beatles and I knew that ultimately it would be a good place, based on my history with them. Male, b. '57

Fans had playfully scrutinized the black and white line drawing and collage of *Revolver* like it was a Hidden Pictures page in *Highlights* magazine. But the layers and details of the *Sgt. Pepper* cover were even more compelling—with bright colors, a crowd scene, psychedelic landscaping, and the latest iteration of the Beatles—a band within a band, in garishly colored satin military garb. "I wanted a Pepper uniform so badly. My Grandmother took me to a costume shop in town, and we brought the album to show them what we were looking for. They had never seen such a thing. I don't think I knew the costumes were marching band style. I just loved that the Beatles were wearing colorful, shiny clothes" (Male, b. '55).

Studying the crowd of people on the cover, trying to identify them, and wondering what it all meant were the goals of Paul's "magic presentation," and fans responded:

I remember looking at the cover and wondering who all the people were. They put stuff in there for me to find, or to figure out. They were doing it to be playful. I'm not really a game person, never was, but you were always trying to figure out what they were up to. Male, b. '55

I remember looking at the cover with friends, pointing at someone and saying, for example, that's Gandhi. Everyone could name at least one or two people. We always stared at the cover when listening to the music. Like reading the back of the cereal box while you ate your Rice Crispies. Male, b. '55

As with the photo collage on *Revolver*, fans appreciated that the Beatles were acknowledging their earlier selves, this time with the wax figure moptops, "like they're saying 'we've come a long way.'" A sense of "I saw them come up," and "I grew up with them" was setting in after three years. Their self-referencing habit enhanced fans' feelings of an ongoing relationship and kept younger impressions of them in mind as fans watched them mature, making the relationship seem even more family-like.

Fans remember DJs advising them to listen to the album in its entirety—prescription-like instructions that somehow made the record seem even more special and challenging.[11] Fans recognized that the Beatles wanted them to pay attention to the words; to follow along and think about the meaning if they wanted to. Why else would they be printed right there on the back of the cover?

The magic presentation created sensory overload and demanded interaction, even before a sound was heard. Then the sound drew them in even further:

I was out with my parents, and they went into a store and left me in the car. So I turned the radio on and heard "Lucy in the Sky with Diamonds." The lyrics and the texture were mesmerizing. It was so different from the innocence of "A Hard Day's Night." Everything was getting serious. It seemed in tune with my getting older; their lyrics and my life seemed to parallel each other. Male, b. '53

I got *Sgt. Pepper* for my twelfth birthday. My Dad and I looked at the cover and played it all the time in the living room. We loved it. My eight-year-old sister loved it too. It was a family experience. Female b. '55

A Splendid Time

Listening to this record was, as with the previous Beatle albums, an experience unlike any other. These were not merely more sophisticated lyrics (again), more diverse themes (again), and a unique soundscape (again). Fans had learned to recognize and expect artistic development, but the way the entire album played with levels of reality was a whole new thing to ponder. It's the band they've "known for all these years"— or is it? And who is this Billy Shears? Where would this performance be taking place?

Billy sounds like Ringo, singing another idealistic, whimsy-filled song in the spirit of "Yellow Submarine." Both songs, with their positive, communitarian refrains, evoke a utopian world where love is the only thing that matters—though fun is very important too. The young fans on Beatle break, venturing to take a dip into *Sgt. Pepper,* said, "With a Little Help From My Friends" was one of the few songs they liked. Proto-hippie and Beatle friend Peter Fonda said the song inspired him to "sing out of tune" and create *Easy Rider,* with "a little help" from friends Dennis Hopper and Terry Southern.[12]

"Lucy in the Sky with Diamonds" literally asked fans to "picture themselves" inside the song, to experience an acid trip. It wasn't like the "Rain" trip, which looked outward and questioned conventional behavior, or the "Tomorrow Never Knows" trip, which looked inward and explored states of consciousness. This trip focused on the pure delight of heightened senses and fantastic imagery. How could the title not be code for LSD? Sometime later, John showed the world the drawing of his son's friend Lucy—proof that the letters in the song's title were a coincidence. The controversy gave fans more to speculate about, but the song by any other name would have been just as acid-soaked. As one male fan, age seventeen at the time, recalled, "If nothing else got you interested in trying pot or LSD, that would."

The listener, floating through the cavernous train station as "Lucy" fades to silence is suddenly redirected by the insistent staccato guitars of "Getting Better," and told, in Paul's familiar, sweetly authoritative, voice, that "it's getting better all the time." And what exactly is "it" that has gotten better? I'm done with uncool teachers, I'm not angry and hiding my head in the sand (like a Nowhere Man), and I'm no longer cruel to the person I love. I'm becoming a better person. The song induces a positive, proactive state of mind whether or not one can relate to the examples. The reminder that things "can't get no worse" doesn't negate the song's optimism. As was often the case, Paul's glass is half full and John's is half empty.

Despite the song's positive vibe, one female fan, age sixteen at the time, recalls her negative reaction: "The lyrics in 'Getting Better' about violence bothered me because I had come from an abusive home. A friend told me to be more open-minded about it, but my gut reaction was negative."

This is the second Beatle song to evoke violence against women—albeit in a completely different context than the first. "Getting Better" refers not only to physical abuse but also to the controlling, nuanced emotional abuse of keeping "her apart from the things that she loved." The lyrics call out an all too common practice and implicitly, intentionally or not, admonish against it—certainly a first in pop music.

For fans following events in San Francisco, or news of smaller hippie enclaves sprouting up across the country, "She's Leaving Home" was part of the story. Despite the song's Englishness, it captured a dynamic that was happening in households across America. In its review of *Sgt. Pepper*, *Time* magazine quotes a fifteen-year-old boy who "left home to become a hippie" and "interprets the Beatles' songs as a put-down of his parents: 'They're saying all the things I always wanted to say to my parents and their freaky friends.'"

Younger fans remember "something scary" about the vocal in "Being for the Benefit of Mr. Kite!" Though apparently about a circus, the cacophonous carnival music was "frightening in some way," conjuring up images of "mean clowns." Reading along with the handy lyrics, there are exclamation points—not yet overused in 1967—adding a touch of fun to what fans were hearing.

Frightened or not, fans listened. "It's the Beatles." Not the Beatles of "She Loves You," not the Beatles of "Ticket to Ride," not the Beatles of "Rain," or even the Beatles of "Tomorrow Never Knows." Each record brought opportunities to engage more cerebrally—or not. It was often a richer meal than many fans were ready for, but they still nibbled around the edges. The lyrics on *Sgt. Pepper* also spoke to fans' Anglophilia—as did much on the album. Having the lyrics was especially nice because some of these songs had words and place names fans had never heard before.

The "weirdest" sounds and words were in George's "Within You Without You," which used no electric instruments. The song's Indian instrumentation, droning sound, and esoteric lyrics made it the least accessible song on the record. For some, it was "the most amazing thing" they'd ever heard, but many thought it was "a waste of space." Some young fans "always skipped it"; others found it "intriguing." One male fan, age ten at the time, said it was like "being in church and so you had to pay attention because it was important."

"Within You Without You" was inspired by Vedantic philosophy, but draws on principles from several traditions—universal truths—including the Beatles' own brand of spiritual humanism. The lyrics recount a conversation and, along the way, present the most extreme and overt spiritual entreaty the Beatles had put forth yet.

Picking up from where "The Word" left off, Harrison's song preaches the transformative power of love and connectedness. Like Lennon's "Rain" and "Nowhere Man," it asks the listener to take a side: "Are you one of *them*," or are you on board with what "*we*" were talking about? It counsels that "peace of mind" will come—and who doesn't want that?—if you "see beyond yourself" and realize you are but a small piece of an infinite connectedness. The song says to listeners, of all ages, "Think about who you are, think about your place in the universe, and think about what's important."

The spiritual gravitas of "Within You Without You" is relieved by "audience" laughter at the end, changing the ambience and pulling the listener into a smaller space, closer to the music, without echo. Still in a music hall, we hear "old-fashioned" music—and the clean, tight sound and colorful clarinets put you front and center.

Though very different from the preceding track, "When I'm Sixty-four" also offered fans new things to consider. Both songs asked fans to leave where they were and go someplace else for a few minutes. The utter cuteness of "When I'm Sixty-four" was an accessible, theatrical diversion after "Within You Without You." The suggestion to "fill in a form" sounded clever and modern, adding depth to a light, old-fashioned song by suggesting the future. Subtle psychedelic time shifting, 1920s style.

The aural space opens up again with "Lovely Rita," another offering with a very English feel that, as one male fan (b. '50) put it, "elevates a meter maid with a humdrum job." The singer's studied recollection of the "boy-meets-girl" details, right down to who paid the bill, adds intrigue to the encounter.

Although John thought Paul's "novelist" songs were "stories about boring people doing boring things," fans weren't bored. With listeners creating the imagery in their own heads, *Sgt. Pepper* became the encompassing, multimedia experience Paul intended it to be. Listening to "Lovely Rita," for example, several fans recall discovering the sound of a cork popping after the word "dinner," and could picture the two—or three—of them on the settee in the parlor. A female fan recalled sitting in her grandmother's living room listening to *Sgt. Pepper* at age six: "I felt transported into a semi-dream state. I loved the melodies. It fed my imagination, especially 'A Day in the Life.'"

The album asked a lot of fans but gave them a lot to work with. By pointing out the mundane and asking them, as one female fan (b. '47) put it, "to pay attention to the little people," the world is reframed. *Sgt. Pepper*'s mundane observations were more detailed and personal than the wide-angle reactions to inclement weather in "Rain" one year before. As with "Eleanor Rigby" the year before, listeners met people with names on *Sgt. Pepper*. Where fans heard the early boy-meets-girl songs as "little stories," these were mini theatrical performances, presentations within presentations within presentations.

Despite its carnival atmosphere, the record was calm, even mellow, compared with the new American music of the moment. While bands like the Doors and Jefferson Airplane exuded tense, edgy urgency, fans found *Sgt. Pepper* dense and contemplative, its heaviness tempered with humor, humanity, and whimsy. It took itself as seriously as you wanted to think it did.

A female fan, age seventeen at the time, "sensed that the album encompassed truth and beauty" in its "send-ups of everyday life; mocking middle-class existence."

Though some fans thought more highly of it at the time than they do now, they all remember the album as an important event in their lives:

As a musician, its biggest impact was that pop music could be a vehicle for thinking philosophically. Male, b. '50

Even at twelve I was an "artsy" kid. I am still in the graphic design business. I went to music college, I went to art school. *Sgt. Pepper* sparked that in me. Male, b. '55

Reading the words on *Sgt. Pepper*, you could see how words and music go together. It encouraged me to listen to the words by other artists. You knew that if it was arty you have to pay closer attention or you'd miss something. Male b. '48

One older fan who enjoyed the record was beatnik-cum-hippie Allen Ginsberg, who said the Beatles, "conveyed a realization that the world and human consciousness had to change."[13] Similarly, radical activist Abbie Hoffman said the album "summed up so much of what we were saying politically, culturally, and artistically; expressing our inner feelings and our view of the world in a way that was so revolutionary."[14] As one female fan (b. '54) put it, "It made me aware that things didn't have to be as they were."

The weight of *Sgt. Pepper* and fans' growing understanding of the Beatles as artists didn't diminish interest in the Beatles' personal lives. To the contrary, for fans still on "the journey," *Sgt. Pepper* deepened their interest in all things Beatle. A female fan, age sixteen at the time, recalled: "We were still interested in their personal lives and their girlfriends. There was lots of discussion about *Sgt. Pepper*—it was a big part of our lives. My friends and I would meet and hang out at the park on a Sunday afternoon, and we'd listen to the album." A female fan five years older also remained engaged: "We followed the Beatles' comings and goings very closely in college, in the news and in interviews."

The Drug Thing

By the summer of 1967, drugs had become a focus of the cultural conversation, along with the war and the hippies. Many fans recall that *Sgt. Pepper* was "obviously drug influenced," and some, regardless of age, thought "it wasn't a good example." A male fan, age ten at the time, remembers: "It still kind of sounded like them but I wasn't sure if I should be liking it. It seemed like they had made a record for druggies; they seemed like different people. Suburbia was scared by hippies" (Male, b. '57).

Any doubt about the record's drugginess or the Beatles status as Hippies-in-chief was quickly put to rest when Paul publicly acknowledged using LSD. His comments, first published in the UK, were reprinted in the June 16 issue of *Life* magazine in an article called "The New Far-Out Beatles."[15] McCartney hadn't simply used LSD— he was an LSD enthusiast: "After I took it, it opened my eyes. We only use one-tenth of our brain. Just think what we could accomplish if we could only tap that hidden part. It would mean a whole new world."

A female fan (b. '49) remembers, "People thought they heard drug references in everything, which made it easier to deny the Beatles were using drugs, until the *Life* magazine article." She continued: "I didn't want to believe it; I admired him and I was disappointed. It upset me because Paul was one of my heroes. I grew up with alcoholics, so I didn't like anything like that. They were my beacon, making me feel better; I wanted them on a pedestal. I didn't want to hear anything negative about them. I could focus on them and be happy" (Female, b. '49).

Paul's acknowledgment further fueled speculation that "Lucy in the Sky With Diamonds" was code for LSD, and some radio stations didn't play it. Some stations wouldn't play "A Day in the Life" because of its "I'd love to turn you on" refrain.

Parents had come to accept the Beatles' presence in their kids' lives, though many still bemoaned time spent Beatleing as opposed to schoolwork or other activities. Bedroom walls plastered with photos, obsessive conversation about the band and their music, and longer hair and colorful clothing on their sons had become normalized. And many parents liked the Beatles' music, or at least had a favorite song or two. Even the most anti-Beatles parents had acquiesced an album or two ago.

Yet many fans recall their parents were upset by the McCartney interview and warned them "not to copy everything they do." A male fan, age eleven at the time, remembers, "My friend's dad said they were singing about drugs and wanted us to turn the music off." Another male fan recalls: "I was only seven when *Sgt. Pepper* came out, but I was aware of how important people thought it was. I remember being in the backseat of my grandparent's car and hearing 'Lucy in the Sky with Diamonds' on the radio, which my grandmother said stood for LSD. My grandfather said he kind of liked the music, and I said, 'The

Beatles wouldn't use drugs!' Then the DJ came on and said the same thing. It seemed that the Beatles and *Sgt. Pepper* were just as important to the grown-ups as something called 'the dmz' and 'hochee men'" (Male, b. '60).

With the war escalating and the generation gap quickly widening, the unprecedented mass popularity of these four musicians gave them unprecedented cultural authority. Lennon had observed a year earlier that the Beatles were more popular with young people than Jesus, and some fans brought religious metaphors into their recollections. As one male (b. '56) put it, "By this point, everything they did was like it was handed down on golden tablets from on high." Another male fan (b. '50) said, "We trusted them; they seemed like good people, and they had an angelic quality."

Fans recall that, "schools and churches started to talk about the dangers of drugs." *Time* magazine warned of "potential chromosomal damage and long-lasting psychotic aftereffects from LSD."[16] A male fan, age eleven at the time, remembers, "Some kids tried pot and LSD in 1967; I had the vague sense this wasn't a good thing; I ignored it and enjoyed the music." Another male fan, age eighteen at the time, remembers noticing the "glint in their eyes on the gatefold and thinking they were on drugs." He continued, "I was very straight, but I was interested in their development; I loved the music and went along for the ride." Some fans found it hard to reconcile what they were learning about drugs with what they saw and heard around them: "I was led to believe drugs were dangerous and criminal. Paul's admission disturbed me. My parents talked to me about it because they were afraid I would emulate him. By age thirteen or fourteen I knew people who were taking drugs, doing what the Beatles were doing. Why weren't they in prison? Why didn't they have fried brains? My heroes were doing something I was told was bad. It was unnerving" (Male, b. '54).

Young fans had been emulating the Beatles since the beginning, and that didn't change when they learned of the Beatles' drug use. McCartney's remarks and the follow-up interview, in which he defended his honesty and naively blamed the press for spreading the news, changed the conversation about LSD. If the wise, talented, successful Beatles used drugs, maybe drugs weren't all bad:

> I knew they used drugs. It didn't upset me. I tried LSD once and didn't like that you can't turn it off. Male b. '50

> LSD never interested me, but pot did. I would attribute that to the Beatles. Female, b. '54

> We saw drugs as assistance for spiritual enlightenment; we thought they were something good; cooler than alcohol; more peaceful. Male, b. '50

The drug culture was oozing into the mainstream, from The Monkees to the *Smothers Brothers*—and making young people all the more curious about what a drug experience would be like. In this context, *Sgt. Pepper* was a personal, communal, and cultural "event," and fans' three-year relationship with the Beatles made Paul's comments more compelling.

Many fans perceived the Beatles as more credible, more authentic, and more "on your side" than parents, churches, or schools. In an article called "Pop Music: The Messengers," *Time* magazine observed, "Kids sense a quality of defiant honesty in the Beatles and admire their freedom and open-mindedness; they see them as peers who are in a position to try anything, and who can be relied on to tell it to them straight— and to tell them what they want to hear."[17]

In language similar to that used in their review of *A Hard Day's Night* three years earlier, the magazine noted the Beatles' "refreshing distrust of authority, disdain for conventions and impatience with hypocrisy." In 1964, the press didn't see the significance of Beatle attitude because they didn't see the band through fans' eyes or fans' life circumstances. They also didn't know how long the Beatles would last or how uniquely important they would become to their millions of fans. Now, the significance emerges: "When the Beatles talk—about drugs, the war in Vietnam, religion—millions listen, and this is a new situation in the pop music world."[18] What *Time* and other cultural observers didn't fully appreciate was that this type of influence, this type of relationship, was a new situation in the world, period.

Though many fans are reluctant to say anything negative or critical about the Beatles, many do believe they influenced some young people to use drugs. This is not to blame or necessarily fault the Beatles, but merely to avoid historical whitewashing. Several fans remember "hearing stories" about kids who had "bad trips," or worse. A male fan, age nineteen at the time, recalled his "brother's best friend committed suicide after taking LSD."

Many young people, with their normal insecurities and fluid identities, tried hallucinogenic drugs a few times. Some had an experience they didn't like and stopped. Some, like the Beatles, benefited from the experience, or at least enjoyed it. But others, with more fragile egos, undiagnosed mental health problems, or other emotional vulnerabilities, embarked on acid trips and, physically or mentally, never returned.

The Summer of Love

Two weeks after the release of *Sgt. Pepper*, The Monterey International Pop Music Festival kicked off the "Summer of Love" and reconfirmed San Francisco as the seat of the counterculture. Estimates vary, but somewhere between fifty-five thousand and ninety thousand young music fans turned out to hear Jefferson Airplane, the Mamas and the Papas, the Byrds, the Association, the Who, Quicksilver Messenger Service, Simon and Garfunkel, Janis Joplin, and others. The event marked the first American appearance by the Jimi Hendrix Experience and introduced Otis Redding to a large, mostly white audience. It was also Ravi Shankar's first performance before a rock crowd.

Though none of the Beatles were at the event—despite rumors to the contrary—they did play a significant role behind the scenes. The Beatles were friends with the Byrds and the Mamas and the Papas, the prime movers behind the event, and Paul sat on the festival's planning committee. They also created artwork for the festival's program. They were big fans of Jimi Hendrix—having just seen him perform a surprise homage to them in London—and were largely responsible for him being on the bill. Many British and American bands wanted to perform, but drug-related visa problems, miscommunication, and insufficient coolness in the eyes of planners kept significant acts off the stage.

In addition to their behind-the-scenes role at the festival, the Beatles also had a sanctifying presence. Festival staffers wore badges that read, "A splendid time is guaranteed for all," and David Crosby, on stage with the Byrds, quoted McCartney from the recent *Life* magazine interview: "If we gave LSD to all the statesmen and politicians in the world, we might have a chance at stopping war." The crowd cheered.[19]

One of the most important bands emerging from San Francisco at this time was Jefferson Airplane, whose "Somebody to Love"—from their breakthrough album *Surrealistic Pillow*—became a number five hit. The song introduced a strong, assertive, female voice to Top 40 radio, and the album further turned the attention of the nation's youth westward.

Rock, pop, folk-rock, psychedelic—whatever it was called—there was a lot of new music to listen to that summer. Beatle fans were diversifying, but whether they were also listening to the Doors or Donovan, Motown or Moby Grape, the Beatles remained the "main course":

Not everyone was listening to the same thing anymore—there were more options—Cream, Hendrix, Simon and Garfunkel, the Doors, the Monkees. But the Beatles were a common denominator regardless of what else you listened to. Male, b. '58

I had a dear friend who smoked pot, loved the Grateful Dead, wore Eastern dresses, and knew nothing about politics. I was political and countercultural and I didn't use drugs. But we both liked the Beatles. Female b. '46

All You Need Is Love

On June 25, three weeks after the release of *Sgt. Pepper*, the Beatles represented the UK in *Our World*, the first live, international satellite TV hook-up. An estimated four hundred million people watched them perform "All You Need Is Love," dressed in designer hippie chic, surrounded by a studio orchestra and a crowd of friends, also in psychedelic duds, including a visibly humbled Mick Jagger. Written hastily after weeks of procrastination, the song's simple words and universal message were perfect for the occasion and perfectly defined the moment. Released in mid-July, "All You Need Is Love," was number one a month later. The song ascended the charts while "San Francisco (Be Sure to Wear Some Flowers in Your Hair)" was enjoying a four-week stint in the top five. Performed by Scott McKenzie and written by John Phillips of the Mamas and the Papas to promote the Monterey Festival, the song became an international hit and is credited with fueling the migration of one hundred thousand "flower children" to San Francisco. The global siblinghood of Beatle fans who watched the Beatles on *Our World* couldn't have missed the conspicuous red flower in Paul's hair—a shout out to hippies everywhere.

In its July 7 cover story, "The Hippies: The Philosophy of a Subculture," *Time* magazine described these "internal émigrés" as "young and generally thoughtful Americans who are unable to reconcile themselves to the stated values and implicit contradictions of contemporary Western society" and are seeking "individual liberation through means as various as drug use, total withdrawal from the economy and the quest for individual identity."

The article, significant in that it framed America's perception of the youth movement while also fueling it, observed, "The cult is a growing phenomenon that has not yet reached its peak—and may not do so for years to come." According to *Time*, "the most striking thing about the hippie phenomenon is the way it has touched the imagination of the 'straight' society," and that "hippie slang has already entered common usage and spiced up American humor."

As for the movement's leaders, readers are told that, "Except for a few spiritual gurus and swamis, the hippie movement is leaderless and loose." Yet, the in-depth article cites the Beatles as "the major taste-makers in hippiedom," mentioning the new "psychedelic" album, and reminding the nation that "Beatle Paul McCartney admits to taking acid trips." According to the article, hippies are "fed up" with many aspects of American society, including the draft. Hippies, however, were not the only ones protesting the war.

By mid-1967, five hundred American soldiers were dying in Vietnam every month, yet 40 percent of Americans still supported sending more troops.[20] When a coalition of eighty antiwar groups planned a demonstration at an LA hotel where President Johnson was being honored, the police anticipated two thousand protestors at most, but ten thousand showed up. The LAPD was unable to disperse the crowd, and a violent clash followed—foreshadowing the rapid growth of the antiwar movement and further clashes with law enforcement.[21]

The Summer of Love was also marred by race rioting, making it a "long hot summer" for residents of American cities large and small. Riots broke out in Newark, Detroit, Atlanta, Boston, Cincinnati, Buffalo, Tampa, Birmingham, Chicago, New York, Milwaukee, Minneapolis, New Britain, CT, and Rochester, NY.

While burning, looting, and the ongoing civil rights issue may not have directly touched the lives of most Beatle fans, they heard fifteen-year-old Janis Ian sing about interracial dating in "Society's Child." The controversial song, depicting a white girl breaking up with her black boyfriend under pressure from parents, school, and friends, reached number fourteen in July, quite a feat for a song banned on many radio stations. Though primarily about race issues, the song, like the rest of Ian's album, was an insightful, heartfelt critique of liberal hypocrisy and its toxic impact on young people, especially girls.

When George and Pattie Harrison visited Haight-Ashbury in August, two months after the release of *Sgt. Pepper*, they were disturbed by what they saw and couldn't wait to escape the scene. The community spirit and positive vision Paul saw when he visited four months earlier was gone. Dirty, strung-out runaways were thrilled to see George and his small entourage, all of whom were eager to retreat to the safety of their limo. Disappointed that George declined their offers of drugs and complied only briefly with their request to play the guitar, the agitated, grotty throng rocked the car back and forth and nearly turned it over. The flowers had wilted. Haight-Ashbury was no longer a youth paradise, though teenage runaways continued to get press attention.[22]

Listening to the Pre-Fabs

Eight months after the debut of their TV show, the Monkees—now writing their own songs and playing their own instruments—released their third album, *Headquarters*. The album went straight to number one, a position it held for only one week before it was overtaken by *Sgt Pepper*. *Headquarters* remained in the number two position for eleven weeks.

The Monkees wanted to show the world they could do it, and they did. *Headquarters* is a competent, thoughtful record, with multiple Beatlesque flourishes and outright shout-outs to "the four kings of EMI." It is playful, clever, and irreverent, as expected. Like their TV show, it presents its countercultural message with a mix of goofiness, simplicity, and earnestness. Many young Beatle fans on their Beatle break preferred *Headquarters* because "*Sgt. Pepper* was a little hard to grasp":

> You saw the Monkees on TV and you saw their personalities; the Monkees included me in their clubhouse; I could enter their world. The Beatles' world was too hard to figure out. You didn't get to hear the Beatles talk; they stopped interacting with you. Male b. '57

> I saw *Sgt. Pepper* in the record store, but I couldn't relate to it. I didn't hear the music and there were no singles from it. I didn't necessarily want to get it. I thought the Beatles were leaving me

behind. It was okay because I was listening to *Headquarters*. Male, b. '55

The other Monkees hit of the summer, "Pleasant Valley Sunday," peaked at number three in August. The song opens with a Beatle-like guitar intro, and then gives the listener a "Penny Lane"–like tour of a neighborhood and its inhabitants. The inhabitants of Penny Lane are presented as quirky, but no judgment is passed on them. In contrast, the listener sees the inhabitants of Pleasant Valley through the cynical, bored eyes of an idealistic young person on the cusp of adulthood, turned off by consumer culture; the kind of young person who might be thinking about running away.

An Exit and an Entrance

In late August a full-page petition appeared in the *Times* of London calling for major reform of Britain's marijuana laws. The petition was signed by over sixty prominent British citizens, including all four Beatles and Brian Epstein.

The Beatles' drug use goes back at least as far as their days in Hamburg, when "prellies" allowed them to stay up all night to "mach schau." But by this point, with fame, fortune, and power beyond anything they could have imagined back on the Reeperbahn, they saw drugs as a tool for mind expansion—a way to tap into the other 90 percent of the brain. Drugs were also seen as a vehicle for finding spiritual enlightenment. Epstein's drug use, in contrast, was more about getting through the lonely, anxiety-filled days and nights at the vortex of global celebrity while confined in a closet. He died of an accidental prescription drug overdose just as the Beatles were embarking on a new spiritual quest. Many fans remember "wondering what would happen after Brian died."

The Beatles learned of Brian's death on the final day of a weekend meditation retreat with Maharishi Mahesh Yogi, whom they had met only days earlier. After two days of meditation and living in a spartan college dorm—an already disorienting situation—the stunned Beatles, with no time to process what happened, faced the press to comment on their shocking loss.

The Maharishi entering their lives at the precise moment of Brian's exit seemed significant. Some fans remember seeing John and George on the news, visibly shaken, answering questions about their plans, and whether the Maharishi had given them any advice for coping with the sudden passing of their friend and mentor. The Beatles renounced the use of drugs at this time, though the renunciation would prove to be short-lived.

Brian had been there from the beginning, but because the Maharishi was new, unusual, and had entered their lives at a vulnerable moment, fans felt very protective. Many remember feeling the Beatles "might be taken advantage of" or that "the Maharishi was trying to take over." Some wondered if the Maharishi was "sincere," although some of these memories may be shaded by knowledge of how the Beatles relationship with the Maharishi evolved and ultimately ended.

Some fans, of all ages, thought the Beatles' involvement with the Maharishi was "ridiculous." A female fan (b. '49) understood "they needed a break from the insanity" but didn't understand why they "reached out to this scrawny little man." Others thought it made sense because they "needed guidance" or "just didn't want to be bothered anymore." Some remember "reading more about it" at the time and thought the Beatles "were lucky to have the money to travel to places like India and seek truth, not caring what anyone thought."

Many younger fans remember thinking "it was all very exotic; part of their mystique," but others thought it was "weird," and one, age eleven at the time, said she felt "alienated from them." Another female fan (b. '53) wondered, "Why don't they just pray?"

Some fans, college-age at the time, knew people who meditated and understood what it was about. One female fan (b. '47) saw it as "an extension of the Eastern direction that had been there since *Help!*" A few older fans went to Transcendental Meditation Society meetings "with fifty dollars, a handkerchief, and a flower." Others remember oranges instead of flowers.

It's been several decades since the health benefits of meditation have been recognized by Western medicine, and many doctors routinely advise their patients to meditate for stress reduction and overall well-being. It's likely that the Beatles' interest in meditation was a catalyst in the widespread acceptance of the practice. But more pertinent to the fan experience at the time, regardless of whether they were intrigued, "turned off," or neutral about the Maharishi, was that the Beatles had once again given fans something new to think about, talk about, and have an opinion about. A male fan, age seventeen at the time, said the Beatles "made everyone think about aspiring to spiritual enlightenment."

Crayons to Perfume

Though many fans were bewildered by the Beatles new music and spiritual quests, they continued to follow the comings and goings of the hippie Fab Four and other pop acts in *16* magazine. Though often dismissed as unimportant, the magazine regularly reached over four million girls between eleven and fourteen—and their older and younger brothers and sisters.

In November 1967, a profile of *16* editor Gloria Stavers appeared in the *Saturday Evening Post*, revealing the enormous power the so-called "Mother superior of the inferior" held over the music industry and young music fans. Years later, music critic Dave Marsh credited Stavers with "basically inventing rock and pop culture journalism."[23]

Record company execs sought Stavers' advice on how to promote their artists and wouldn't make a decision until hearing from her. Talent agencies counted the number of pages devoted to their clients, and even Bob Dylan, not a "fave rave" of typical readers, would play his new songs to her over the phone to get her reaction.

Stavers, age thirty at the time, said "she has a button in her head" that she could push and "become thirteen again" and claimed that "no other magazine can reach these children" the way she could. Stavers had enormous respect for the intelligence and emotional concerns of her readers, who wrote hundreds of letters a week bemoaning the fact "nobody takes them seriously." She noted that her readers were "strangely unaware of their tremendous economic power," but aware of their "mass power," because they "hear the constant adult talk about 'teenagers.'"

The savvy editor spoke of the "flower children" wanting to "flood the adult world with love," saying, "there's a crusade going on whether parents know it or not," and that "the rebellion against the parent generation shows all the signs of being a very solid mass movement."[24] These teenage letter writers, whom Stavers referred to as "the future mothers of America," would soon find other ways to express their frustration at not being taken seriously. And many of Stavers' older readers were graduating to a new publication.

Numerous "underground newspapers" had been established nationwide by 1967, many in San Francisco. All these publications reported on music and the counterculture, though each had its own flavor of antiestablishment politics. Out of this primordial soup emerged *Rolling Stone* magazine.

Twenty-one-year-old Jann Wenner was active in the Free Speech Movement at Berkeley and wrote a column called "Something's Happening" for the Berkeley student newspaper. After a stint at the very left-leaning *Ramparts*, Wenner dropped out of school, borrowed $7,500 from family and friends, and cofounded *Rolling Stone* with Ralph J. Gleason, jazz critic for the *San Francisco Chronicle*.

Describing the magazine's mission in its first edition, Wenner wrote, "*Rolling Stone* is not just about the music, but about the things and attitudes that music embraces." The first issue, in newspaper format, came out on November 9, 1967, with a cover story on the Monterey Pop Festival and a photo of John Lennon as Private Gripweed from *How I Won the War*.[25] Many young fans, male and female, read *Rolling Stone* and *16* on a regular basis, passionately engaging with both the lightness and the heaviness of what was going on around them.

Step Right This Way

The *Magical Mystery Tour* album, released in late November, included four songs from previous singles, plus two songs released as a single the same day, "Hello Goodbye" b/w "I Am The Walrus." The other five songs were from *Magical Mystery Tour*, the Beatles' fifty-three minute avant-garde film, conceived and directed primarily by Paul McCartney and scheduled to be broadcast on American television in March.[26]

The day before the album and single were released, a promo for "Hello Goodbye," filmed only two weeks earlier, was shown on the *Ed Sullivan Show*. Before introducing the film, Sullivan read a brief telegram, allegedly from the band, with regrets and Christmas greetings, allowing him to claim relevance through his ongoing chumminess with the much-transformed Beatles.

The film begins with a curtain going up to reveal the Beatles in their *Sgt. Pepper* suits, performing on a stage with a psychedelic Art Nouveau backdrop. It had been five months since the album's release, but they are still obviously in *Sgt. Pepper* mode. John and Paul are clean-shaven, but otherwise there is no new look, no new iteration. Facial hair had become "a new variable in their appearance," but it would never be as startling as it was the first time fans saw it.

Obviously miming the song, the Beatles look, for the most part, self-conscious, uncomfortable, and bored. When they vamp for the camera, intermittently, it is parody. Paul, of course, is the most animated. At times, it seems he is trying to muster enough performance energy for all four. George looks particularly unhappy to be there, almost angry, in his tri-cornered feathered chapeau. There are no microphones and few tight close-ups.

About a third of the way through, there's a cut to the four of them posed in their iconic collarless jackets, waving with excess enthusiasm, and, through facial expressions and shrugs, commenting on the absurdity of it all. Cutting back to the stage, Ringo is shaking his head, as in the early days of Beatlemania. But with his hot pink suit and facial hair, the gesture doesn't express glee and exuberance; instead, it underscores the absence of those once defining Beatle qualities. Another quick cut to the gray-suited early iteration, then back to the stage. John notices Paul's sudden stomping to the beat and apes the move with exaggeration.

They bow in unison, the song transitions to its extended outro, and the film winds down chaotically, abandoning any pretense of a performance in real time. Maori dancers suddenly appear, there's yet another cut to gray-suited Fabs, and then quick cuts to all of them on the same stage, changing their clothes, moving equipment, dancing, and performing bursts of silliness for the nonexistent audience. The curtain goes down on the Beatles' wacky in-joke, and Sullivan says, "That was very. . . that was very thoughtful of the guys to prepare that for us," and tells the audience "Hello Goodbye" is the band's latest hit record. The song went to number one about a month later and held the position for three weeks. Though the A-side is upbeat and cheerful, they look severe and annoyed on the picture sleeve.

The "Hello Goodbye" film is the first new footage of the group since February, and it was the first new music since the summer's "All You Need Is Love" and "Baby You're a Rich Man." The Beatles seemed distant in the film, even when fooling around. The self-referencing told fans "We've changed but it's still us," and the simple, playful lyrics seemed to support that. But the heavy-handedness of it—especially after using the same self-referencing technique earlier in the year on the *Sgt. Pepper* cover and at the end of "All You Need Is Love"—seemed to almost mock rather than neutrally or nostalgically recall their former image.

The *Magical Mystery Tour* album was seen by many fans as a "continuation of *Sgt. Pepper*" in that it was, as one male fan (b. '48) put it, "progressive, psychedelic, and cacophonous; it was otherworldly and allowed you to visit different places in your mind." Another male fan (b. '49) saw it as a "sequel to *Sgt. Pepper*" in that it "invited you somewhere."

Fans had come to expect every album to be significantly different from the one before, but *Magical Mystery Tour* violated that pattern. Those who had been closely following their development and loved *Sgt. Pepper* were "a little disappointed" because they expected another "game changer." Those who were less thrilled with *Sgt. Pepper* were also disappointed at the similarity. A male fan, age twelve at the time and on a Beatle break, recalled, "It looked like the same Beatles as on *Sgt. Pepper*, I wanted melodies but didn't think I would get that there." And then there was the issue of "not enough new songs."

The album's cover, with its four different typefaces, was colorful and flashy like the previous one but lacked thoughtfulness and precision. Fans thought the pictures inside were "weird," but of course "you gave anything a second look and listen because it was the Beatles." The opening song invited listeners on a magical mystery tour; but they were already on a magical mystery tour with the Beatles—and about to start the fourth year. As a male fan (b. '53) put it, "you accepted the disappointment along with the enchantment."

Fans remember the "creepy images" of "I Am the Walrus" but "loved singing it" and were "glad the words were there." There was something empowering about singing along with John's nasty rant—"it didn't matter what it meant." Though John wrote the supposedly meaningless lyrics to confound those who look for meaning in his songs, the sounds and imagery of the carefully crafted nonsense lyrics express a generalized disgust at the establishment, much in keeping with the moment. Fans didn't know anything about the origins of the song until much later, but they heard Lennon cleverly railing against the world, and they joined in.

"Blue Jay Way," the only Harrison song on the collection, was a haunting, dirge-like production with otherworldly sounds that captured fans' attention. Recalling the song, a female fan, age twelve at the time, said: "It attracted and repelled me. I tried to keep up with them, but that song pushed me beyond where I was emotionally and intellectually." The more fans were "pushed beyond" where they were, the more they let the Beatles in, the more intertwined they became in fans intellectual and emotional development.

Also reacting to "Blue Jay Way," a male fan, age fourteen at the time, said, "The combination of music and lyrics made it spooky and mysterious, and of course you always want to solve a mystery."

When asked about the goal of the mystery, what he would learn if he solved it, he explained: "It puts you on the same wavelength with them; they were geniuses and it brought you closer to them. You wanted to understand so you could feel connected to them."

Young fans who stuck with the Beatles, through facial hair, "creepy circus music," and spooky cellos, were drawn to them as a source of stimulation and psychic nutrition they couldn't get anywhere else. Having an older sibling or friend as a "Beatle buddy"—someone to listen and discuss them with—also made them, indirectly, more accessible. Fans listened with activated minds, digesting the next new set of ideas and sounds, letting the Beatles take them to new stages of emotional and intellectual development.

The band had become so omnipresent and important to the culture as a whole that "trying to keep up with them" allowed young fans to feel connected to people and ideas far beyond their own neighborhoods. Fans signed on to the Beatles' vision. In the ways that ultimately mattered, engaged Beatle fans were cool no matter how old they were.

The *Magical Mystery Tour* album made the mystery theme explicit, but the many fans who describe themselves as "lucky" to have "followed them from the beginning" or as lucky to have become "aware of things when the air was filled with Beatles" had been working on Beatle mysteries since *Revolver*, if not before.

In some sense, the Beatles were no less mysterious on the *Ed Sullivan Show* in 1964 than they were in 1967—but fans worked out, internalized, and grew from that early mystery, changing the culture in the process and planting the seeds for the Summer of Love. The loud screams of the much-maligned and misunderstood pubescent girls in the *Sullivan* audience and in the bleachers at Shea woke up a generation.

Together, *Sgt. Pepper* and *Magical Mystery Tour* included everything the Beatles recorded in 1967 and are rightly seen as a pair. The band's acid-fueled alternative consciousness was manifest on these records, thus presenting fans with myriad enigmas and ambiguities to explore. High or straight, with friends or alone, in bedrooms or college dorms, it was an experience so stimulating as to be "mind-blowing."

The hastily conceived and self-indulgent *Magical Mystery Tour* film outraged television viewers in the UK when it was broadcast the day after Christmas—on the national Boxing Day holiday—and was nearly unanimously described by critics as the Beatles' first failure. Lacking the discipline and professionalism Epstein might have provided, the film can be seen as the product of four wealthy, powerful man-children to whom no one, not even the head of the BBC, could say no. Plans to show the film on American television were scrapped. Although fans in metropolitan areas had opportunities to see the film a few years later, many didn't see it for decades.

Not Just the Hits

By the end of 1967, the trend toward more explicit lyrics and adult themes in pop music was becoming a concern for radio station managers across the country who didn't want to "feel responsible for provoking their typical listener, described as "a twelve-year-old with the mind of a six-year-old" into a life of promiscuity, drug addiction, and maybe, an awareness of the new music."[27]

Writing in 1967 about the issue of censorship on Top 40 radio, critic Robert Corliss noted that in the early days of rock and roll, songs were banned because of "unsavory incidents in the lives of the singers, but not until the Beatles did they find material worth censoring." The handholding of early Lennon-McCartney hits was not a concern. The concern started with the pop music renaissance and thematic maturation those early hits initiated.

Top 40 radio stations faced a dilemma: they didn't want to offend their listeners or frighten sponsors; yet they programmed for the largest possible audience—most of whom wanted to hear "Let's Spend the Night Together," "Society's Child," and "Light My Fire."

Corliss predicted artists would present objectionable themes with more subtlety, and quoted lines from Peter, Paul and Mary's "I Dig

Rock and Roll Music" to support this view. But the mass economic power of this generation, of which *16*'s Gloria Stavers said her readers were unaware, was forcing a change in the entire radio industry, as broadcasters with FM licenses began programming "underground radio."

These new FM stations were a boon to greater artistic expression and encouraged the emphasis on the album, as opposed to the single, an approach that began with *Rubber Soul*. Listeners would hear a new breed of "laid back" DJ—quite unlike Arnie "Woo Woo" Ginsburg and Cousin Brucie—rapping between deep cuts about politics, drugs, and other social issues.

Calm Before the Storm

As the year drew to a close, an estimated hundred thousand people— a cross-section of America—rallied in DC to show their opposition to the Vietnam War. Students protested the on-campus recruitment efforts of the military and napalm manufacturer Dow Chemical, along with the war. Draft cards were burned at induction offices across America. Protestors attempting to exorcise evil from the Pentagon used flower power to disarm law enforcement, thereby creating a new symbol and catchphrase for the counterculture.

President Johnson announced progress in the Vietnam War; two weeks later his secretary of defense resigned over LBJ's refusal to accept his advice to de-escalate. Teenage boys and young men increasingly sought sympathetic counsel as they weighed the option of "resisting" or "dodging."

In defense of the counterculture, anthropologist and World War II–era conscientious objector David P. McAllester pointed out that what most frightens the establishment about young people is that they are "blatantly practicing" what their elders have taught them: "We counsel them at their mother's knee to love thy neighbor, and they burn their draft cards. We urge them to be creative and original and suddenly they are—with hair, clothing, art, dance, and music that we can't stand the sight or sound of. We bid them know themselves, and they launch investigations of ideas, and of their own bodies, that seem to us to threaten our whole way of life."[28]

A male Beatle fan, age eight in 1967, remembers, "The nuns talked about the Beatles when 'All You Need Is Love' was out, but they weren't critical. They said Jesus spoke of love too."

CHAPTER SIX
We All Want to Change the World
January 1968–December 1968

More and more guys only two or three years older than I was were coming home in body bags or without arms or legs. It was pretty upsetting to think that your boyfriend or your brother, if you had one, might be headed to Vietnam. Especially if you were lower middle class or working class, chances were not good that your brother or boyfriend would go to college and be able to get a deferment.

Female, b. '51

BY 1968, THE BEATLES' MOST PROFOUND and enduring impact on their original fan base was more or less established. There were of course more musical surprises to come, more enigmas to explore, and more happenings in the Beatles' personal lives for fans to ponder, discuss, and debate. For those still on the journey, those four Beatle-filled years significantly affected their development. Those too young to have fully appreciated *Rubber Soul*, *Revolver*, and *Sgt. Pepper* in real time revisited those records repeatedly and absorbed their richness.

Though their records and appearances were less frequent, and there were more artists for fans to explore on the radio, in their record purchases, and in magazines, the Beatles still remained the focus. And young fans who "got off the Beatle bus" would be getting back on soon.

For Beatle fans of all ages, 1968 would feel different from 1967—darker and less colorful; less hopeful, more violent. They didn't hear anything new from the Beatles until later in the year, but they watched and participated in the events of 1968 with Beatle-informed consciousness. In this year of turbulence and surreal violence, fans especially appreciated the diversion, encouragement, and insight the previous four years of Beatles had brought them. Even if they momentarily stopped focusing on the band and their music, they knew they were there. The Beatles had become "part of the atmosphere."

Social Sorting

Fans got a New Year's treat in early January with *Look* magazine's special issue on "Sound and Fury in the Arts" which featured a pullout portfolio of Beatle portraits by no less than Richard Avedon. They enjoyed and had come to expect photos of the Beatles in newspapers and magazines from time to time, but the dramatic *Look* spread was more than a casual photo op—this was obviously art.

The color and detail in each solarized portrait seemed to reveal glimmers of truth about its subject, while maintaining, if not adding, mystery. The intense black and white pullout, a "group" photo, shows four tired, highly styled, self-conscious young men.

"Hello Goodbye" was at number one while fans carefully removed the staples and hung these very special portraits on their walls. The penultimate goodbye to the psychedelic era held that position for three weeks—lots of New Year Beatle cheer—before being displaced by one-hit wonder John Fred and His Playboy Band's "Judy in Disguise (With Glasses)," which held the position for two weeks. The insipid tribute to "Lucy in the Sky with Diamonds" kept *Sgt. Pepper* in listeners' minds and may have gotten a few younger fans to go back and listen to the song they had found a little spooky six months earlier. "Judy" was knocked out of the number one position by the Lemon Pipers' "Green Tambourine," a song with earnest hippie imagery that also owes a debt to the previous year's psychedelia, which had turned both plastic and sour by year's end.

Linda Ronstadt had her first top twenty hit with "Different Drum," written by Monkee Mike Nesmith. The sound of a female voice on AM that didn't belong to Diana Ross was still a rare thing. Ronstadt's heartfelt yet powerful statement of a woman's desire for independence and freedom in a relationship was something new.

With the coming of FM, music fans now had options beyond Top 40 radio. Many quickly came to see the AM format as inferior; it's what you listened to in the car with your parents if you had no choice, if they let you. FM radio was a new world for open-minded music fans and seekers who required more. Listeners enjoyed album tracks by a wide range of artists across rock's quickly multiplying sub-genres and were exposed to sounds and ideas that were new and exciting.

Listening to FM set fans apart from friends who were content listening to Top 40, who "didn't need anything other than what they were forced to hear." Emerging and diverging music preferences began slowly separating kids who, for the past four years, had been huddling in someone's rec room listening to the latest Beatle record. Social groups were shuffled as young people sorted themselves. AM was for the younger or less sophisticated listeners, who "weren't interested when someone told them about a new thing related to music, or dress, or politics."

FM listeners were exposed to countercultural politics along with the Grateful Dead, and Jimi Hendrix, Cream, and the Velvet Underground, and they were also more likely to try marijuana and other drugs—part of the social sorting process. Because these drugs were illegal, even casual users came to see themselves as outsiders and hung around with others who were similarly inclined—the "freaks" and the "hippies." Fans recall "cool, younger, teachers" who would talk with them in small groups about the issues of the day or sit with a group of kids—"the hippies and the freaks, not the jocks"—and listen to records with them.

Even young teen listeners tuned in to the youth culture by turning on FM. This new radio transported you to a place where cool people listened to important music and talked about important things. They seemed to be talking *to* you, not *at* you; and there weren't any grown-ups around.

Young people were now getting countercultural messages directly from FM radio and from *Rolling Stone,* or one of the hundred-plus underground newspapers that were in circulation by 1968. Network television, in a more sanitized and ambivalent way, also brought the counterculture and the growing antiwar movement to a mass audience. A year after the Be-In put hippies on the front page, *Rowan & Martin's Laugh-In* debuted on NBC, appropriating the evocative countercul-ture suffix, a Hollywoodization that both trivialized and advanced the movement's agenda.

Though *Laugh-In's* creative team purposely included writers of all political persuasions and often featured retro rat-packers vainly seeking new relevance—including the show's two hosts—*Laugh-In's* quick-cut, mix-it-up style, mod fashion, flower-power set design, and topical humor gave the show a decidedly left-of-center feel. The peace button on Dan Rowan's lapel contributed to that vibe as well.

Youth culture attitudes toward drugs and sex had slowly been creeping into mainstream media since 1965 and *Laugh-In* brought it to a new level. Like the hipper and more poignant *Smothers Brothers Comedy Hour, Laugh-In* flirted with the network censors. Unfortunately, the combination of sexual boundary-pushing, prefeminist consciousness, and vaudeville slapstick created a mindless grooviness that too often found humor in playfully assaulting women wearing as little as the cen-sors allowed. Beatle fans enjoyed the show's plastic hipness, as did the Beatles themselves, who watched it on BBC2.[1]

Political comedy had been heating up, reflecting growing antiwar sentiment. But when North Vietnamese and Vietcong troops staged the Tet Offensive in late January, antiwar sentiment surged. From a strictly military standpoint, the long battle was a victory for the US and the South, but President Johnson and his best spinners couldn't hide the fact that the US military was unprepared for jungle warfare and had underestimated the enemy's skill and determination. In the six weeks following the Tet Offensive, LBJ's overall approval rating went from 48 to 36 percent; approval of his handling of the war went from 40 percent to 26 percent.[2]

While the Beatles' were meditating in Rishikesh and preparing to bring their innovative business plans to fruition, fans of all ages watched as the love and optimism of the previous year slowly began to fade. The war was dividing the country, with six hundred thousand soldiers in Vietnam, nineteen thousand American deaths, and no end in sight.[3] Male Beatle fans born in 1950 or before faced the prospect of being drafted—many were scared, angry, and confused.

By March, *Newsweek*, NBC, CBS, several *New York Times* columnists and even the right-leaning *Wall Street Journal* had all reached the conclusion that the war was unwinnable.[4] The media's ambivalent response to the counterculture and antiwar movement continued, and in February 1968, CBS reversed its position from five months earlier and allowed Pete Seeger to perform "Waist Deep in the Big Muddy," on the *Smothers Brothers Comedy Hour*, an antiwar song that pointedly referred to LBJ as the "big fool." In late March, LBJ announced he would "neither seek nor accept the presidential nomination" for a reelection run.

Mind the Gap

If "hippie" was the buzzword of 1967, the following year was all about the "generation gap." The constant media chatter about the generation gap and student protestors had an undertone of bewilderment reminiscent of Beatlemania press coverage four years earlier. In both cases, the establishment witnessed reactions in young people that they couldn't understand. And in both cases, they favored convoluted explanations, avoiding the need to examine what their sons and daughters were actually responding to.

The press had ultimately concluded that the Beatlemania of 1964 was a harmless diversion, but if they had seen it through young people's eyes, they wouldn't have been so flummoxed by the generation gap and the unrest on college campuses four years later. In fact, student protestors were described in almost the exact same language as that used to describe the Beatles in the laudatory reviews of *A Hard Day's Night* discussed earlier: "anarchists," "not giving a damn for prejudices of their elders," and "never for a moment blinded to the really flagrant foolishness of the adult world around them."[5]

For those who saw the youth movement as a generation of young people raised on Dr. Spock's indulgent parenting practices, campus unrest was nothing more than a temper tantrum. Another common reaction to the protestors was to dismiss their "tortured probing of conscience" as "idealistic."[6] In other words, students may have high moral purpose, but they're naive and need not be taken seriously.

Some suggested that young people were protesting the draft and social injustice because they felt guilty about their own relative privilege. Another riff on the "affluence" observation was that protestors should appreciate how much better they had it than their parents' generation and tend to their studies.[7] The main reason for the protests—forced conscription into an unwinnable war—was rarely addressed.

Four years earlier, when Dylan told America "your sons and your daughters are beyond your command," the truth of the observation was not merely that they could no longer tell their children what do, but that young people had a greater stake in the future, and, using the moral compass and the education their parents had given them, were developing new value systems.

These new values were not only about war and peace, and race. An in-depth report on the new "arrangement" of unmarried college-age couples living together noted that "Victorian and Protestant ethics are being replaced by a whole new set of values, and a new emphasis on honesty and integrity in personal relationships."[8] Reasons given for the trend include access to birth control, alienation from parents, recreational drug use, "the love philosophy of the hippies," and "the influence of the Beatles and Bob Dylan."[9]

Antiwar candidate Eugene McCarthy's "Clean for Gene" volunteers, many of whom were in conflict with their real fathers, were willing to shave their beards, cut their hair, and lengthen their skirts because, according to some observers, the "paternal looking iconoclast was an ideal surrogate."[10] Again, simpler motivations were overlooked.

Some observers were a bit more insightful. Regarding McCarthy's appeal to young people, a *New York Times* editorial said the candidate's "fresh approach" to Vietnam shows that it's possible to "close the generation gap and to counter the alienation of America's young people." The editorial quotes McCarthy volunteers who "would have turned to violent protest" if Senator McCarthy had not entered the race.[11]

Big business was also watching the protestors. David Rockefeller, then head of Chase Manhattan Bank, told corporate leaders they "could not afford to ignore" the generation gap, and though young people's attitudes "are both uncongenial and deeply disturbing, they are realities and angry denunciation will not cause them to vanish." Rockefeller urged business leaders to embrace the qualities their "youthful critics" said they lacked—"open-mindedness, intellectual honesty, and commitment to responsible social progress."[12]

A week before student protests rocked his campus and spread like wildfire to others, Columbia University president Grayson Kirk called on the US to get out of Vietnam "as soon as possible" because none of the country's other problems could be solved until the conflict was ended. But to Establishment Kirk, the most pressing problem was that "young people in disturbing numbers appear to reject all forms of authority," and have "taken refuge in a turbulent and inchoate nihilism whose sole objectives are destructive." Speaking for many with generation-gap jitters, Kirk warned, "I know of no time in our history when the gap between the generations has been wider or more potentially dangerous."[13]

From the students' point of view, those who condemned their idealism were simply accepting defeat while claiming to be realistic. As articulated in the SDS's 1962 *Port Huron Statement*,[14] students envisioned a society that appealed to the unfulfilled human capacity for reason, freedom, love, and creativity—a vision consistent with the Beatles' message that emerged in the intervening years.

On April 30, in a move that would come to symbolize the generation gap, a thousand helmeted police officers swarmed onto the Columbia University campus and began dragging away protestors, kicking and beating many along the way. Hundreds of students were arrested and dozens injured.

Cultural luminaries outside of business and politics were also asked to comment on the generation gap and student protestors. Leopold Stokowski—who early on encouraged young Beatle fans to embrace self-expression, seek ecstasy, and find joie de vivre—was once again displaying his empathy for the younger generation: "The revolts in the schools are mainly positive. . . . Much in education today is routine and dry. If the students are protesting dead attitudes, they are right." Sounding more like a tripping flower child than an octogenarian maestro, he continued: "What older people today must try to grasp is that everything is changing all the time. . . . Everything is in a state of vibration—sun, earth, ideas, everything—and expanding outwards from the center."[15]

In a valedictorian speech at Williams College, a young man observed, "The generation gap is something America over thirty has invented to excuse itself from listening." The young woman giving the valedictory speech at Radcliffe said, "We do not feel like a cool, swinging generation—we are eaten up inside by an intensity we cannot name."[16]

Making Ends Meet

Before leaving for India, the Beatles recorded "Lady Madonna" b/w "The Inner Light" for a mid-March release. The B-side, weirdly reminiscent of the Hollies' 1966 hit "Stop Stop Stop," would be the band's final installment of the previous year's Indian-influenced psychedelia. The "Lady Madonna" promotional film was shown on ABC's *Hollywood Palace* in late March, revealing new, simpler Beatles.

The back-to-basics, Fats Domino-influenced rocker continued the band's self-referencing habit in the "see how they run" refrain. Only a tad less perfunctory than the "Hello Goodbye" promo of four months before, the film actually showed viewers the "Hey Bulldog" recording session with a "Lady Madonna" soundtrack. Looking alert and energetic, the Beatles enjoy beans on toast before getting down to work in the studio—in the most ordinary and drab clothing fans had ever seen them wear.

McCartney's ode to single mothers peaked at number four in April. Bobby Goldsboro's "Honey," most memorable for the hilarious Smothers Brothers "Honey House" parody, was number one at the time and held the position for an inexplicable five weeks. Gary Puckett and the Union Gap's "Young Girl," one of their six interchangeable top twenty hits about deflowering virgins, was number two.

In early April, Simon and Garfunkel released *Bookends,* an artfully produced, self-conscious album that begged comparison with *Sgt. Pepper* and evoked the Beatles in several ways. A few seconds shy of thirty minutes, the tidy collection explored themes of time and aging with intelligence, wit, and poetry—and featured a cover with a Richard Avedon photo on the front and a Pepper-like spread of lyrics on the back.

The *Bookends* listening experience is theatrical, visual, and continuous like *Sgt. Pepper,* with named people and places, but the feel is as American as *Pepper* is British. Riddled with pop culture references, snide asides, and double-entendres, the album is wistful and longing, though not outright sad. Like *Pepper,* the sound is multilayered and multitextured, with effects that converge playfully with the lyrics.

Black Beatle Fans?

The day after *Bookend*'s release, Martin Luther King Jr. was assassinated in Memphis. Violence and riots followed in the days ahead, resulting in forty-six deaths. King had become a major voice of opposition to the Vietnam War, believing, like many, that "The promises of the Great Society have been shot down on the battlefields of Vietnam."[17]

A female Beatle fan, age twelve at the time, recalls, "I was watching *That Girl* and it was interrupted with a news bulletin that King had been shot. I remember thinking there would probably be more riots." A male fan, age eighteen at the time, also recalled the King assassination: "It was of a piece with the rest of the civil rights movement. It didn't hit me that much."

Most young Beatle fans did not feel personally connected to King but saw his assassination as part of the encroaching chaos—another act of violence that bubbled up from where chaos and violence frothed just below the surface. Beatle fans, like many other white Americans, had very little contact with "Negroes," and so their impressions were formed, for the most part, by the images they saw on television: stereotypes on sitcoms and dramas, singers on variety shows, athletes on playing fields, and depending on one's perspective, as oppressed citizens or rioters; maybe both.

When the Beatles were still a touring band, their refusal to play for segregated audiences had symbolic but little practical significance. Beatle fandom has always been a largely white phenomenon. Harvard Law School professor Randall Kennedy remembers laughing at "all the white people going crazy" when they arrived and saw reaction to their cover of the Isley Brothers' "Twist and Shout" as "yet another instance of white people finding they could only identify with other white people."[18]

According to black poet and critic Larry Neal, "Everything about them smacks of boyhood," and in the black community, "a manly image is highly valued and there is no place for little boys."[19] Similarly, cultural critic Benjamin DeMott wrote in 1968, "The Beatles' smoothie, nice-lad manner never much engaged lovers of mainstream soul."[20]

With the assassination of Martin Luther King Jr., black youth lost an inspiring leader, just as they had three years earlier with the assassination of Malcolm X. Along with black activists like Stokely Carmichael and musician James Brown, sports hero and conscientious objector Muhammad Ali—who publicly said, "No Vietcong ever called me nigger"—stepped into the void, bringing his antiwar and black pride messages to college campuses across the country. Fours year earlier, the Beatles had been pressured into doing a photo-op with then underdog

Ali, still called Cassius Clay. Iconic photos capture the moment when five ambitious and charismatic young men, still years away from their destinations, stopped to play when their paths briefly crossed.

The Apple Cart

Back from India and in the middle of recording the next album, Lennon and McCartney flew to New York to promote Apple, which John described as "a business concerning records, films, and electronics. And as a sideline, whatever it's called . . . manufacturing, or whatever." Seeming a bit impatient with the usual inane questions, and perhaps a bit uncomfortable in the new role of businessman, John continued: "We want to set up a system whereby people who just want to make a film about anything, don't have to go on their knees in somebody's office. Probably yours."

Some fans remember seeing John and Paul on the *Tonight Show* with Joe Garagiola sitting in for Johnny Carson, an interview that Lennon remembered as one of his most unpleasant. One female fan (b. '51) remembers, "I just happened to turn it on and there they were! Usually it was actresses or people my parents liked."

Paul coolly shared the magnanimous goals and innovative vision of the enterprise: "We're in the happy position of not really needing any more money. So for the first time, the bosses aren't in it for profit. If you come and see me and say, 'I've had such and such a dream,' I'll say, 'Here's so much money. Go away and do it.' We've already bought all our dreams. So now we want to share that possibility with others."

Always ready to add a bit of edge, John elaborated on Paul's effort to explain the project: "The aim of this company isn't really a stack of gold teeth in the bank. We've done that bit. It's more of a trick to see if we can actually get artistic freedom within a business structure."[21] In response to a reporter's question, John and Paul both reiterated their opposition to the war, with John noting that they came out against it "years ago."

Student protestors, capable of envisioning alternatives, were derisively called "idealists" by a defensive establishment that could comprehend only business as usual. In the middle of all this, John and Paul present Apple, their countercultural, alternative business model and it seemed to make perfect sense. Not that campus protestors were going to become entrepreneurs—at least not right away—but it was yet another suggestion, from the Beatles to their fans, that alternatives, once imagined, might be possible.

Apple aggressively recruited new talent by placing ads in youth-oriented music magazines. That they received more material than "five men in five years couldn't listen to" should have surprised no one.[22] No talent was recruited through this campaign, and even considering the artists who came in through the inner circle, their success at bringing new talent to the world fell short of expectations.[23]

It's beyond the scope of this book to delve into the irrational and capricious decision-making at Apple in the early years. Suffice to say it was a worthy concept, poorly executed, and, however imperfect, it was a template that would be used with more success decades later by others in the music industry. The problem wasn't their idealism; the problem was that the four principals and their inner circle lacked both interest and knowledge when it came to running a business.

The Beatles were explaining their new way of doing business to the world at the precise moment the world's under-thirties became fed up with business as usual. While John and Paul were on the Apple press junket, tens of thousands of students protested and clashed with police in the streets of Paris. Student fervor spread to the workers, resulting in more confrontations with police and general strikes that almost brought France to a standstill.

Inspired by Columbia and the Sorbonne, student protests spread to twenty different countries.[24] These protestors, despite differences in culture and language, grew up in the global village. They were united in their disgust with imperialistic wars like Vietnam, and in their desire to live more freely and meaningfully. Another thing they had in common was the Beatles. The global siblinghood had been listening together for four years.

What's with the Hair?

Less than a year after the Haight-Ashbury scene crested, hippiedom had come to Broadway, in *Hair: The American Tribal Love-Rock Musical*. Initially controversial, the show celebrated freedom, diverse sexuality, drug use, and racial and gender equality, with the war and opposition to it playing a central role. The show, like student protests, spread throughout the world.

During rehearsals for the show's London opening—which had to be postponed until theater censorship was abolished by the Theatres Act 1968[25]—the *Guardian* asked director Tom O'Horgan about the nudity in the show. O'Horgan explained that nudity "was a celebration of freedom, a casting off of false values."[26] A few months later, one of the *Guardian*'s more famous readers would use nudity to make a similar statement.

Establishment reaction to the counterculture throughout the sixties, even when it showed up on the Broadway stage, continued to clearly echo early reaction to the Beatles and *A Hard Day's Night*. At a loss to explain "what was so likeable" about *Hair*, New York Times drama critic Clive Barnes said, "I think it is simply that it is so likable."[27] John J. O'Connor of the *Wall Street Journal* said the show was "exuberantly defiant."[28] Richard Watts Jr. of the *New York Post* wrote that, "it has a surprising if perhaps unintentional charm, its high spirits are contagious, and its young zestfulness makes it difficult to resist."[29] It may seem difficult, by definition, to call a Broadway show countercultural. Yet, if open-minded audiences enjoy it, the countercultural agenda is advanced.

When the Beatles arrived on the scene four years earlier, their hair got more attention than their music, and the style caught on immediately. For male fans, longer intervals between haircuts turned into arguments with parents. Soon, acquiescing parents and their long-haired sons faced school administrators. Sometimes hair was cut and sometimes students were suspended—not exactly a punishment for the rapidly increasing population of long-haired boys.

Facial hair was also a dress code violation. A male fan, age seventeen, grew mutton-chop sideburns after seeing the "Lady Madonna" promo film and picture sleeve: "The principle told the gym teacher to take me downstairs and shave my sideburns. I couldn't believe they were doing this. My mother went down to the school and gave them hell; she defended me. I started growing them back right away and no one said a word."

The freedom and identity expressed through hair, the most personal and natural of adornments, could not, as a practical matter, be silenced. Several male fans between eleven and seventeen in 1968 have very unpleasant memories of parents, some of whom had been fairly tolerant, suddenly forcing them to cut their hair. One fan, age thirteen at the time, recalls: "I had very long hair at a young age and it drove my parents crazy. My hair was very important to me, but it was a source of almost constant friction in my suburban Boston family. I distinctly remember after some event, maybe they had found some pot, the folks insisted that I get it all cut off. Since I was a minor, there wasn't much I could do about it, so I submitted. I still haven't forgiven that transgression."

Another male fan, same age, recalls, "Somehow they finally forced me to get a haircut. As soon as we got home from the barber shop, I hid in my room with a towel over my head and cried for hours. I was so angry."

Long hair had unmistakable cultural meaning, and continued to show up in unlikely places. By the time Robert Kennedy entered the presidential race as the other peace candidate, he had skipped a few haircuts. When asked about the tumult and adulation he encountered on the campaign trail, including women tossing undergarments, Kennedy, a bit overwhelmed by it all, laughed and said, "I'm a Beatle!"[30]

Kennedy was also a fan of the most outspoken Beatle. Talking about the eclectic mix of guests Robert and Ethel would invite to their McLean, Virginia, mansion, veteran TV journalist Roger Mudd recalled a dinner party where he was seated next to John Lennon.[31]

Robert Kennedy was a calculating politician—he needed the support of young voters and knew a more casual style would add to his appeal. But if his long hair was intended as statement of solidarity with the youth movement, he seemed sincere. In late May, he told a journalist for the *Simmons College Review*, "American youth do not accept the failures of today as a reason for the cruelties of tomorrow; they make me realize even more that a greater effort must be made to meet their demands." He said, "The students have demonstrated to me that they believe in a special mission for their generation," and that their political involvement will "give this nation a new dedication, a new commitment, and a new spirit."[32]

Ascendant Evil

Less than a week after he made those comments, two months after the King assassination, Kennedy was thanking supporters for his victory in the California primary and looking ahead to the nomination. He was shot while walking through the kitchen at LA's Ambassador Hotel, on his way to meet with reporters. The nation and the world waited, stunned with shock and disbelief, not knowing if his wounds were critical. Even if he survived, supporters wondered, would he have brain damage? Could he still be president? Kennedy was officially pronounced dead twenty-six hours later.

Kennedy supporters were devastated and felt "politically lost; many not sure if they would vote at all."[33] Many older Beatle fans supported Kennedy but were not yet old enough to vote. A male fan, age eighteen at the time and fearing the draft, recalled, "Bobby grew his hair, was antiwar, reached out to the poor, and identified with the counterculture. He was going to stop making us kill or be killed."

Beatle fans were growing up in an increasingly violent society—with the first Kennedy assassination and the televised Oswald shooting days later being early memories for many. But two assassinations in rapid succession, the televised war, race riots, and student protests meant unprecedented exposure to violence over the preceding months—and the people being killed and hurt were, for the most part, the good guys and the powerless. When a TV show was interrupted, this generation was conditioned to assume someone important had been shot.

A female fan, age seventeen, vividly recalls: "I got tears in my eyes when I heard Ted Kennedy's eulogy at Robert's funeral, the part about 'he saw wrong and tried to right it, saw suffering and tried to stop it.' That really got to me. I think the way Teddy's voice cracked got to me as much as the words did."

Ronald Reagan, outspoken critic of the counterculture since the Free Speech Movement days, quickly blamed the murder on "a growing permissiveness in the nation."[34] Experts talked about "America's addiction to guns," and one noted that the US is not a "melting pot" but a "pressure cooker."[35]

Servicemen in Vietnam reacted with anger, bitterness, and confusion: "Everyone's asking what the hell we're here for when we can't even deal with things back home." Another said, "He was a hippie, that's why most of us liked him." A twenty-two-year-old military policeman wondered, "I don't know if it's because I'm over here or not, but I seem to accept a violent solution to things; it's almost taken for granted now; there's violence in diplomacy, in race relations, in politics."[36]

A diverse crowd of one hundred thousand filed past Kennedy's coffin at New York's St. Patrick's Cathedral. In place of a military guard, his coffin was guarded by a shifting group of six men or boys, including Robert McNamara, then president of the World Bank, a fourteen-year-old black junior high school student, and SDS founder Tom Hayden.

Pope Paul VI's vicar, upon arrival in New York for Kennedy's funeral, said, "Perhaps it is about time that serious steps be taken by governments to arouse the conscience of the people that better living is not based on violence but on love and understanding."[37] While the governments of the world abdicated this responsibility, global pop stars filled the void.

Exemplary Hippies

Young music fans could tune out the turbulence, pick up *16* magazine, and still see pictures of the Beatles and their wives, or girlfriend in Paul's case, and read about their clothes and forthcoming music projects. The Monkees and Paul Revere and the Raiders were also covered. A lucky reader could win Davy Jones's puppy; for the edgier or older reader, a "dream day" with Jim Morrison.

But politics was creeping into the pages of teen magazines, too. The June 1968 issue of *Teen Screen* printed a poem by a thirteen-year-old female reader entitled "To a Hippy" and received hundreds of letters in response. Under the headline "Hippies: Sinners or Saviors," a hippie defender, also age thirteen, explained the difference between the "dressy or part-time hippie and the true, peace and love hippie." She says the first type is much more common but the latter group "does the best job and wins the least credit." She offers an example: "I believe that the most famous examples of this type are the Beatles. They know what they are talking about and have found where it is at."[38]

The letter writer is too young to have run away to San Francisco, but she wasn't too young to fall in love with the Beatles in 1964. For girls and boys her age, the Beatles were not love objects, as they were for girls only two or three years older. Theirs was a different kind of love. And it didn't matter that these fans were too young to be "real hippies," because the media's obsession with hippies the year before and with the "generation gap" and "student protestors" now, provided an electronic guidebook that allowed interested young fans to understand the tumult, cultural divide, and emerging lifestyles impressionistically and to experience all the "now" vicariously. They were "with it" in the McLuhanesque sense, interacting with "cool" media that invited projection, engagement, and cocreation of meaning.

For four years, these children were exposed to new ideas and new sensibilities—through music, hair, and groovy clothes. Their ears and minds had been opened. But the countercultural aspects of all that fun and grooviness seemed more benign then. Fashion and musical taste were means of self-expression, not matters of life and death. Now, suddenly, these forms of expression had become political statements.

Even if fans didn't understand what was happening, they could sense the divisive "us v. them" of the generation gap, and they knew where the Beatles stood. Many fans assumed, based on their positive feelings toward them, that the Beatles would be on the side of good. It was a simple equation: Beatles = Good, Beatles = Counterculture, Counterculture = Good.

This is why fans "just knew" where the Beatles stood on the issues of the day—even before they expressed their views in song. It was in the clothes, the hair, the attitude, and their constant imploring of fans to think, feel, and see. Fans felt the Beatles were "on their side" before the media even realized there were sides.

This is not to say that all Beatle fans were antiwar or countercultural in their outlook. A male fan (b. '52) knew the Beatles were antiwar but "didn't agree with them." He explained: "I still wanted them to be my heroes, so I ignored it. I didn't have to agree with them—it was about the music." A female fan (b. '51) from a "definitely conservative background" wondered, "Why did they start talking about politics? Why didn't they just focus on the music?"

Nowhere in the media was the Beatles countercultural role made more explicit than in *Rolling Stone*, also read by fans who'd been with the Beatles from the start. Jann Wenner and music critic Ralph Gleason, both "superfans," viewed the band as spokesmen for the counterculture and relied heavily on coverage of them to sell their countercultural magazine, whose editorial focus was more music and lifestyle than politics. According to one insider, Wenner's "rule of thumb" was "when in doubt, put the Beatles on the cover."[39] Negative comments about the Beatles were rare, and as factions within the counterculture criticized the Beatles—as would happen later in the summer—*Rolling Stone* came to their defense.[40]

Another Girl

John Lennon and Yoko Ono corresponded by mail while John was in India, and it was just a matter of time before they became an "item"—that is, noticed by the press. Their first public event was on June 15 at Coventry Cathedral, where they planted acorns for peace. Later that week, they attended the premier of the National Theatre's stage production of *In His Own Write*. Eyebrows were raised, and the item appeared in the next day's papers.

Less than two weeks later, the high profile couple's *You Are Here* exhibit opened at Robert Fraser's London gallery and included a launch of three hundred sixty-five white helium balloons, each with an attached note saying, "You Are Here," and an invitation to write to John at Fraser's gallery. The exhibit was panned by the critics, but more importantly, the press and the public, especially in the UK, were cruelly critical of John and his new companion.

American fans were bewildered by John's relationship with Yoko and thought she was an "odd bird." Male fans were more likely to have formed an impression of Yoko based on her looks, thinking she was "not attractive" and wondering why John was with her when "he can get any model he wants." Several male fans remember thinking "she looked like a witch in her big black hat," and fans of both sexes thought he was "under her spell." Before long, fans who were ambivalent or willing to give her the benefit of the doubt felt she was "changing John, not for the better."

Not only did Lennon have the audacity to be open about the relationship while still married to the pretty Liverpool blonde the public was used to seeing at his side—also the mother of his child—but his transgression was exacerbated by the fact that Yoko was not a conventionally attractive woman and was an avant-garde artist of a different race. The press and fans felt entitled to their opinions, and most disapproved. The more fans saw of Yoko, the less they liked her.

More Beatle relationship news came later that month when Jane Asher announced that her engagement to Paul was off and their five-year relationship was over. A female fan, age sixteen at the time, was "surprised" by the split: "We used to read about Paul and Jane all the time in *16* magazine; I thought for sure they would get married. I think he wrote a lot of songs for her." Their breakup, like that of John and Cynthia, signaled major change in Beatle world. And while millions of fan fantasies were buoyed by Paul and Jane's breakup, one fan in particular was positioning herself to take Jane's place.

Another noteworthy transition in Beatle world that July was the closing of the Apple Boutique, which had opened only eight months before. The corner shop, with a three-story-high colorful mural emblazoned on the building's exterior before abutters insisted it be whitewashed, was plagued by Apple's signature extravagance and poor management and attracted more shoplifters than shoppers.

Somewhat uncomfortable with the public's perception that they were seriously in "the rag trade" and consistent with their rejection of materialism and their appreciation of a good happening, the inventory was given away, after all the insiders had their pick. A rare look at the boutique's interior could be seen in the 1968 Oscar-nominated comedy *Hot Millions*, starring Maggie Smith, Peter Ustinov, and Bob Newhart.

Making It Better

It had been five months since the unsubstantial "Lady Madonna" and its unremarkable promotional film when "Hey Jude" b/w "Revolution" was released—the first single with a Granny Smith apple on the label instead of the familiar orange-and-yellow swirl. At seven minutes and eleven seconds, longer even than Dylan's "Like a Rolling Stone," the song was so long that some AM stations faded it out at three and a half or four minutes, though many played the entire mantra-like ending.

These new Beatle songs seemed to be commenting on a violent year, up to and including the riots occurring on the streets of Chicago at the moment of their release:

I didn't want to watch the Democratic convention because it seemed extremely boring, just a bunch of old fart windbags droning on. The next thing I knew, the riots in Chicago were on every channel! A lot of the kids getting their heads bashed in by the police looked like they weren't much older than I was. It was pretty upsetting to watch. Female, b. '51

I used to watch the conventions gavel-to-gavel and Chicago was no exception, so I saw all that was going on, both inside the hall and on Michigan Avenue and in Grant Park. It absolutely outraged me and, in fact, still does. By the end of things on the final night, I was almost physically ill. It was hard to believe this was happening in my country. Male, b. '49

For young fans watching the bloody chaos of Chicago, after two assassinations and nightly footage of violence from college campuses, inner cities, and the jungles of Southeast Asia, "Hey Jude" was encouraging and optimistic. The intimacy of Paul's voice was comforting—instilling confidence and offering advice, as if prepping the listener for an important mission. A male fan, age sixteen at the time, remembers, "It was an amazing song that made you feel good."

The simple instrumentation—including an exquisitely expressive tambourine—builds and builds, as does the talk of making things better, simultaneously plodding and rocking, until "better, better, better" erupts into the first of many ecstatic screams and the "sing along" begins. The insistent *nah nah nah nah*'s reiterate the message of empowerment and unity with hypnotic urgency.

"Hey Jude" was the best song they ever did; it's saying don't be so down, keep your head up, it's good to be alive. Male, b. '48

I was in a band, and we played "Hey Jude" at dances, including the whole ending. We thought people would get sick of it but they didn't, they loved it! Male, b. '53

Punctuated by Paul's wild, authentic euphoria—some of his best vocal expressions to date—it only took a few listens before his outbursts became thoroughly familiar, adding, if not lyrics, texture, punctuation, and temporal orientation to the four-minute coda.

The uplifting ballad plus chorale went to number one in late September—displacing Jeannie C. Riley's rant on small town hypocrisy, "Harper Valley PTA"—and held the position for nine weeks, becoming the Beatles' bestselling single.

Stripped of noisy and distracting psychedelia, this Beatle iteration was more accessible to young fans, and "Hey Jude" welcomed many back. A male fan, age twelve at the time, ended his Beatle break: "'Hey Jude' was a reminder that we shouldn't have doubted them, that they are still the greatest. I was extremely moved by it. It's like they were saying, 'Get a load of this.'" A female fan, age eleven at the time, also ended her Beatle break when she heard the song speaking directly to her: "The Beatles became important to me again after 'Hey Jude.' There was a divide between us and the parents, but the Beatles understood us."

For another male fan, age fifteen at the time, the song is inextricably linked with the war: "A boy on our street was killed in Vietnam, and a group of us watched as military people pulled up in a car, got out, and knocked on the door to tell his mother. We had a radio with us, and 'Hey Jude' was playing. I remember that day every time I hear the song."

When asked by a reporter if the Beatles were going to do any antiwar songs, John flippantly said all Beatle songs were antiwar songs—and certainly that case could be made given the recurring themes of love, reason, and reciprocity. But "Revolution" was the band's first song that directly responded to world events. And, more importantly, it spoke directly to fans about what was happening in their lives. Lennon had been watching the bloody unfolding of 1968 from the banks of the Ganges, and now it was time to say something.

Preteens and young teenagers heard "a good rock and roll song" and "didn't think about the lyrics." A female fan, fourteen at the time, liked "Revolution" because "it was the first Beatle record in a long time that you could dance to."

Fans listening to the lyrics heard the Beatles aligning themselves with the mission of "changing the world"—clearly on young peoples' side—though the particulars were unclear and not important anyway. The message for these fans was that social change was complicated, serious business, but everything was going to be "all right." The song disparaged haters and espoused nonviolence, with sonic aggressiveness. The final "all right" seemed to say, "Can we stop talking about this now?" At this level of understanding, "Hey Jude" and "Revolution" carried the same message, delivered in the familiar Lennon-McCartney yin-yang.

Fans just a few years older heard all of the above but with more detail. They heard a Beatle song that juxtaposed words from social studies class with the admonition to "free your mind." Teenagers tried to find meaning in Lennon's musings, just as they tried to understand the surreal events of 1968. Though no "real solutions" or answers were offered, this trusted and beloved commentator was telling them it's going to be "all right."

Radicalized older fans and other observers on the left found the song simplistic and naive, especially in light of growing opposition to the war falling on deaf ears, and the excessive use of force just used against protestors on the streets of Chicago.

The Whole World Is Watching

The violence around the Democratic convention was a sharp contrast to the "love" vibe of the previous summer. A young female fan, age twelve at the time, recalls, "My parents were watching it, saying how awful it was. I went over to take a look. I thought something must have gone terribly wrong. It made me uneasy to see real violence like that." Nobody understood how this could be happening in our country. How did it come to this?

According to Tom Hayden, there was a realization in late 1967 that "the establishment does not listen to public opinion" and that "available channels have been tried and discovered meaningless."[41] The body count was escalating along with the war. Oblivious to the seething anger felt by young men who couldn't vote but were forced to be cannon fodder in an unjust and unwinnable war, the establishment dismissed protestors as naïve, spoiled, and rude.

The only viable peace candidate was assassinated. Volunteers who faithfully "worked within the system" for Kennedy and McCarthy were outraged that the party machine nominated the uninspiring Hubert Humphrey and rejected the peace plank—ignoring the fact that 80 percent of primary voters had voted for an antiwar candidate.[42] Young people were wondering what happened to our democracy.

Protest organizers, a coalition that included the SDS, the national Mobilization Committee to End the War in Vietnam, and Yippies— Abbie Hoffman and Jerry Rubin's effort to politicize hippies through the use of street theater—were not planning violent protests but "were determined, at the least, not to be intimidated."[43] There was an enormous amount of anger amid the theater.

According to writer and eyewitness Todd Gitlin, "A critical mass of people in the New Left still cherished nonviolence and felt a terror of real bloodshed," but pervasive violence in the culture, including the war, had left them "churning in a sea of rage," such that "many of the middle-class young were stunned into a tolerance, a fascination, even a taste for it."[44] A small but apparently sufficient number of protestors could not be dissuaded from their readiness for violence.

For many Chicago demonstrators, 80 to 90 percent male, it was, as Tom Hayden later said, "A matter of finding out how far you were willing to go for your beliefs, and finding out how far the American government was willing to go in suspending the better part of its tradition to stop you."[45]

On the other side, law enforcement outnumbered demonstrators three or four to one, including twelve thousand Chicago police with "shoot to kill" orders.[46] One in six demonstrators was actually a government agent of some kind, often acting to incite what an in-depth study concluded was a "police riot." The violence peaked on the evening of August 28 in front of the Hilton Hotel, in full view of TV cameras, two days after the release of "Hey Jude" and "Revolution."[47] As one fan, age sixteen at the time recalled it, "The kids flipped out because Humphrey got the nomination and Daley sicced the cops on them. I didn't like how anyone was acting, but I was, frankly, more worried about gas money for the weekend."

What Would John Do?

That the left heard "Revolution" as an inadequate response to recent events speaks to the enormous authority and responsibility they gave the Beatles. By the summer of 1966—after Lennon's Jesus comment and after Dylan's motorcycle accident—the "voice of a generation" baton passed from Dylan to the Beatles. They were now widely acknowledged as leaders of the counterculture, especially Lennon. His disdain for intellectuals, authorities, and ideologues, combined with his intermittent self-loathing, made him uncomfortable in the role. But he was also an impassioned communicator with deeply held views, well aware of the power he wielded over a large and impatient generation. Despite his ambivalence, he had used the platform of his celebrity in song and in interviews on several occasions—"Revolution" being the most recent.

The *New Left Review* called the song "a lamentable petty bourgeoisie cry of fear," and the *Berkeley Barb* wrote, "Hubert Humphrey couldn't have said it better." Ramparts called it "a betrayal."[48] Robert Christgau wrote in the *Village Voice*, "It is puritanical to expect musicians, or anyone else, to hew to the proper line, but it is reasonable to request that they not go out of their way to oppose it."[49] What most angered radicals was that Lennon seemed to be abandoning politics in favor of personal liberation, believing that real change begins with the individual—"free your mind."

A female fan, in college at the time, recalls: "'Revolution' was anti-communist of course, dismissive of radicals who admired the Chinese revolution, but the song was more critical of radicals who opposed the war than it was of the power structure prolonging the war. I hoped he would have turned his gift for critical irony on the power structure instead of potential allies in the antiwar movement."

The New Lefties who took issue with the song were radicalized older fans. Their criticism seems to rest on three assumptions: 1) Lennon has a responsibility to address the issue, 2) he has a responsibility to take a position, and 3) that the position be theirs. The most interesting part of this controversy is not what John said or what his critics preferred he had said, but that they were criticizing him for not properly performing his role.

These assumptions are not unreasonable, given the connections these older fans felt with the Beatles—one personal, one generational. A personal relationship had been growing for four years, each fan listening to Beatle music alone in his or her room as an awkward teenager, feeling supported. The Beatles spoke to these fans' political imaginations and countercultural impulses through *A Hard Day's Night*, the Jesus affair, public antiwar statements, and overall Beatle attitude.

The other relationship is collective—the generational consciousness fans developed around the Beatles. The war was a crisis for this generation, and they wanted the Beatles to help them through it.

As disgusted as John was by the war and the power structure, he was, ultimately, immune from it. With historically unprecedented fame and extraordinary wealth, Lennon didn't face the same existential concerns as his fan base. He wasn't facing a draft board and he wasn't questioning the commitment he made to four years of "irrelevant" education. His wealth allowed him to be impacted by events only to the extent he chose to be. He was off buying an island or tranced-out in front of the TV. John Lennon "*read* the news today," but he didn't live it.

Lennon was empathic and intelligent, and his political consciousness was evolving. But fame excused him from having to live in the real world as a young adult and from having to put his principles to the test.

He couldn't feel the frustration and rage felt by Tom Hayden and the others in Chicago.

Framing the controversy in this way, John's New Left critics can be seen as disappointed fans. But the profundity and scale of the Beatles phenomenon imbues "disappointed fans" with a deep, elusive meaning, getting to the singularity of the connection first-generation fans feel toward the Beatles and the role they played in fans' lives.

The Beatles weren't the only top tier British rock band whose reaction to international student protests was heard during the showdown in Chicago. But the Stone's "Street Fighting Man" got a very different reception. Many critics who dismissed "Revolution" praised Mick & Co. for the song—inspired by a March 1968 Vietnam War protest at the American embassy in London, at which Jagger briefly put in an appearance but left before violence erupted.

"Street Fighting Man" is Stones rock and roll at its best, more brash and edgy than "Revolution." And the lyrics, incorrectly and selectively heard, seemed a bit more radical. Most radio stations wouldn't play it. But the bravado is just that—the signature Stones tune is actually quite cynical and ultimately expresses hopelessness and futility with regard to radical change. "Revolution," in contrast, engages with the issues, advocates nonviolence, and leaves open the possibility of change, starting with the individual. Like its inspirational A-side, "Revolution" is of a piece with the recurring Beatle theme of realizing potential—personal and societal—through insight and love.

Rethinking Gender Roles

Less than two weeks after the Democratic Convention in Chicago, a demonstration took place at the site of yet another time-honored American ritual of selection. Four hundred feminists protested the Miss America pageant in Atlantic City, and showed the world how this one event symbolized the many ways the culture oppresses and devalues women. Established as a scheme to keep tourists in Atlantic

City after Labor Day, the pageant was in its forty-seventh year when Americans were asked to think about it differently.

Using the hippie and yippie street theater approach to protest, demonstrators tossed various objects of female oppression, such as mops, false eyelashes, pots and pans, and bras, into a huge "Freedom Trash Can." Contrary to widespread reports, no bras were burned—a reporter's analogy between the women's protest and antiwar protestors' draft card burning, also theatrical, was the source of the still surviving bra-burning meme. Several women entered the pageant hall and unfurled an enormous banner emblazoned with WOMEN'S LIBERATION. The protest drew international media attention, the phrase caught on, and the second wave of feminism was born.

It had been five years since Betty Friedan's *Feminine Mystique* identified "the problem with no name," and four years since young boys fell in love with the Beatles and wanted to look like them and be as "cool" as they were. Four years since these androgynous artists singing about love replaced traditional male heroes like athletes, astronauts, Davy Crockett, and cowboys.

The Beatles represented a new model of masculinity but women's roles hadn't changed. In fact, the confluence of base-line sexism, pop culture permissiveness, and readily available birth control made for greater exploitation and oppression of women.

With their long hair, girl group harmonies, and pop lyrics evincing higher IQ and EQ than anything that came before, the Beatles breached the gender dichotomy from the beginning. Although John repeatedly said they "sold out" when they fulfilled Brian's vision of what they should look like, it was a decision that would not only allow them to fulfill their vision of "making a lot of money" and being "bigger than Elvis," but it would ultimately advance a transformation in gender roles.

As discussed earlier, girls liked boys who were Beatle-like—who were free and had enough imagination to venture outside the confines of male stereotypes. These were young rebels with the best of causes: Freedom. The girls who screamed at the concerts were also expressing freedom. And fans of all genders were listening to intelligent lyrics, in which relationships were authentic and "working it out" was valued. And regardless of how the Beatles conducted their personal lives and the expectations they put on their wives and girlfriends—Pattie Boyd said Beatle women were basically baggage—their look and their music together constituted a different male persona and suggested, at least aspirationally, more satisfying relationships.

However, women faced a particular kind of struggle, and there were more constraints to be liberated from. And because men couldn't undo years of socialization by growing their hair long and wearing flowered shirts, women had to raise men's consciousness—as Yoko was eventually able to do with John.

By 1968, the civil rights, antiwar, and youth movements converged in an urgent cultural debate, at times violent, over personal freedom and values. Women entered the debate at the Miss America protest in Atlantic City. Many of the girls who wrote letters to *16* magazine, those girls whose greatest frustration was not being taken seriously, would fuel second-wave feminism.

Men in Ruffled Shirts

Fans hadn't seen the Beatles for seven months—since the underwhelming "Lady Madonna" promotional film—when the "Hey Jude" film was broadcast on *The Smothers Brothers Comedy Hour* in early October. With hip, antiwar humor and sympathetic references to the counterculture, this Sunday night variety show bore little resemblance to *Ed Sullivan*. The Beatles saw the Smothers Brothers as kindred spirits and the perfect MCs to introduce their latest incarnation.

The film opens with a full-screen close-up of Paul at the piano. He looks directly at the viewer, with a sweet flirty intensity that is sometimes too much to look at. He seems to be illuminated from within. He's clean-shaven, confident, and wearing a raspberry velvet jacket. Cuddly Paul was now cuddly in a new way to the seven-, eight-, and nine-year-old girls who collected Beatle trading cards in 1964—even those who had been distracted by Davy Jones.

Significantly, this broadcast was the first time fans saw John's hair parted in the middle, shoulder length, and stringy. Many male fans remember trying to adopt this look—"If John Lennon did it, it was okay"—with varying success. This change in appearance was even more dramatic than the leap from "Rain" to "Strawberry Fields." Clean-shaven and chewing gum, John was carefully costumed: short-sleeved lavender Henley shirt, black vest, and orange snap-on bowtie—a clownish look overall. Or perhaps this is the first outward evidence of his transition into the wise and clever Fool.

Unlike in earlier TV appearances, live or on film, the set here is relaxed, casual, and uncoordinated. George, also clean-shaven, is in a brown silk, blousy shirt and dark green corduroys; muted earth tones. Ringo, in contrast, is wearing a lime green suit, with a white ruffled shirt, and mustache. Perhaps Ringo didn't get the memo, having just returned that day from a brief retirement.

As the song spills into the coda, there's a rush of people to the stage—lucky fans—closing in so tightly the band's movement is almost restricted. Viewers had been listening to this song for over a month, imagining a happy crowd singing along. Now they can actually see the happy crowd—and a thirty-six-piece orchestra. The Beatles mustered enough performance energy to create some chemistry among themselves, and the band's rapidly growing fissures were not apparent. They seem quite present and quite pleased.

They were back on the *Smothers Brothers* the following week, on film, performing "Revolution" to a backing track, with no audience. Their positions on the stage are as fans first saw them four years earlier, but little else about it could be described that way—except of course that it was the Beatles, and essentially familiar.

Paul, looking well fed, wore the Henley shirt this time, with black pin-stripe dress pants. George is wearing an orange mock turtleneck sweater and the same green corduroys. Ringo is in a bland off-white sweater. John seems to have dressed up for his emphatic lead vocal, in black dress pants, black silk shirt and black vest, with another Fool tie, this one light blue with white polka dots. It was a powerful performance of a powerful song.

Fans could practically count the fillings in John's mouth as the camera closes in, and for the first time, they hear the equivocating "in" after the "count me out"—which they would hear again, on a slower version, the following month.

Fans paying attention noticed the addition. Does he want to be counted "in" or "out" of efforts to "change the world" that involved "destruction"? Would he give money, his voice, or his body to the cause? Why the change, and what is he trying to say?

John was miffed by the left's reaction to the single when it came out, and always found comparisons with the Stones' tedious and inane— especially this one. But he was also defensive and very ego-invested in the controversy. Clearly his thinking about revolution and social change were in flux at the time, and of course he did get involved briefly in radical politics in the post-Beatle years.[50]

A male fan, age twelve at the time, remembers hearing "Revolution" when it first came out and loving the song's intensity, but he didn't think about what it meant, or about the war. He recalled: "I accepted that our government knew what they were doing; I didn't think about it that much. I was thinking about the Beatles and the Red Sox and how to not get suspended from school for clowning around."

A female fan, age fourteen at the time, recalls her history teacher explaining the difference between a "liberal" and a "conservative" and then passing out "a little test to find out what you were." She "proved to be a liberal" and remembers thinking, "If the Beatles took Mr. McGillicuddy's test, they would score liberal too."

A Bloomin' Book

Fans of all ages had always been interested in learning as much as they could about the Beatles' personal lives, their childhoods, and how they became the Beatles. No surprise then that they devoured Hunter Davies' *The Beatles*, published in late 1968. Still the only authorized biography of the band and number forty-nine in Amazon's Top 100 Beatle books forty-five years after it was published, the hefty book gave readers a more or less accurate though incomplete account of the group's early life and rise to fame.

For many young fans, it was the first book they read that was not required reading for school, and its length was no deterrent. It seemed like a grown-up book—several young fans remember their shock at seeing the word "fuck" in print—"that's a word you're not supposed to say," recalled a male fan, age eleven at the time.

In the *Rolling Stone* review of Davies' book, twenty-two-year-old Jann Wenner wrote, "I find the first part uninteresting, because it is the tale of young boys growing up in any town anywhere."[51] But the superfan editor was ten years older than many of the fans reading the book. It's the "any town anywhere" aspect that allowed younger readers to relate to the lads' youthful frustrations, conflicts with parents over clothes, alienation from school, and uncertainty about the future.

Of course, there was much in the book fans couldn't relate to. But after living and breathing Beatles for four years, reading about all the talent, work, perseverance, and luck required to turn these four young men into "The Beatles" made them seem more human. At the same time, it allowed fans to think about the story with a sense of wonder and see "the incredible weirdness of it," which, Wenner noted, people rarely considered.[52]

Asked who would buy a Beatles biography, the executive editor at McGraw-Hill's trade book division said, "We assume we will get the readers around twenty."[53] In other words, the publisher expected fans who'd been with the Beatles since age sixteen to buy the book, not realizing that those who'd been with them since age seven and eight, now eleven and twelve, would also be buying it and lending it to their friends.

Beatles v. Blue Meanies

In November, Richard Nixon, one of the bluest of Meanies, was elected thirty-seventh president of the United States. His law and order message was effective in a violent, turbulent year, and too many young people old enough to vote but disillusioned after Chicago stayed home on election day.

Less than two weeks later, *Yellow Submarine* was released, fulfilling the Beatles three-film commitment to United Artists. Too busy and not interested in doing another film, they reluctantly agreed to a full-length animated feature. Al Brodax, originator of the Beatle cartoons, was involved with the project, which lowered the expectations of older fans, who found the cartoons insipid and "difficult to watch."

But fans had vivid memories of the "cool," "colorful," film, sitting in the theater with friends or parents. Many recalled being in "a car full of kids" and getting dropped off at the theater. For ninety minutes, they watched cartoon Beatles with exaggerated Liverpool accents, yet these characters seemed consistent with the personalities they'd come to know.

The combination of Beatle music, innovative animation, pop culture imagery, and a Beatle-inspired twist on good versus evil gave the film unique appeal. Pitting the Beatles, love, music, reason, knowing, color, and flowers against Blue Meanies replicates the generation gap and evokes a similar "us versus them" as their other two films, especially *A Hard Day's Night*. There was a sense in which fans saw the Beatles as superheroes since their first *Sullivan* appearance, but *Yellow Submarine* made it explicit.

For many, the Beatles appearance and the multilingual "All Together Now" sing-along tacked onto the end of the cartoon was the high point of the film, several recalling how "cool it was to see 'All Together Now' in all those languages." The childlike lyrics of unity and love reiterated the Beatle message and again reinforced the band's place in global generational consciousness.

The *New York Times* praised the film as "delicate, friendly, and unpretentious," saying "it presents the strongest case for animated feature films since *Fantasia*." Interestingly, the reviewer also notes that the film would not have been "of great importance" without "the imprimatur of the Beatles, with their special talent, power and grace."[54]

By this point, any Beatle-related project would be considered important—and there would be three more this month.

The same reviewer called it a "family movie in the truest sense," and concluded *Yellow Submarine* "would delight a child, or a head, or anybody who loves and admires the Beatles," even though they appear only briefly at the end.[55] The matter-of-fact acknowledgment of the film's appeal to druggies spread to fans as well. According to one older fan, "word was to see it stoned," and many age fourteen and over did.

A young female fan (b. '61) said she and her friends played games "where we were trying to escape the Blue Meanies." But college students also enjoyed the cartoon. A male fan, only seven at the time, recalls, "My brother was in college and kids in the dorm were playing 'Yellow Submarine' very loud over and over and my brother had to ask them to turn it down. They took his blue bathrobe and turned it into a Blue Meanie costume."

Writing in *The New Yorker*, influential film critic Pauline Kael said the film's "Pop flourishes" and "inventiveness" deliver the "pleasure of constant surprise" which is "the fun of good animation."[56]

Kael's phrase is noteworthy in that the "pleasure of constant surprise" was one of the essential Beatle elements fans had been responding to, indeed, had become addicted to, over the previous four years. But Kael misses the point when she says, "yesterday's outlaw idols of the teenagers" had become "a quartet of Pollyannas for the wholesome family trade." The Beatles largest and most tuned-in audience still saw them as "outlaws." *Yellow Submarine* didn't change their message—it simply wrapped it in dazzling animation.

The film and its title song are now children's classics and have been the gateway to the Beatles for three generations. In addition, the Yellow Submarine has become a worldwide symbol of social harmony.

Keep on Trying

Fans were getting used to seeing John with Yoko, and now they were seeing George out and about without the other three. In mid-November, the quiet Beatle made a surprise visit to the *Smothers Brothers Comedy Hour*. Tommy Smothers told George he and his brother "thought the 'Hey Jude' video was the best presentation" they'd ever seen of the band, and were "glad it was on their show." George, in a significant TV moment, responded, "Yea. So are we!"[57] Any fan watching now knew with in-your-face certainty that the Beatles were in agreement with the Smothers Brothers' position on the war and other issues.

The Beatle Seal of Approval was purposefully given to the Smothers Brothers and their agenda—a contrast with the approval they unwittingly and mistakenly gave the Maharishi. Beatle fans who didn't understand what the war was about or had not taken a position had a realization: "I noticed the cool people and people I admired, like the Smothers Brothers, and the Beatles, were against the war. After a while, the establishment view offended my sensibilities. I knew what was right and what was wrong" (Male, b. '54).

Looking cool in an orange ruffled shirt, green pants, and leather jacket, Harrison told the brothers he had "something very important to say on American television" and joked with them about their ongoing battles with network censors. He urged them to "keep trying to say important things." George's cameo wasn't only a surprise to fans—it was also a surprise to the show's hosts. Tom Smothers recalled: "The Beatles were the biggest thing in the entire universe. And to have George Harrison just stop on by to wish us luck and say 'Go on, keep doing it,' it was a real coup."

John Being John

While George was sprinkling Beatle dust on the Smothers Brothers and helping the antiwar movement, his soundtrack to the movie *Wonderwall* was released—the first solo Beatle effort and the first Apple LP.

In November, John and Yoko released *Two Virgins*, with front and back nude photos of them on the front and back cover, respectively. Most fans were "mildly amused" by the cover. Some appreciated its "authenticity." Perhaps, for Lennon, the cover was a reaction to the lack of authenticity he felt he had to maintain in the band's early years.

Many fans simply saw the *Two Virgins* cover as "John being John." They had come to know John as "antiestablishment" and "more willing to push the boundaries," and they "admired him for it." A male fan, age fourteen at the time, remembers, "We knew he was a joker and a punk, that's what we loved about him. The cover didn't surprise us."

Also in November, the couple were arrested and charged with possession of a small amount of cannabis, a stressful incident they believed resulted in Yoko's miscarriage. Their arrest and conviction would shadow their lives in other ways for years to come. In the midst of all this activity, John and Cynthia were officially divorced.

In the early days, fans learned about Beatle happenings by reading *16* magazine, or from friends who did. And while some young fans still read teen magazines, *Rolling Stone* had become the source for serious news about the new serious Beatles. A male fan (b. '52) recalls, "You couldn't be seen reading *16* anymore. If you read *Rolling Stone* and had it in your locker at school, you were cool."

In late November the magazine published a lengthy interview with John conducted two months before, in which he expressed apparently genuine surprise at the public's negative response to Yoko, their relationship, and his embrace of conceptual art. *Rolling Stone* featured the bare-bottomed back cover of *Two Virgins* on its front page.

The interview includes many casual references to drug use, which, by this point, was no surprise to anyone. While not all fans used drugs at the time, and many never did, many recall "head shops" with names like "Nirvana," "Dreamers," and "Bell, Book, and Candle" suddenly appearing in their cities and towns, especially if there was a college campus nearby. Fans remember merchandise such as "black lights, posters, flower stickers, John Lennon glasses, pipes, and bell bottoms." Male fans remember "special stores" where they'd go to buy "Nehru jackets and flowered shirts—things guys didn't wear until the Beatles wore them." Female fans recalled "macramé vests." As one female fan (b. '47) said, "Before mod and hippie clothes, we looked like mini versions of our parents."

The White Album

Eight months after the *New York Times* reported on the trend toward album covers employing "graphics, sculpture, lithography, etchings, paintings, abstruse photography and combinations of all to grab the customer's eye," the Beatles released *The Beatles*.[58] Fans quickly renamed it, making it easier to talk about and refer to.

They were "thrilled that it was a double album," but of course that meant it was more expensive. Several mentioned not being able to buy it right away, and a few remember paying for it "with lots of coins." One lucky fan, age eight at the time, whose parents also loved the Beatles, recalls, "I was the only kid on the block who had the *White Album*. It was eleven bucks in '68!"

Bringing home a new Beatle album continued to be a memorable moment, "sort of like a ritual, with great suspense." Gazing at the album cover was always an important part of the experience, and even though this album didn't offer much to gaze at, fans didn't mind. "It was the Beatles," and as one female fan (b. '51) put it, "Who else would have the nerve to do this?"

Album designer Richard Hamilton was a well-known London Pop artist whose work the Beatles admired. He believed pop art should be truly popular, so when the Beatles approached him about designing an album cover, he realized it could sell as many as five million units, and immediately obliged. [59] The record sold more than two million copies in the first ten days of its release and was number one for seven weeks.[60]

The simple white cover, described by Beatle historian Ian McDonald as "one of the laziest ways iconic status has ever been achieved," with its crookedly embossed eponymous title and serial number, was both art and a comment on art. For fans, it was the outermost layer of another intriguing, interactive package from the still Fab Four:

It's like they were saying there are so many songs here that all we have to do is put a white cover on it. The important stuff is on the inside, not the outside. Eventually I understood that it was an artistic statement. Male, b. '55

The design was mysterious, but in a different way than *Sgt. Pepper* was mysterious. Maybe there was something hidden in it. I sensed that they were playing with us in some way. Female, b. '54

Not only were fans getting two records of new Beatle music at the same time—a first—but the package also included a color portrait of each Beatle "with eyes that followed you," and a poster. Some hung the pictures and the poster; others wanted to "keep it in pristine condition."

The poster, also designed by Hamilton but with much input from Paul, used images contributed by the four band members. The poster was designed so that each section would be seen as a "subsidiary composition." In other words, thought was put into what fans would see at every stage of unfolding and folding.[61] Recalling the poster, a male fan (b. '53) said, "They obviously wanted to involve us in it and spend time with it. There's a lot to look at."

Except for a few very small images on the poster, the *White Album* includes no group shots, paralleling the lack of cohesiveness fans say they heard in the music—although that impression might be based more on hindsight and decades of commentary. The image of Yoko in bed with a naked John is more prominent than any image of the group.

The album, which at one point had the working title of *A Doll's House*, takes the listener into many different spaces, creating a corridor with surprise-filled rooms, like the early sequence in *Yellow Submarine* when Ringo is collecting the other Beatles.

Some fans, young and old, found the album "scary" and "totally weird." One female fan (b. '61) recalled, "I didn't get it and I wasn't drawn to it; some of the lyrics were disturbing." Another female fan, ten years older, recalled, "The music and the lyrics changed from happy-go-lucky to 'out there.' I didn't care for their look or the lyrics.

I preferred the earlier, more happy stuff." For some, it was just a matter of getting used to it: "My older brother bought the *White Album* when he came back from Vietnam. I was sort of afraid of side three and four. I thought it was a bit weird and didn't like it. But then I heard it coming from my brother's room and I liked it" (Male b. '57).

Many fans have vivid memories of the *White Album* as both off-putting and appealing. The Beatles were once again luring them out of their comfort zone with the promise of an intriguing experience:

> I listened to it a lot on a portable record player in the corner of the living room, with all the other records spread out across the floor. I skipped "Revolution 9" because it scared me. And I didn't like the raucous ones like "Birthday" and "Helter Skelter." I didn't like screaming. I studied the pictures and the poster. I wanted to get the whole experience; I studied the whole package. Male, b. '61

> I was babysitting and brought it with me. I listened to it alone. It's a very vivid memory. I was confused by it and loved it. It was unsettling. There was lots of different stuff on it. I didn't understand "Piggies" or "Bungalow Bill." Each time I listened, I tried to figure it out. Female, b. '56

Despite being unsettling for some, the *White Album* marked the end of the Beatle break for many. As one male fan (b. '57) who'd been spending a lot of time with the Monkees put it, "It's like we had a quarrel and made up." A female fan (b. '56) recalls, "I didn't like the Walrus stuff; it wasn't friendly. But they won me back with 'Hey Jude' and then the *White Album*. I loved every song." Another recalled: "This was a different Beatles again. They're still a little scary to me, with Paul naked behind a pole and some of the lyrics, but I think I was at an age when I was ready for something with an edge" (Male, b. '56).

Fans remember the album as "a lot to take in," "a smorgasbord," or a "hodgepodge of totally different songs to explore." A male fan, also getting reacquainted with the Beatles after a fling with the Monkees, remembers, "It was the Beatles challenging us with their weirdness. Those thirty songs sparked a lot of conversation among us twelve-year-old kids." A female fan, age thirteen at the time, recalled, "The album played a huge emotional role in my life, and the variety of it blew my mind. I remember internalizing the album. I thought a lot about them and their music."

Many fans remember it "took a while to get to know this album," but one female fan, age fourteen at the time, was determined to get to know it right away: "I sat in a room and played it over and over and memorized the words in one afternoon. No one could believe I knew all the words so quickly."

Time said, "The album's thirty tracks are a sprawling, motley assemblage of the Beatles' best abilities and worst tendencies."[62] The record had many critics at the time, including George Martin, who thought the band should have selected the best fourteen tracks and made it a stronger, single album. And while many fans have come to this conclusion over the years, most were thrilled by hearing thirty new Beatle songs at once.

Though the album was seen as part of the "back to basics" movement launched by Dylan's *John Wesley Harding*, most fans simply took it as the latest Beatles iteration. Younger fans who came back from Beatle break with the *White Album*, especially female fans, liked that it had songs they could dance to. Fully one-third of the album gave them the opportunity to dance to Beatle music—and to reconnect to the original thrill and fun of Beatleness.

As Beatle records required closer listening and ventured away from 4/4 rock, some fans, male and female, who joyfully danced at age seven, eight, and nine suddenly thought dancing was "uncool." The new self-consciousness of puberty also kept many off the dance floor.

Danceability aside, it's not surprising that the Beatles "won back" young fans with this expansive collection. The record is rife with amusing characters both human and animal, silly, singable choruses, nature imagery, and numerous direct appeals to the child in every listener. At the same time, the album seemed to reflect the chaos and bad energy of the world outside the studio. There was more violence on this record than on any other Beatle album.

Fans especially loved "Back in the USSR," although they had "no idea what he was talking about," the rousing "Birthday," the "purity" of "Cry Baby Cry," and the sweetness of "I Will" and "Martha My Dear." Several recall feeling slightly uncomfortable as bewildered parents overheard "Why Don't We Do It in the Road" and "Happiness Is a Warm Gun" blaring from their rooms. Even the youngest fans knew what "it" referred to, and though "happiness is" evoked the *Peanuts* comic strip, the dark passion and drug talk was hard to miss.

"Glass Onion" mentioned five other Beatle songs and brought the band's self-conscious self-referencing to new heights. Fans liked the playfully enigmatic song, and it enhanced their feelings of connection to other fans and to the Beatles; even the youngest fans were "in the know."

"Revolution 9" was the track mentioned most often when recalling original impressions of the album. Many "couldn't understand why it was there," and even those who understood it as "experimental" didn't like it. Several young fans said the song "scared the daylights" out of them, and they usually skipped it when playing the record. Some didn't like the eight-minute cut but listened to it anyway because "you don't skip Beatle songs."

Fans who listened to "Revolution 9" heard a wide range of disparate sounds, snippets, and voices, but the most discernible bit was Yoko's voice, which contributed to fans' growing impression that "she was a bad influence." Fans assumed the track's very existence and placement on the record had something to do with her, which was their first inkling that she was "too intrusive." Also, after the *Two Virgins* cover on which the couple "become naked" and showed they had nothing to hide, it seemed like John was referring to her as his monkey, which somehow added to fans' weird vibe about her.

Not that John should have cared whether or not fans liked Yoko, but it's understandable that many didn't. For those fans, she was a cloud in sunny Beatle world. All fans accepted "John being John," but they saw a change in him when she appeared, and, like Paul and others who loved him, they felt weirdly threatened by John's metamorphosis. Fans' unease with Yoko, however small-minded it may have been, triggered protective feelings, just as the Maharishi did.

Contrary to John's defensive assertion, fans didn't want the Beatles frozen in time as the moptops. In fact, watching and learning from their evolution was a key part of what made growing up with them so enriching and nurturing. But as fans grew with the Beatles, they came to cherish them and developed genuine feelings of protection toward them, as one would with family.

In the November *Rolling Stone* interview, John talked about why he would get knocked more often than his bandmates. He says, "I seem to open me mouth more often, something happens, I forget what I am till it all happens again."[63] He doesn't say what he is and the interviewer doesn't ask. But he seems to be alluding to the no-win reality of his unprecedented reach as a communicator and to the unprecedented and inherently problematic relationship between him and his global fan base.

Fans love talking about the Beatles, but the records, events, and experiences most fans want to talk most about are pre-*Pepper*. Not that fans didn't love the *White Album* or the music that came later, and many coming back from Beatle break were thrilled to rediscover them. But the *White Album* period and beyond was a different experience from what came before, with different energy and different meaning for fans. They were still "along for the ride," still "on the journey," but there would be no more brilliant ascents.

The Stones' *Beggar's Banquet* was released less than two weeks after the *White Album*, with a remarkably similar white cover. Once again, the Stones seemed to be mimicking the Beatles and fueling the Stones versus Beatles conversation. But most record buyers didn't know at the time that *Beggar's Banquet*'s original cover, anything but white, had been censored by their American record label.

Many Beatle fans were also Stones fans, and although they recalled *Beggar's Banquet* coming out shortly after the *White Album*, "a new

Stones album wasn't a major event, it was just the new Stones album."
As this male fan, age thirteen at the time recalls, "I think I understood
intuitively at a very young age that there was something mythic and
epic about a new Beatle album."

Beatle fans grew up *listening to* the Stones, but they didn't grow up
with the Stones as they did with the Beatles. Fans continued to see the
essential differences between the two bands. A male fan (b. '59) recalls,
"The Beatles and Stones were rival gangs—I liked the Beatles more,
and they were funny. Anything they did was fascinating to me." Many
female Beatle fans continued to find the Stones repellent. The Beatles
created a safer space; they accepted you.

As the year drew to a close, Elvis Presley's *Comeback Special*, with an
awkward shout out to the Beatles, was broadcast on NBC, and the first
televised interracial kiss was seen on *Star Trek*. And for the first time,
humans saw a consciousness-raising image of the whole Earth beamed
back from a space-ship that had been to the dark side of the moon.

The following month, the Beatles would perform live for the
last time.

CHAPTER SEVEN
The Last Leg
January 1969–May 1970

They informed how I thought about the world.

Female, b. '55

FANS WERE STILL EXPLORING the expansive *White Album* as the new year began. Many who started listening to the Beatles in 1964 were now adolescents and had come to rely on them for a unique type of support: "*The White Album* played a huge emotional role in my life. I remember feeling and internalizing the album, and I thought a lot about them and their music. I was struggling with adolescence. I didn't like Catholic school, I felt misunderstood, and I felt restricted, especially as a girl. The Beatles made me realize that if I could just stick it out, there was something bigger out there" (Female, b. '55). Another female fan a year older recalled: "*The White Album* was musically contagious, and it was goofy, like John's sketches or poetry. I mostly listened alone. Other kids didn't get it. I hated school. I was lonely, obnoxious, snobby. I had a few friends, but music became my friend. I hung the *White Album* poster and pictures on my bedroom wall."

While some older or more astute listeners sensed lack of cohesion on the *White Album*, most didn't assume the Beatles were coming apart, and had little reason to. But the new year brought conflicting reports about their performing and recording plans. Nineteen sixty-nine also brought a "don't sell or else" ultimatum to record dealers in Union County, New Jersey, where thirty thousand copies of *Two Virgins* were confiscated as pornography.[1]

The *Yellow Submarine* album was released early in the year, with only six Beatle songs, and only four of them new. George Martin's symphonic film score fills the remaining tracks. Though disappointing in the same way as the other two albums associated with Beatle films, the album did reach number two on the US charts, kept from the number one spot by the *White Album*. Fans and critics recognized the brilliance of "Hey Jude," and it was nominated for Song of the Year. However, the Recording Academy continued to snub the Beatles and gave the Grammy to O. C. Smith's "Little Green Apples."

Fans didn't know conflict was developing within the group, but they saw Paul and John making serious commitments to other partners. On March 12, while George and Pattie were getting busted for marijuana possession, Paul married Linda Eastman in a simple civil ceremony. Female fans, many in tears, crowded the couple as they left London's Marylebone Registry.

Paul had been a fantasy love object, a "safe boyfriend" for young teenage fans. Many of these girls had grown up in five years and had little or no emotional reaction to the McCartney-Eastman marriage— other than feeling "happy for Paul." They had outgrown the personal fables of adolescence. Some fans, a little younger, "stopped fantasizing about Paul when he married Linda," and they didn't cry either.

The girls who did cry were the youngest of the first wave of fans, now young adolescents, with richly embroidered fantasies about the only bachelor Beatle. They cried because they were suddenly confronted with the reality that, contrary to their personal fables, they would never be Mrs. Paul McCartney. Not surprisingly, the press reacted to the crying fans with amused dismissiveness, but to the girls whose hearts were aching, forced to leave fantasy behind, there was nothing funny about it.

Eight days later, in an act described by one fan as "part of the competition between John and Paul," John and Yoko got married in Gibraltar. The marriages of these close friends, so close in time and without the other present, was their simultaneous declaration, to each other and to the world, that they were no longer primary partners. John and Paul both found someone else to perform with.

While Paul and his new family retreated to his farm in Scotland, John and Yoko continued exploiting their mutual love/hate relationship with the media to promote peace, and themselves. The couple, with beaming smiles, appeared on the cover of *Look* in mid-March. Betty Rollin's lengthy feature story, in which she described Yoko as "pushy," "ambitious," and lacking a sense of humor, did nothing to endear Yoko to fans.[2]

Bed Peace

John and Yoko knew the world press would accept an invitation to join them in their honeymoon suite—Beatle John and his Japanese conceptual artist wife were just too compelling for the press to ignore. They were getting used to John and Yoko's politico-artistic events, and so were fans. The very antics that precipitated John's fall from grace with the establishment-fueled media interest.

With Beatlesque panache, the couple quickly captured the world's attention—they were entertaining, interesting, fun to watch, and seemed to be saying something important. With disarming playfulness and charisma greater than the sum of the parts, they were theatrical and stylish, in their black and white and hair, John looking larger than life, towering over Yoko by nine inches. They communicated a fierce sense of purpose with unabashed earnestness, while keeping all observers enthralled and a little off balance.

The press didn't know what to expect at the Amsterdam Hilton, but in light of *Two Virgins*, *Hair*, and *Oh! Calcutta!*, they assumed it would be something arty and sexy. They weren't expecting Mr. and Mrs. Lennon to hold court for a week, in nice pajamas, talking about peace as though it were a consumer product one could choose.

Technology and demographics had given John Lennon the largest platform any communicator ever had in the history of the world. He understood this, and felt a responsibility to use it for good. But the immediate impetus for the couple's antiwar activity was a response to a letter activist filmmaker Peter Watkins sent to numerous high-profile communicators in Britain, reminding them of their responsibility to use the media for world peace. Lennon described it as "getting your induction papers for peace!"[3]

The bed-ins were consistent with the approach espoused on the "Revolution" single: change the world by changing people's heads one at a time, and, therefore, collectively. Change the way people think about war and peace. And along the way, catch children at the dawn of their political consciousness and bring them to an antiwar, nonviolence worldview.

Most fans reacted to the bed-ins as they did to *Two Virgins*—another instance of "John being John." They were neutral about it but wary of Yoko's influence. A male fan (b. '52) recalls, "The bed-ins were meaningless, but I think Yoko was dragging him off the rails." A male fan (b. '54) recalls, "Yoko seemed to be encouraging these types of things."

Fans' perception of Yoko's influence on John was in some sense accurate. But what they saw as "wacky" or "off the rails" was her helping him become the artist and communicator he wanted to be. Younger fans recall an older sibling, cousin, or neighbor who "tried to explain Yoko," and, over the course of many "intellectual conversations," they became "more accepting of her."

Fans understood the bed-in as an antiwar statement, but were skeptical about its effectiveness. A female fan, age twelve at the time, found the whole thing "pretty silly." She recalls, "I didn't see how this would stop the war, but I knew they were trying to shake thing up."

The couple's nonviolent message resonated with fans. A female fan (b. '51) recalls, "Violence scared me; calmer ways of protest appealed to me." A very young female fan (b. '61) who grew up near a military base also recalls the couple as a catalyst for conversation: "The bed-ins led to what were really philosophical discussions among a group of children, trying to figure out what 'Make Love Not War' means; we associated that phrase with John and Yoko. Our church also talked about love and said war wasn't right, yet everyone had a brother or a father or someone in Vietnam. It was very confusing."

It was around this time, she recalled, that some of her friends were no longer allowed to listen to the Beatles: "A lot of my friends were from military families, and many parents thought John was anti-American. I think some parents were afraid John would get their kids to be against the war. We had a very rudimentary understanding of politics, but the Beatles absolutely influenced us. It seems like the war and the Beatles were all we talked about. If we wanted to put a Beatle record on the little Close and Play record player, some kids would have to leave or disobey their parents."

Older fans were less likely to focus on Yoko's influence one way or another, and there were mixed reactions to the bed-in overall. But many recognized the courage involved. A female fan (b. '46), very involved in the antiwar movement, thought, "John looked foolish," although she thought they were "personally brave" to open themselves up to so much criticism. A male fan (b. '47), not involved in the movement but "committed to never living in the straight world," thought "the bed-ins were great" and that John and Yoko were "courageous crusaders."

Across the age range, many "appreciated that they were using their position to call attention to something, rather than just being celebrities" and thought it was "brilliant." As one female fan (b. '53) put it, "Anytime any Beatle breathed the world stopped and listened."

No Discernible Pattern

As the antiwar movement continued to grow, the draft weighed heavily on the minds of male fans. Many recall considering their various options: educational deferment, go to Vietnam and hope for the best, try to get into the National Guard, get married, purchase a letter from a reputable psychiatrist, pretend to be gay, ingest something to raise blood pressure or otherwise make you unfit, or leave the country.

In the spring of 1969 alone, three hundred colleges and universities, involving a third of American students, saw large demonstrations, including strikes, building takeovers, and class disruptions. A few involved bombs, arson, and trashing of property.[4] Massive antiwar demonstrations were held in cities across America throughout April, a month that would mark the peak troop strength of the war—over a half million. Peak troop strength was manifested at home by a level of divisiveness many cultural observers believe had not existed since the Civil War.

On one level, the divisiveness was abstract and impersonal: protestors v. police; young people v. the establishment, doves v. hawks. But fans felt and saw the divisiveness in their daily lives. Neighborhood kids who Beatled together grew apart. A female fan (b. '54) recalls: "A group of us were sitting around listening to the *White Album*, and one of the kids was talking about a letter from his brother, also a Beatle fan, in Vietnam. He said there was a photo of him posing with dead bodies. He thought his brother was a hero and was there for a good reason, but I thought the war was wrong."

In May, the Beatles released "Get Back" b/w "Don't Let Me Down," their first record since the *White Album*. The back-to-basics single, credited to "The Beatles with Billy Preston," marks the first time an American had played on a Beatles record. The record was described in an Apple ad campaign as "The Beatles as nature intended."

The A-side was a fun, upbeat rocker, another Paul "story song," with amusing characters and scenarios, gender confusion, and marijuana. It had a catchy chorus, was fun and easy to sing along with, and fans who still enjoyed dancing to Beatle records appreciated it for that reason as well.

In late May, "Get Back" knocked the 5th Dimension's "Aquarius" out of the number one spot—a position the anthemic *Hair* tune had held for six weeks—and stayed in the spot for five weeks until Henry Mancini's "Love Theme from Romeo and Juliet" assumed the position.

John's B-side, which many fans now think was the better of the two songs, was a plea to Yoko for lasting love and redemption that sounded like it came from the deepest recesses of John's being. It was one of his most emotionally authentic vocal performances to date. Billy Preston's keyboard work added a memorable interlude to the song, subtly evoking the piano break of "In My Life." By this point, fans could no longer think about John without thinking about Yoko. They had a distinct identity like no other Beatle couple had, an identity separate and apart from the Beatles.

Around this time fans learned that John had legally changed his middle name from Winston to Ono. Many remember this because, like much about John and Yoko, it had an element of spectacle and asked fans to think about something familiar in a new way. A female fan, age seventeen at the time, recalls: "I thought it was cool that he was taking her last name as part of his name. Men don't do that; it's always the woman who changes her name. There was something respectful about it, like he was honoring her" (Female b. '52).

In May, John and Yoko released *Unfinished Music No. 2: Life with the Lions*, another album of avant-garde music that also included the fragile heartbeat of the baby they lost the previous fall. Reviewing the album in *Rolling Stone*, a publication always ready to bless any Beatle-related project, Ed Ward said the album was "utter bullshit" and "in poor taste."

The album, whose title parodied the BBC Radio comedy *Life with the Lyons* and was a commentary on the couple's relationship with the press, sold about sixty thousand copies in the US. Lennon, somewhat delusional about the album's commercial potential, was furious that Apple did nothing to promote it.[5]

One of those sixty thousand, a male fan, age sixteen at the time, recalls, "I bought *Life with the Lions* because it was made by them; it was by an artist whose records I bought." A male fan, age thirteen at the time, remembers seeing the album—with the couple in the hospital on the front and their drug bust on the back—at his local record store, but "didn't trust it based on 'Revolution 9,' *Two Virgins*, and Yoko."

At this point, most fans knew a John and Yoko record was likely to be less satisfying than even their least favorite Beatle album. But they followed the couple with great interest, parallel to the Beatles, which meant exposure to new forms of art and communication. John and Yoko were a compelling spin-off, tickling fans' Beatle-cultivated appreciation for spectacle. The couple's flirtatious dance with the media was historically unprecedented, even in a post-Beatlemania world.

While fans watched or read about John and Yoko's globe-trotting, new Beatle music was on the way and there were rumors of more projects in the pipeline: the delayed *Get Back* album, and maybe a film. Fans relied on *Rolling Stone* for information about Beatle happenings, but that spring the magazine reported "no discernable pattern" in the band's activities.[6]

An Anthem Is Born

In late May, John and Yoko staged their second weeklong bed-in, this time at the Queen Elizabeth Hotel in Montreal. Having been denied entry to the US, they chose a location close enough to attract the US media. According to Lennon, "The States are afraid we're going to go over there and rouse the kids up, which we don't intend to do at all; we intend to calm it down."[7] An estimated three hundred fifty US radio stations reported on the event.

While in bed in Montreal, John spoke with student demonstrators at Berkeley, actively involved in an ongoing, increasingly violent dispute over the use of People's Park. In a phone conversation broadcast on KPFA radio, an angry, frightened young man asked John what he would do in that "out of control" situation. John expressed his support and urged the protestors to avoid a confrontation with the police. "Don't play their game" he tells them. "Entice them, con them, you have the brains and you can do it." Yoko tells them to extend their hand to the police, to "open their minds up and give their love."[8]

The couple was criticized for giving advice at odds with the traditional practice of nonviolent resistance. But more significant than the advice they offered was the fact that when these politicized fans were on the front lines in a war against Blue Meanies armed with clubs, guns, and tear gas, they were on the phone with Beatle John Lennon, asking him, perhaps challenging him, to provide practical advice.

Robert Christgau, in his own ambivalent fan relationship with Lennon, said the call "firmed up" Lennon's "newfound status as a pompous piece of shit."[9] *New York Times* reporter Gloria Emerson and cartoonist Al Capp, among others, were also sharply critical of the Lennons at the time, in a very personal, nasty way. These critics missed the point. John and Yoko didn't have all the answers and never claimed to, but they were willing to be "the world's clowns" if it would draw attention to their antiwar message.

Asked by a reporter what the couple hoped to achieve with the bed-in, the phrase "give peace a chance" fell out of John's mouth, along with other verbiage. He liked the phrase and saw its potential. The couple had been talking for over a year about plans to "package peace in a new box."[10] The bed-ins were the promotional campaign; now the product had a catchy jingle that would be heard and sung by millions.

With a little help from their friends—including Tom Smothers, Norman Mailer, Timothy Leary, Petula Clark, Murray the K, and Allen Ginsberg, "Give Peace a Chance" was recorded in their hotel room on a rented multitrack recorder. With its organic, tribal feel, the song's structure creates a contrast between the everyday blah-blah-blah people chatter about and the overriding urgency of ending war. A male fan (b. '49) recalls, "It was a different kind of message than 'end the war now.' It's a gentler message, but very powerful."

This Plastic Ono Band debut record, with Lennon-McCartney songwriting credit, was released in July and peaked at number fourteen in September. The same week the single was released, *Rolling Stone* ran a review of "the Beatles next album, *Get Back*, due in July," which includes a "beautiful Paul McCartney ballad titled 'Let It Be.'" Fans were watching John and Yoko do their thing, and new Beatle music was on the way.

In June, between "Get Back" and "Give Peace a Chance," the Beatles released "The Ballad of John and Yoko" b/w "Old Brown Shoe."

The A-side, featuring only Lennon and McCartney, is a wordy chronicle of John and Yoko's wedding plans and global escapades for peace. The chorus decries their treatment by the press and, once again, John evokes Jesus Christ when talking about himself. This time there would be no apologies. Many radio stations, including New York's WMCA, banned the record.[11]

Ian McDonald said the song was "so outrageously egocentric, it's difficult to know whether to deplore its vanity or admire its chutzpah."[12] Fans seem to have had a similar reaction. A female fan, age fifteen at the time, recalls, "I thought it was a little weird that he was singing about them like that, but I liked the song." A male fan, thirteen at the time, said, "Only Lennon would have the balls to sing about being Jesus and getting crucified."

John wanted this song recorded and released quickly and called on Paul to play drums and bass; Ringo had a prior commitment and George was out of the country. Their energized collaboration that evening, and the positive feelings around it, suggests a critical moment in their personal and professional relationship. Paul was expressing acceptance of John's new partner, and helping him record a Beatle A-side about it. The world was giving John a hard time, but Paul was there for him.

It's been observed that the songwriting credit on "Give Peace a Chance," released in July, was John's way of thanking Paul for playing on "The Ballad of John and Yoko," released in June. However, years later, John said he regretted feeling "guilty enough to give McCartney credit as co-writer" on his "first independent single" instead of giving it to Yoko, who had actually written it with him."[13] It's not clear, however, what he would have felt "guilty" about, or how he defines "first independent single."

John also points to his choice of George's "Old Brown Shoe" for the B-side, recorded during the *Abbey Road* sessions, as a kind gesture toward its writer.[14] This makes the single significant to John's relationship with the other two as well. He clearly wanted to involve all the Beatles in the project even though it wasn't conceived as a Beatle project. In fact, it was basically a vanity project for him and Yoko. But the group involvement reaffirmed Lennon's leadership in the band and reaffirmed the band as an ongoing entity at a time when, as one male fan (b. '49) recalls, "there was conjecture that they were breaking up, plus there was all that controversy about her."

Fans liked the rock and roll novelty song enough for it to peak at number eight in mid-July. Not all those who bought the record were lucky enough to get it with the picture cover, but those who did saw a beautifully posed group portrait of the four Beatles and Yoko. John and Yoko, dominating the photo, are seated in the front row on Alice in Wonderland statuary. The couple is similarly dressed in black, both wearing ties. The other three stand behind them, in the back row, not looking particularly happy to be posing with a fifth Beatle.

The June single may have satisfied John's desire to keep the couple on the world stage and it may have, secondarily, filled a lingering need for Beatle brotherhood. Yet, from the fan perspective, the package, musically and iconographically, situated Yoko within the Beatles in a new way.

Summer Spectacles

Later in the summer, young gays, lesbians, and drag queens in New York City, angered at their relentless, brutal harassment by the NYPD and united in their determination to no longer live in hiding, fought back and launched the gay rights movement at the Stonewall Inn in Greenwich Village.

An early promise of the decade had been realized a few weeks later when the world watched a human walk on the moon. A male Beatle fan, age fourteen at the time, remembers watching the event and seeing people all over the world watching it with him: "It was a moment shared by all humanity. I remember thinking what an amazing accomplishment it was; it seemed like a new beginning of some kind."

For many, pride in America's accomplishment was overshadowed by the morass of Vietnam. A male fan, age twenty at the time, recalled,

"I knew this was us supposedly winning the space race, but it had nothing to do with me. The war and the draft were more important."

In August, a charismatic, psychotic Beatle fan, who at one time aspired to be a rock and roller and had even auditioned to be a Monkee, was identified as the leader of a murderous cult. Charles Manson was neither the first nor the last Beatle fan to ascribe cosmic meaning to the band and interpret their songs in idiosyncratic ways—though most who consider the Beatles in these expansive terms take it to the light side, not the dark side.

Manson was an angry, disturbed individual with a criminal record that predates the Beatles and the hippie movement. He was the first high-profile, deranged Beatle fan to emerge from the vast swath of the population that had been psychologically intimate with them since the beginning.

Fans were saddened to see the Beatles appropriated by a delusional monster, and the murders seemed to implicate the Beatles in something bad. Manson was an aberration, but his hippie lifestyle, so much a part of the story, gave straight America another excuse to be both more fearful of and more hostile toward hippies and the counterculture. Fans remember their fascination with the murders:

I felt weird that I was more interested in it than I felt I should be. Manson was a fascinating character, that he could do this by remote control. We talked about it a lot. It was the first mass slaughter and it was tied up with the counterculture. I remember there was a Beach Boy connection. Male, b. '52

The Beatles got into everyone's head, but he's a fucking madman. A piece of me felt what a pain in the ass it must be for them to be dragged into this. For them to wake up and read this, it was even undignified for them to have to comment. Male, b. '47

The violence of Chicago the summer before and the violence of this psychotic killer fueled the erroneous perception, two years after the Summer of Love, that violence was an accepted part of the hippie lifestyle and countercultural value system. In fact, violence, in general, at home and abroad, seemed to be on the rise—thus making messages of peace and nonviolence more compelling, especially to young people.

Music and Mud

A week after the Manson murders, young people would have an opportunity to show the world that violence was not a countercultural value when a half-million young people gathered at Max Yasgur's dairy farm in upstate New York for the Woodstock Music and Art Fair. Young fans too young to be "real hippies" were still tuned in to the event and felt a connection with the people there:

> I remember seeing that red poster at the card shop where we bought our Beatle records and magazines. I remember thinking how cool it would be to be able to go to something like that. I wanted to be part of it, but I was too young, although I was already a pot smoker. Female, b. '56

> I didn't know about it before but I saw it on the news and read about it after. I wish I was there. The hippie thing was appealing to me. I grew my hair, listened to FM radio. Woodstock was all the people who felt like I did. Male, b. '54

A female fan (b. '51) who did go to Woodstock remembers, "There was no food, bathrooms were few and far between, there was mud and trash everywhere. I guess it was uncomfortable, but we didn't care. It was fun." A male fan (b. '48) remembers driving up with his brother: "We went up there with the clothes on our backs, on the second or third day. It was a music event and we weren't going to be able to hear any music, so we left. I wasn't there to be part of this groovy community—I found it overwhelming. Being in a crowd that size scared me." Pete Townshend said the "alternative society" was "basically a field full of six-foot-deep mud laced with LSD."[15] Perhaps. But efforts to avoid romanticizing the event, then or now, should not diminish its significance. Given the size of the crowd and the unusually stressful conditions, including lack of basic necessities, the absence of violence was truly remarkable. An objective view of human behavior would have predicted otherwise. The instant sense of community and the peacefulness of the event manifested a consciousness that aspired to something better.

Woodstock organizers invited the Beatles to play, but they declined. John offered the Plastic Ono Band, and event organizers declined. Even if they had put the band on the bill, John couldn't have performed at Woodstock because he wasn't allowed in the US at the time. But Beatle presence was felt. Richie Havens performed three Beatle songs, and Joe Cocker and Crosby, Stills, and Nash each performed one.

Lennon observed the event from his Tittenhurst estate and later noted it as "the biggest mass of people ever gathered together for anything other than war! Nobody had that big of an army that didn't kill somebody or have some kind of violent scene, like the Romans or whatever. And even a Beatles concert was more violent than that, you know, and that was just fifty thousand."[16] John was heartened by the peaceful crowd at Woodstock and believed the message of peace, love, and nonviolence was having an impact.

As this summer of happenings, both good and bad, drew to a close, fans were back at school. Many were sporting longer hair and scruffier clothes, provoking further confrontations with school administrators. Also, more young people were refusing to participate in the Pledge of Allegiance, a passive form of protest that satisfied their need to express opposition to the war and to explore the limits of their rights as students and citizens.

In September, *Rolling Stone* did a track by track review of the Beatles' *Get Back* album, calling the record "a model of simplicity, in concept, music, philosophy, and politics."[17] The same issue featured an item on John and Yoko's plans to bring their message of peace to the people of the Middle East from a private ship off the Mediterranean coast.[18] While the "Peace Cruise" didn't happen, the *Get Back* album did. Sort of.

Radio stations around the country were playing acetates of the *Get Back* sessions—what would later become *Let It Be*—mixed the previous spring but never released. Boston's WBCN played the album on September 22, and the entire broadcast, including commercials and discussion, was captured on numerous bootleg recordings.[19]

Also in September, four years after its debut, the Beatles cartoon series was canceled. In those four years, millions of very young children had watched the cartoon with their older brothers and sisters, who had been the youngest in the first wave of fans, and now this new group, age six to ten, was in the fan pool too.

Oh That Magic Feeling

Fans who read *Rolling Stone*—and all their friends and siblings and siblings' friends— were expecting "some sort of roots album" called *Get Back* or *Let It Be*. But in early October *Abbey Road* appeared, named for the location of the studio where they'd been working together since the beginning.

It had been almost a year since the last album, and two of the last three singles, one in June and one in July, were very "John and Yoko." The latter, "Give Peace a Chance," was actually a Plastic Ono Band release. A new Beatle album was always "like a special holiday," but fans especially appreciated this one. It was reassuring after all the John and Yoko stuff and murmurs of discord among the maturing Fabs.

A few days later, the double A-side "Something" b/w "Come Together" was released. As weirded out as some fans might have been by John's antics of late, the powerful, exhortative "Come Together," with what one snarky reviewer called "Look Ma, I'm Jesus lyrics," knocked The 5th Dimension's cover of Laura Nyro's "Wedding Bell Blues" out of the number one spot, a position it had held for three weeks. The insistent chorus of "Come Together" resonated with the spirit of generational unity demonstrated at Woodstock less than two months earlier.

"Something," George's first A-side and the first Beatle single in almost four years to feature anything resembling a traditional love song, hit number three. Singles, affordable and frequent, had always fueled fan enthusiasm. Many recall the period from late 1964 to mid-1966—with its spate of fresh and surprising 45s—as the most joyful time of their Beatle fan experience. This new double-A side offered a great new song, or two, to fans of all ages, all expectations, and all degrees of allegiance. Here was a romantic ballad, heralding George's arrival as a Beatles-caliber songwriter, and a swampy rocker that one male fan (b. '47) heard as "Lennon singing to our breed, to the freaks who said 'no' to a straight lifestyle."

Abbey Road was less of a "package" than the last few albums—no gatefold, no inserts, no printed lyrics. But it did have an enigmatic image that would become, like previous Beatle album covers, "indelible" in fans' consciousness—so indelible that a certain shade of green tree-tops against a certain shade of blue is often described by fans as "an Abbey Road sky."

The carefully posed but casual photo by Iain MacMillan, with its vanishing point, soft symmetry, and absence of lettering, presented a simple but richly detailed scene. They're a foursome, yet each wears his own costume within his own personal space, making no eye contact with each other or the viewer as they cross the tree-lined residential street. If the image invited viewers in, it was to the infinite space beyond them.

John's reddish-brown mane and now familiar white suit got a lot of attention. A male fan (b. '54) recalls, "Some kids thought the Beatles were freaks, but we liked how Lennon looked." Several referred to John's "Jesus" or "rabbi" look, having seen it full-face in news reports of the bed-in. As a male fan, age eleven at the time, said, "The Beatles' changing appearance was something I followed almost as much as their music."

Paul with cigarette was not unusual; it was quite common to see all of them smoking. In fact, Paul was with ciggie in one of the early Dezo Hoffman photos emblazoned on numerous products marketed to children, just weeks after the Surgeon General's report on the dangers of smoking. But bare feet were unusual and would soon suggest something more than Beatle quirkiness.

George's American hippie garb reflects his time hanging out with Bob Dylan and the Band in upstate New York and gigging with American rockers Delaney and Bonnie. The non-fashion, utilitarian full denim look, already popular with some fans, became a uniform for many in the early seventies. George's footwear also caught on. A male fan (b. '54) recalls, "I went out and got a pair of desert boots after that album came out."

The photo was taken on August 8, 1969, scheduled for earlier in the day than the group usually arrived. Despite careful planning, the shoot was delayed briefly when the group and MacMillan asked the police—who were unable to oblige—to move the Volkswagen Beetle that they thought would mar the photo.

Some of the youngest fans remember *Abbey Road* as the first album they bought with their own money, which made it even "more special." A female fan (b. '55) recalls her first encounter with *Abbey Road*: "I was at a department store with my mother and I went off to the record department, as usual. I heard 'Come Together,' 'Something,' and 'Oh! Darling' and realized it was a new Beatle album. I found my mother and asked her for $3.99 to buy it—I think I was able to talk her into it because it was on sale. I walked into the house and showed it to my brother and sister. Between the three of us it was playing all the time. We eventually wore it out and had to get a new one."

Fans of all ages, male and female, sometimes developed rituals as part of their listening experience. A female fan (b. '54) remembers, "For some reason, with *Abbey Road*, I resolved to keep track of how many times I listened to it. I also filled out the discography in the Hunter Davies book as the records came out." A male fan (b. '61) recalls, "I tried to write down all the words and if I came across one I didn't know I wrote it down phonetically. In 'Octopus's Garden,' I heard 'near a cave' as 'irricade.' I knew the word 'cascade,' so I thought an 'irricade' was some sort of waterfall beneath the sea."

The Beatles had matured but were still inviting fans of all ages to fantastic places like an "Octopus's Garden" where "they can't be found";

where "every girl and boy" would feel "happy and safe" and there'd be "no one there to tell us what to do." It's "us against them," again.

Fans enjoyed the dark humor of "Maxwell's Silver Hammer," several recalling Paul's chuckle during the phrase "writing fifty times I will not be so, oh oh oh." A female fan, age eight at the time, recalls liking the song, but wondered, "Why is someone getting killed, these are the nice Beatles?" It appealed the way "When I'm Sixty-four" and "Honey Pie" appealed—with a familiar, Paulishly articulated vocal, and clever rhymes that were sing-along mouthfuls. Vague images of Rose and Valerie in the gallery always played along with it.

Abbey Road felt and sounded like a collaborative effort in a way that the *White Album* didn't. Ensemble playing, unique complementary harmonies, and a tighter braiding of the four Beatle essences gives *Abbey Road* a more Beatley sound and feel, with more concentration of Beatle energy.

Time praised the entire album's "cheerful coherence" and called it the band's best work since *Sgt. Pepper*, singling out Harrison's "Something." *Rolling Stone* published positive and negative reviews. The latter, by Ed Ward, was especially nasty, offering *Time's* praise of "Something" as proof the song was "vile" and derided the band for the song's commercial appeal. Though Ward was apparently too hip to appreciate the song, fans loved "George's beautiful song for Pattie."

Ward called side two "a disaster," and singled out the "Sun King" portion of the medley, calling it "a Muzak-sounding thing with Italian lyrics" that is "probably the worst thing the Beatles have done since they changed drummers." But fans enjoyed the "floaty sound" and many remember trying to figure out those "Italian lyrics," sometimes with help: "We asked my Italian grandmother to translate 'Sun King.' We played it for her over and over again. It drove her crazy trying to make sense of that gibberish. I guess we didn't get the joke."

George's side two opener, "Here Comes the Sun," was an album favorite. Fans liked its "optimistic message" and many commented on the album having "two great George songs."

Fans "especially loved side two," as did the *New York Times* reviewer, who said the fifteen-minute medley was "the most impressive thing they've done since *Rubber Soul*" but thought the rest of the album ranged from "mere gentle tedium to cringing embarrassment."[20] Another *New York Times* review called it "a sincere, simple and powerful collection of songs . . . much less flossy and grandiose" than the *White Album* but "endlessly more satisfying for just that reason."[21]

Many remember hearing Polythene Pam made "good use of the Pill" rather than "the *News of the World*," not having recalibrated their ears for John's scouse delivery. A female fan, age fifteen at the time, recalls, "I remember my sister and I wondering what it meant that someone could steal but not rob. What was the difference?"

Fans talked about "side two of *Abbey Road*" as though it were a song unto itself. The band had never done anything like that before—no other Beatle album had a chunk that big. Fans didn't think about how the medley was put together—they were listening to fifteen minutes of Beatlemusic, as crisp and clear as the sunny fall days when they first listened.

Each element of the medley was intriguing and textured, but the words had no clear meaning. Meticulously and artfully stitched together by Paul McCartney and George Martin, the music became a coherent whole on which the ambiguous, or perhaps meaningless, lyrics also cohered and became meaningful to fans because of what they brought to it.

In the medley, fans heard a concentrated, well-measured blend of those four Beatle essences, coming to them from the toppermost of the poppermost. Some of the songs seemed to be about the challenges of life at that apex and what lies beyond. But many fans, now in high school and college, or finished with school and starting careers and families, were contemplating their own futures and found personal relevance in the evocative lyrics. Everyone had weight to carry.

Just as not all critics liked *Abbey Road*, neither did all fans. A young listener, age nine at the time, thought the songs were too long.

"I got bored," she recalled. But the nine-year-olds bored by it at the time listened again a year or two later and felt differently. And because they'd been revisiting and "growing into" earlier Beatle records in the interim, they came to appreciate the chronology and could experience the entire body of work as a seamless whole.

A male fan, age fourteen at the time, recalls, "I responded to *Abbey Road* in a less visceral way than I responded to them in the past, although there were some worthwhile moments. 'Hey Jude' ignited me. I was waiting to be wowed again and I wasn't." Another male fan, age fifteen at the time, recalled, "Something was lost after *Sgt. Pepper*; they were still great, but something was lost."

And in the End

What was lost, or different, was that the Beatles were no longer on their ascent—that trajectory ended with *Sgt. Pepper*, the full flowering of their creativity. *Pepper* brought the band to a new level of personal and professional satisfaction. They were fully self-actualized millionaires in their mid-twenties, with the world at their feet. Thus began their search for higher meaning, greater awareness, and new challenges.

The Beatles had achieved what they set out to achieve. The next leg of their journey didn't have as clear a path as the one that led them to realize their one sweet dream. There was no exit strategy. They had matured, but they were still four young men finding their way. Each meandered where his interest took him, and that was, not surprisingly, away from each other. And for the two principals, it was toward new primary partners. The synergistic "Maclen" energy had dissipated.

That the foursome could collaborate and play as a band in the midst of the conflict and mixed emotions they felt toward each other at the time speaks to their maturity, talent, and commitment to their craft. Always self-conscious, and now with the added burden of legacy consciousness, they were able to leave the noise outside the studio and focus on their art, knowing it was for the ages. *Mojo* describes the album as a "triumph of immaculate, if temporary, unity."[22]

As fans were exploring *Abbey Road*, one of the results of John's meandering away from the Beatles, "Give Peace A Chance," was sung by over a half-million demonstrators in Washington, DC, and millions more around the country and the world—including future US president Bill Clinton at Oxford, England—on October 15, Vietnam Moratorium Day.

Pete Seeger led the crowd at the DC protest, adding "Are you listening, Nixon?" and "Are you listening, Agnew?" between the chorus. Lennon later remarked, "I saw pictures of that Washington demonstration on British TV, with all those people singing it, forever and not stopping. It was one of the biggest moments of my life."[23]

Some older fans who'd been involved in the antiwar movement and found John and Yoko's politics "flaky" or "naive" were "very glad the song had caught on" and, like all fans, felt the Beatleness when they heard the phrase used by protestors or saw it in headlines.

Emboldened by older friends and siblings, the climate of protest, media harping about the generation gap, and "cool" teachers, high school students also participated in moratorium activities, although their protests were not limited to the war. Many recall when confrontations over dress codes finally led to change. According to a male fan, age fifteen at the time: "A few months into the school year, I didn't have to wear a tie anymore, we could pretty much wear anything. But a lot of kids were suspended along the way."

High schools across the country honored recent graduates killed in action, but these tributes, like most expressions of troop support at the time, were interpreted as support for the war, and fueled the divisiveness: "We had a half-mast recess for two former students who were killed in Vietnam. Everyone was standing around the flagpole. I remember two girls, sisters of one of the boys who was killed, were sitting on the ground when everyone else was standing. I guess they were protesting but it seemed disrespectful to me at the time" (Male, b. '53).

The Wedding Album

Less than three weeks after *Abbey Road* was released, John and Yoko, the first reality media stars, released *Wedding Album*, the third in their series of experimental recordings. The elaborate box set included a sixteen-page album of press clippings, numerous photos of the couple, and playful inserts, such as a picture of a slice of wedding cake, a bag labeled "Bagism," and a reproduction of their marriage license. Those who bought the pricey album thinking it would someday be a valuable collector's item—a mindset already in place by 1969—were correct.

The many who passed on the *Wedding Album* heard John and Yoko on their single "Cold Turkey" b/w "Don't Worry Kyoko (Mummy's Only Looking for a Hand in the Snow)," released the same day. McCartney had declined Lennon's offer of the A-side for a Beatle record, and John's decision to put it out as a Plastic Ono Band record marked his first solo songwriting credit, and a turning point in the Lennon-McCartney partnership.

A male fan (b. '54) recalls buying the record "without hearing it" because "it was John Lennon." The five-minute grunge rocker featured one of John's most raw and intense vocals, revealing a vulnerability that made 1965's "Help!" seem almost trite by comparison. A female fan, age fifteen at the time, remembers, "My brother had that 45 and I didn't like it. I didn't want to think about John on heroin or in pain."

Many were disturbed when they learned about John's heroin use; young fans were frightened by it. Some attributed the habit to Yoko's influence and it became another reason to dislike her. The song didn't get a lot of airplay and peaked at number thirty early in 1970. The B-side provided the first opportunity to hear Yoko sing. Most fans didn't take the song seriously and found it "hilarious" or "irritating"— yet another reason to dislike Yoko.

Turn Me On, Dead Man

Days after *Abbey Road*'s release, during Moratorium week, there was unexpected Beatle news: "I was in History class and one of the jocks said he heard Paul was dead. The teacher discussed it with us for a while. Some people knew about it and knew some of the clues. The jock probably just said it to be cool; he wasn't that into the Beatles" (Male, b. '55).

With passion, velocity, and density of Beatletalk not witnessed since the band's arrival five and a half years earlier, a rumor that Paul died in 1966 spread through neighborhoods and schools. A male fan, age eighteen at the time, recalls, "We just got swept away with it. There was a crazy frenzy about it, the way it spread."

According to the rumor, Paul had been replaced by a look-alike after dying in a car crash, events which the band painstakingly and successfully hid from the public. However, it was revealed that clues about the accident and proof Paul was dead could be found in songs and on album covers, as far back as *Yesterday and Today*. Many of the clues were on *Abbey Road*, one of the most prominent being, ironically, the license plate on the VW Beetle that would not have been there if the band had their way.

Paul Is Dead fever went on for more than two months. Fans from ten to twenty-five, in grade school and grad school, looked at albums with magnifying glasses, identified symbols, and listened to songs, sometimes backward, for clues. And like early Beatleing, hunting for Paul Is Dead clues was a group activity and gave fans much to explore and discuss:

I was at a friend's house, and her friend's older brothers and sisters were talking about the rumor that Paul was dead and playing the records backwards. They were having lunch; grilled cheese and chicken soup. Female, b. '61

There was a Halloween party where someone put Paul in a coffin. We looked for the clues and talked about it. Male, b. '54

I was in college at the time. We played some songs backwards. We followed the clues. We didn't think he was dead, but it was fun.
Female, b. '47

A Beatle spokesman called the rumor "a load of rubbish," but that didn't quell the frenzy.[24] Several thought the band did it as a "joke at fans' expense because they knew people combed for deeper meaning." A female fan, age fourteen at the time, recalls, "I always thought the Beatles were behind it, that it was a publicity stunt. That disappointed me. I lost some of my trust in them. But we looked for the clues."

Very few thought the Beatles were behind the rumor, though, and not all who thought so felt disappointed. A male fan, also fourteen at the time, recalls, "I thought it was a marketing ploy to sell records, and I still do. These things are there. I didn't think he was dead, but I think they did it on purpose. John's a practical joker, they all were." A female fan, age thirteen at the time, said, "The Beatles had a mysterious side and knew how to put in cool stuff that kids would appreciate."

Looking for clues meant going back to earlier albums that many younger fans, including super young fans introduced to the Beatles with *Yellow Submarine* or the Beatles cartoons, didn't know about or thought were "for big kids." Now these ten- and eleven-year-olds wanted their own copy of *Sgt. Pepper.* The Beatles weren't behind the rumor, but it certainly sold records. It also sold special-issue magazines dedicated to the rumor. A New York City radio station broadcast an hour-long discussion about it, and the early morning AM signal was heard in thirty-eight states.[25]

Rolling Stone ran an article called "One and One and One Is Three?" in late October, explaining how the rumor got started and discussing some of the clues.[26] The *New York Times* ran its second article on the persistent rumor in early November, this one titled "No, No, No, Paul McCartney Is Not Dead."[27] For the most part, fans didn't believe Paul was dead, but they still "looked for clues and played songs backwards."

At the height of the frenzy, a *Life* magazine reporter showed up unannounced and unwelcome at Paul's farm, and after a testy interaction—

photos of which were destroyed by gentleman's agreement—was able to get a rare, extemporaneous interview with McCartney, who conjectured that the rumor started because he hadn't "been much in the press lately." He said he'd done "enough press for a lifetime" and that he'd rather be "a little less famous these days."[28] Paul continued, dropping a bombshell that got less attention than *Life*'s black-and-white photo spread proving he was alive: "I would rather do what I began by doing, which is making music. We make good music, and we want to go on making good music. But the Beatle thing is over. It has been exploded, partly by what we have done, and partly by other people. We are individuals—all different. John married Yoko, I married Linda. We didn't marry the same girl."

By late November, when a New York City television station broadcast a mock trial on the rumor featuring famed attorney F. Lee Bailey, the Paul Is Dead fever had run its course, but fans didn't stop looking at the clues, and still haven't. The rumor had been started by a college student and a DJ, but the hundreds of clues that eventually emerged were created and shared by fans, who collectively developed a kind of game that allowed for purposeful Beatleing.

Since the beginning, countless hours had been spent listening and studying album covers—this was simply more of the same. Those with good imaginations created meaning out of ambiguous details to fit an absurd, emotionally charged narrative. But for some, it was more appealing to believe the Beatles had the cleverness and forethought to create these clues, in benignly conspiratorial fashion, than to believe they were created collectively by fellow fans. That the rumor completely defies logic and common sense was irrelevant to the function it served.

When the rumor started, fans had been seeing a lot of John but not much of Paul, George, or Ringo. And they'd seen a lot of John's side projects that were moving, irretrievably, in non-Beatle directions. At the same time, they were reading about delayed Beatle projects, disagreements, and financial wrangling. And then there was the new album—a tidy showcase with a feel of grand finality that explored, especially on "Side Two," themes of maturity, disappointment, and unknown futures while offering aphorisms for the ages. Like any compulsive behavior, looking for and talking about Paul Is Dead clues assuaged anxiety—not about whether Paul was dead but about whether the Beatles were still alive.

Unbeknownst to fans, John told the band he "wanted a divorce" in September but agreed to keep it quiet until some pending business issues were resolved. Paul, who most loved being a Beatle and who most defined himself in that way, was angry and depressed, going through his own cold turkey. Fans were listening to a new album, rediscovering old ones and, expecting another long-delayed release early in the new year, and so Paul's casual remark to *Life* went unnoticed.

A Poke at Her Majesty

In mid-November, the world learned that in March 1968 American soldiers on a "search and destroy" mission massacred the entire village of My Lai, approximately five hundred people, mostly women, children, and elderly. American soldiers raped, tortured, scalped, and otherwise brutalized the villagers; several who refused to participate were later accused of being unpatriotic.

The massacre came to light after a twenty-two-year-old helicopter gunner wrote letters to thirty members of Congress and to military officials, detailing the events. Like the Tet Offensive, the massacre at My Lai exposed unpleasant truths that fueled antiwar sentiment. On November 15 there was another major antiwar protest in Washington; two hundred fifty thousand people assembled and sang "Give Peace a Chance" again.

My Lai caught John's attention, too. He'd been considering returning his MBE in protest for some time. Having been talked into accepting it in the first place, he'd always felt that he "sold out." The massacre helped him make up his mind.

In handwritten letters signed "With Love" to the queen and other government officials, Lennon explained his reasons: "Britain's involvement in the Nigeria-Biafra thing, against our support of America in

Vietnam and against 'Cold Turkey' slipping down the charts." The only other recipients ever to return the award did so in protest over the Beatles receiving it four years earlier.

Including "Cold Turkey" as a reason for the protest may have undermined the seriousness of the act, but some thought Lennon's "quirky" approach was "cool" and "effective." A male fan, age nineteen at the time, recalled, "His irreverence, the silly note, and 'Cold Turkey' made his message more palatable. He was still my guy; he wasn't lecturing you, he was still entertaining."

End of a Decade

Inspired by the spirit of Woodstock and as a thank you to their fans, the Rolling Stones ended their 1969 tour with a free outdoor festival at the Altamont Speedway in northern California. The hastily planned event featured several top acts of the day and drew three hundred thousand people. The festival was marred by violence throughout the day, culminating in the fatal stabbing of a young man, only feet from the stage, while the Stones played "Under My Thumb." *Rolling Stone* called December 6 "rock and roll's all-time worst day," a day when "everything went perfectly wrong."[29] The Stones' new album, *Let It Bleed*, was released a few days later.

December also saw the release of *Live Peace in Toronto 1969* by the Plastic Ono Band, with a lineup that included Eric Clapton, Klaus Voormann, and Alan White along with John and Yoko. The album had been recorded at the Toronto Rock and Roll Revival the previous September. Side one of the record featured three rock and roll covers, plus "Yer Blues," "Cold Turkey," and "Give Peace a Chance."

These six tracks captured John Lennon doing the thing he loved most and did best—playing and singing rock and roll for a live audience. Side two featured two Yoko tracks, in what was emerging as her usual style. Fans remembered this album and its cover photo of one white cloud against a bright blue sky. It also came with a *John and Yoko 1970 Calendar* or a card to order one.

With their unique blend of politics and conceptual art, John and Yoko continued to work the *mundo paparazzi* with their "War Is Over" poster and newspaper campaign, launched in twelve cities around the world. The white posters with simple black lettering declared "War Is Over! If You Want It" and in smaller letters at the bottom, it read "Happy Christmas from John & Yoko."

Young fans might not have understood what the couple was trying to do—can you really wish war away?—but the campaign kept the couple in the media spotlight and was a provocative but hopeful message at the end of a decade that, with all its early promise, had become increasingly violent.

The international billboard campaign, with the stark, whimsical message suddenly appearing in major cities, momentarily connected fans all over the world and reinforced their sense, again, that they were part of a global siblinghood. In that moment of seeing the billboard—with the artistry of its design and message standing out amid the other billboards and myriad stimuli of a Times Square or Piccadilly Circus—a world without war was collectively, briefly imagined.[30] It was conceptual art for the masses.

The carefully engineered campaign combined concepts Yoko had been using on a smaller scale in her pre-John conceptual art with John's pre-Yoko on-the-job training in how the mass media work. As he told *Rolling Stone* at the time: "We're artists, not politicians. . . . We do it in the way that suits us best, and this is the way we work. Publicity and things like that is our game. 'Cos, I mean, the Beatles thing was that. And that was the trade I've learnt. This is my trade, and I'm using it to the best of my ability."[31]

John and Yoko were still not allowed into the US at the time but were once again as close as they could get—on their third trip to Canada since the spring. Many remember reports of the couple meeting with Canadian prime minister Pierre Trudeau, which immediately made him the coolest head of state in the world. The couple did several interviews while in Toronto, which were reported in the US by the Associated Press and *Rolling Stone*. Lennon said the new Beatles album, now called *Let It Be*, would be out in February.

John had never been impressed by authority or status and didn't suffer fools—gladly or not gladly. And though he believed himself to be a genius, he was also insecure about his own intellect and often expressed defensive disdain for educated people he saw as phony. But respect from people he respected meant a lot to him. When Britain's ATV asked three prominent British intellectuals to name a "Man of the Decade," *Naked Ape* author and anthropologist Desmond Morris selected Lennon.

In an interview with Morris broadcast in Britain on December 30, Lennon was positive, funny, thoughtful, articulate, and amiable, with no chip on his shoulder. He seemed healthy and happy. Lennon, now looking at the Beatles through a rearview mirror, with Yoko at his side, accepted the peculiar role he found himself in, and despite some lingering ambivalence about it—all he really set out to do was play rock and roll and be bigger than Elvis—he was trying to figure out how to play the role comfortably, responsibly, and effectively.

Every year since 1964, the Beatles recorded Christmas greetings on flexi discs for fan club members—"loyal Beatle people." These year-end greetings, with chitchat, Beatle silliness, wordplay, and musical snippets, had an informal, natural quality, much like their early interviews on the BBC—four clever kids goofing around on live mics. The individual Beatles recorded their greetings separately for the first time in 1968; this year's greeting, the final one in the series, was, not surprisingly, also recorded separately. December's *Beatles Book*, the official fan club publication fans had been reading since 1964, included a special message from longtime Beatle secretary and friend Freda Kelly, telling readers this edition would be the last.

A year-end review of the decade in the *New York Times* called "hair" the "four-letter word of the sixties" and recounted how schools across the country, and the military, had been trying to formulate policy to deal with long-haired and bearded men, many of whom continued to face treatment at the hands of authorities that ranged from humiliating to inhumane.[32] By this time, many barbers and hairdressers had become "unisex hair stylists."

A powerful symbol of self-expression and a "freak flag" signaling agreement with countercultural values, including opposition to the war, long hair was increasingly met with hostility and violence as the decade drew to a close. The film *Easy Rider*, released earlier in the year, captures the fear and contempt many Americans felt toward long-haired men, hippies, and the counterculture in general.

Shining On

The January release of Badfinger's "Come and Get It," written and produced by Paul McCartney, showed the world that the other half of the Lennon-McCartney songwriting partnership was also busy with extra-curricular activities. The song, which peaked at number seven in the spring, was written for *The Magic Christian*, a British comedy starring Peter Sellers and Ringo. Fans saw another Beatle doing his own thing in late January when Ringo appeared on *Rowan & Martin's Laugh-In* to promote the film.

In early February, *Rolling Stone* named John Lennon "Man of the Year" for 1969. What is interesting about this is not that Jann Wenner would honor Lennon—no surprise there—but that Wenner writes, "It has become impossible to speak of John without at once speaking of Yoko, truly the fifth Beatle, in an era when it sometimes appears that there are no longer even four Beatles," thus alluding to the mixed signals from the group and the very real possibility that they were over.[33]

While recognizing Yoko's collaborative role in all the activities for which they honored John, the bold, countercultural magazine admitted they "felt foolish saying 'Couple of the Year'" yet acknowledged "they surely were."

Elsewhere in the same issue was a lengthy article on the couple's Christmas trip to Toronto and their "peace persuasion campaign," which was to include "the biggest musical festival in history" at Mosport

Park near Toronto in July and the formation of a peace council. John believed, "Everything points to Canada as one of the key countries in the new race for survival. We've had the arms race and the space race and the Cold War—the time has come for the peace race." While none of these plans materialized, the magazine's Beatle fan readership could see that Lennon's energies and focus were not on the Beatles.

This same article included excerpts from the couple's serious but whimsical conversation with media theorist Marshall McLuhan, in which the astute threesome discussed how performers "project moods" through patterns, which, according to Lennon, soon become "boring" and needed to be "broken" or "scrapped" in their "search for the ultimate." He added: "The Beatles pattern is one that has to be scrapped. Because if it remains the same it's a monument or a museum, and one thing this age is about is no museums. And the Beatles turned into a museum so they have to be scrapped or deformed or changed."[34]

Later in the month, *Rolling Stone* alerted its readers that the *Get Back* album was delayed again, but that the band would soon release "an oldies album," *The Beatles Again*, later renamed *Hey Jude* to highlight the song's inclusion on the compilation. A male fan, age fourteen at the time and not a *Rolling Stone* reader, recalls feeling "very disappointed" with the release of *Hey Jude* because "there was no new music on it." A female fan, also fourteen, recalls the album coming out and thinking "it wasn't for real fans."

The quick turnaround of "The Ballad of John and Yoko" was out-done by that of "Instant Karma!," written, recorded, and released within a week. Instant, indeed.

A female fan, age fourteen at the time, recalls, "I remember the first time I heard that song. I liked it immediately; there was something exciting about it. I remember thinking, 'Okay, this is another John Lennon single, but this is more like a real song than the other stuff he had put out. I had no idea what it meant, but it made me think about all those things he was saying." A male fan, age twenty at the time, remembers how the song grabbed his attention: "The giant drums, the raw vocal, the echo, the 'all shine on'; it was just great."

The bouncy wall-of-sound rocker, with its cymbal crashes and booming drums, was a paean to the cosmos and an urgent tribal message from John to fans. It was an encouraging but stern admonition to be responsible citizens of the world and loving members of the human family. It was also a danceable single with handclaps, great pop tambourine, and a John Lennon vocal that was fun to sing along with and made fans feel powerful when they did.

With "Instant Karma!," John called out the cynics who dismissed peace and love as naive and chastised those who criticized him while at the same time looked to him for answers. His urgent, somewhat paradoxical message was that he didn't have all the answers and didn't claim to; however, he made the case that we could do better than we were doing, and since we were all in this together, everyone had a responsibility to make a difference in their own unique way.

John Ono Lennon's first solo single peaked at number three on March 28, a month after its release. The picture cover of this swift communiqué used the same stark graphics as in the "War Is Over! (If You Want It)" poster campaign and featured John with short, freshly cut hair. John told *Rolling Stone* he and Yoko, who also cut her hair, wanted to be able to "mingle with people without being easily recognized" and that short hair was "functional and we need functional things." Lennon said his new look would "probably freak out the world and the rest of the Beatles."[35]

A male fan, age fifteen at the time, with "very long hair" was "disappointed." Another, age fourteen, recalls, "Someone at school told me John cut off all his hair. I wanted to see a picture fast. I didn't understand why he'd do that. It was another surprising thing he did. He's the one who made me not like short hair, he was the reason short hair wasn't cool, and now he's cutting his hair."

Getting Back to Let It Be

It had been almost a year and a half since fans last saw the Beatles on film, a relatively long gap, although there had been three singles, plus

"Give Peace a Chance," "Cold Turkey," and "Instant Karma!" The latter was still moving up the charts in early March when promotional films for the "Two of Us" and "Let It Be," footage from the *Get Back* project, were broadcast on the *Ed Sullivan Show*. The more simpatico Smother Brothers were off the air, having lost their battle with CBS censors on a petty procedural technicality, with pressure from the Nixon White House—a victory for the Blue Meanies.

These films were the first "new" Beatle music and images fans had seen since *Abbey Road,* though the footage was actually recorded fifteen months earlier. Sullivan introduces "theeee Beeeatles!" once again, as he did so many times before. Ed has longer sideburns and the backdrop is a yellow, pink, and red swirly graphic rather than a scalloped curtain.

Paul is in a dark suit and white shirt and fans see him with a full beard for the first time. He is, uncharacteristically, not mugging for the camera, not even in his later, more subtle mugging style. Because these clips were created from the *Get Back* footage, intended to capture rehearsals, not performance, the four don't interact with the camera in the usual way. Fans are watching them play; they aren't being played to.

George is sitting, looking down, playing guitar, and appears to be wearing his favorite green corduroys. After almost a minute into the song, fans see a close-up of John, chewing gum in time to the music. This is John before the rabbinic *Abbey Road* look, before he grew the full beard currently sported by Paul.

Ringo is dressed in black and looks sad, disgusted, and tired. Eventually, there's a hint of a smile from Paul. As a promotional film, the footage has the same perfunctory feel as the dreadful "Hello Goodbye" film two years earlier. As a through-the-keyhole glimpse of the band working, it wasn't a pretty sight. Fans saw four people who didn't seem happy.

The charm of "Two of Us," Paul's love song to his estranged partner of a dozen years, brightens up the dreariness of the clip. Fans heard the familiar yet still exhilarating harmony of the two, though there was no cherub-faced cheek-to-cheek at the mic. John and Paul were as far apart as they could be in the frame, and there was no eye contact between them. Yet, the song's nostalgic lyrics and the sweetness of their tight harmony would stand as a testament to their bond and the wholly unique experience they shared.

The "Let It Be" footage opens with Paul at the piano, as in the "Hey Jude" promo film almost a year and a half earlier, but his energy is different. He looks uncharacteristically self-conscious. Almost two minutes in there's a cut to John and Yoko. Hmmm. She's there? Okay . . .

John and George sing backing harmonies, and there's a cut to Billy Preston, the only one smiling. The Beatles are concentrating on the task at hand and it sounds great, but they are absolutely cheerless.

Fans liked to see the spontaneous fun that always surrounded the Beatles; it made the band seem more human and made fans feel like they knew them better. The loving camaraderie of *A Hard Day's Night* and *Help!* that so captivated young viewers, that integral and essential ingredient of Beatleness, was absent from this footage.

A few days after this broadcast, "Let It Be" was finally released as a single, b/w "You Know My Name (Look Up the Number)." The goofy B-side was a nightclub parody with sparse, repetitive, and slightly suggestive lyrics, a campy jazz feel, and a feisty Brian Jones sax solo. The record appealed to fans because it exuded Beatle fun and brotherhood—and offered comic relief from the quasi-religious earnestness of the A-side.

When "Let It Be" entered the charts in late March, Simon and Garfunkel's "Bridge Over Troubled Water," another earnest inspirational ballad with an arresting vocal, was a few weeks into its six-week stint at number one; "Let It Be" bumped it from the top spot on April 11 and held the position for two weeks.

I Read the News Today

With the best of intentions, Paul had been trying to keep the band together and busy since Brian Epstein died, but the Beatle box could no longer contain these four individuals who had grown up and apart. Creative differences morphed into interpersonal conflicts, and despite all the underlying affection it was getting increasingly contentious.

While John and Yoko were talking about peace with anyone who would listen, Paul was in Scotland, depressed and on the verge of a nervous breakdown. The wrangling had left him especially isolated, and the simultaneous loss of his best friend, collaborator, and band was overwhelming. With Linda's love and encouragement, he assessed the situation, stopped sulking, realized he was Paul McCartney, and produced a solo album. John and George were collaborating with others, as they had when they first started. And Paul was doing it on his own, as when he first started.

When Paul learned that George and John asked Phil Spector to work on the *Get Back* sessions without consulting him, he was, understandably, livid. Adding insult to injury, he was under pressure from Apple to delay the release of *McCartney* so as not to conflict with the release of the long-awaited *Let It Be*, which now disgusted him.

McCartney got his way on the release date—a minor victory in a cold war that had been going on for two years. But after resentfully acquiescing to Yoko's presence in the studio, the Spectorization of *Let It Be* was a professional and personal affront of great magnitude. Spector's treatment of "The Long and Winding Road" was especially galling to Paul, and his reaction was cumulative, immediate, and extreme.

In a petulant, mock-interview style press release included with promotional copies of *McCartney*, Paul announced he has left the Beatles because of "personal differences, business differences, musical differences—but most of all because I have a better time with my family." About John and Yoko's peace activities, he said he loves John and respects what he does, adding, ambiguously, "it doesn't give me any pleasure." Asked if he foresees writing songs with John in the future, he simply says, "No." Asked if his break with the Beatles is temporary or permanent, he says he doesn't know. The final question in the mock-interview was about his immediate plans, to which he responded, "My only plan is to grow up."

Unlike his off-the-cuff comments to *Life* six months before, or John's public comments in Toronto and elsewhere, these words got through and the story of Paul quitting the Beatles was in every major newspaper the following day, interpreted as "the Beatles broke up."

Many remember "a deep sense of loss," at the "very sad news" and "couldn't imagine a world where there was no new Beatle album coming out." The word they used most often was "devastated," like "a friend had died." A female fan, age fifteen at the time, remembers the day vividly: "It was my mother's fortieth birthday party that day; I was devastated, like someone died. I sat in my room and cried. I was heartbroken."

Another female fan, also fifteen at the time, said, "it was like your parents getting divorced; you were never alone in the house and always felt safe, then one day they break up and you're devastated." Beyond the fact of the breakup itself, several were "upset that everyone blamed Paul," and many thought it was especially sad because "this tight group of friends weren't a tight group of friends anymore."

While many said it was "like losing a family member," others took it more in stride, especially if they saw it coming. A male fan, age twenty-one at the time, remembers, "I was in college; my roommates and I saw an item about it in the paper and they were all upset and thought Yoko broke them up. I didn't have any angst over it."

Another male fan, age nineteen at the time, said, "I remember people were upset about it. But really, I was just thinking about trying to get laid and smoking some weed. I loved them, but I wasn't going to mourn the songs I can't imagine or that would never be."

In addition to the "smorgasbord of music" that would still be there, many "held out hope they would get back together" at some point in the future.

The Next Best Thing

Fans were still waiting for the new back-to-basics Beatle album but bought *McCartney* in the meantime. A female fan, age sixteen at the time, remembers, "The big buzz about the album was that Paul played all the instruments. I liked it a lot; it was interesting to see what he did on his own." A male fan (b. '52) remembers, "I liked it because it was McCartney, but I had the sense it was a weaker product than Beatle product, because it was."

A female fan (b. '57) said her "grief" over the breakup was "relieved a little by the *McCartney* album." Like many, she "loved 'Maybe I'm Amazed' and that gorgeous picture of Paul with his baby on the cover." Another female fan recalled thinking he "looked happy in the picture." Fans liked knowing the Beatles were happy, even when they were no longer the Beatles.

As news of the Beatle breakup sunk in, fans of all ages were "opening up to other music" and were listening to Crosby, Stills, Nash, and Young's *Déjà Vu*, Van Morrison's *Moondance*, Simon and Garfunkel's *Bridge Over Troubled Water*, and the Doors' *Morrison Hotel*. Joni Mitchell's *Ladies of the Canyon* and James Taylor's *Sweet Baby James*, heralding the singer-songwriter period of the early seventies, were also mentioned.

Fans' negative reaction to the Beatle breakup was, for many, not about music that would never be created or heard but about losing the comforting presence of these "friendly-faced adults" who had provided them with multifaceted intellectual, emotional, and aesthetic experiences they had come to rely on and which nurtured them in a unique way for six years. As one male fan (b. '55) put it, "I was waiting for the next thing from them since I was nine years old."

Sad Spring

Later that month, twenty million Americans nationwide participated in the first Earth Day celebration, demonstrating in support of environmental reform. In 1963, Rachel Carson's *Silent Spring* made Americans aware that we were poisoning ourselves and the planet with toxic chemicals, and tighter regulation of pesticides followed. But when Americans saw pictures of our finite, fragile planet floating in space, the modern environmental movement was born.

A week after the peaceful Earth Day demonstrations, Americans learned US troops had invaded Cambodia, an action that immediately led to demonstrations not so peaceful. On May fourth, four unarmed college students at the Kent State University were killed and nine others wounded when the Ohio National Guard fired sixty-seven rounds of ammunition into a crowd of protestors. The shootings led to strikes on college campuses and high schools throughout the country, involving over four million students. It was the only nationwide student strike in US history.

After seeing the disturbing images of the event in *Life* magazine, as millions did, Neil Young wrote "Ohio," and, with Crosby, Stills and Nash, released it as single a few weeks later—not quite as instant as "Instant Karma!" but timely nonetheless. Young said the Kent State incident was "probably the biggest lesson ever learned at an American place of learning."[36] The song calls out Nixon by name and was banned by many AM stations, but received significant airplay on FM.

The politics and the music continued to commingle in fans' experience. Kent State was a stunning event, and Beatle fans talked about it. Teens who opposed the war but lived in predominantly prowar communities often found themselves at odds with their parents. But sometimes they found themselves at odds with friends they used to Beatle with. Kent State was one of those times:

> The kid who didn't want to hear you come out against the war in sixty-eight was the same kid, two years later, saying, 'What were the National Guard supposed to do? The students were throwing rocks!' Male, b. '55

> Lots of kids had brothers in Vietnam, and we didn't want to get into arguments about Kent State or anything else. You could see some of these boys when they came home; they weren't the same. You'd hear that someone sleepwalked to the corner store in the middle of the night in his underwear. A few of these guys eventually committed suicide. Female, b. '52

A male fan (b. '52) recalled, "This was really a time of anger and despair. How can the Beatles say 'Let It Be' when they're shooting college students? 'Ohio' seemed more appropriate."

The Beatles' Reality Show

Fans talked with each other about the breakup, passing along information they'd read or heard somewhere—which Beatle said what; who's blaming who. Paul's split, relabeled "the breakup" by the press, became one more interesting thing the band did, and the slow ooze of news about it added even more intrigue. Like the Paul Is Dead frenzy and Beatlemania before that, it launched countless hours of spirited discussion. Fans were piecing together the story; several said they listened to "You Never Give Me Your Money" and the rest of the *Abbey Road* medley with new ears.

Fans felt sad that negative feelings had replaced the obvious love these four guys had for each other, and it was hard to understand why these four good friends who together created such great music would not want to do that anymore. It was with this mindset that fans went to the movies to see *Let It Be*.

Seeing Yoko in almost every scene, many felt the answer had been revealed. Fans had become experts at reading Beatle body language and affect on film, and in *Let It Be* they saw conflict, sniping, and fatigue. As one male fan (b. '53) said, "These are guys I grew up with. It was hard to watch, but it was fascinating."

Yoko's presence confounded the Beatle geometry and iconography that had been seared into fans' consciousness for six years. As one male fan put it, "Who was this strange woman coming into the studio and causing tension?" They saw her as "intrusive" and "out of place." Yoko entered John's life around the same time as the start of the woes that led to the fracture, and so fans assumed she was the cause.

Yoko's "otherness" in terms of gender and race certainly contributed to much of the antipathy toward her in some circles, but one need not be racist or sexist to have found her off-putting or to conclude that she was a significant factor in the band's disintegration. To the contrary, after seeing *Let It Be* it was a reasonable albeit simplistic conclusion to draw, and many did.

The *New York Times* also noticed Yoko's odd presence among the foursome. Describing *Let It Be* as "a revealing close-up of the world's most famous quartet," the reviewer says "the most intriguing feature of the film is Yoko Ono," noting that "except for one playful dance twirl, Mrs. Lennon remains at her husband's side, expressionless and silent, her eyes never leaving him."[37]

The inherent peculiarity of the behavior he accurately described makes it sound like a judgment of some kind. But if the film critic at the *New York Times* thought Yoko was the most intriguing feature of the film, the fans, more emotionally invested and steeped in Beatles than the film critic, took notice as well. Their impressions and feelings about Yoko were informed not only by these images but by the timing— it had only been a month since the release of *McCartney* and Paul's announcement that he'd quit the band.

There is still negative feeling about Yoko among Beatle fans, and quips like "She should have stayed in the bag" are not uncommon. Many blame her not only for distracting John from the Beatles, intruding in the studio, and ultimately causing the breakup, but also for John's heroin use, for hurting Cynthia and Julian, and for the peace campaign many thought made John look foolish. Many feel she was an "opportunist" and doubt her claim that she didn't know who John was when they first met.

Often overlooked in the Yoko bashing is that John had not been happy being a Beatle for quite some time. Being bigger than Elvis came with unforeseen consequences. The thing he loved most, playing rock and roll, had ceased to be fun. When he was reminded in Toronto of how much fun it could be was when he said he wanted "a divorce" from the Beatles.

Paul's overbearingness after Brian died made John's Beatle experience even less appealing. The strong bond they had as teenagers was still there, as were the extraordinary experiences they shared being Beatles, but they were, simply, growing apart. Their interests and visions were diverging before John met Yoko. They still loved each other, but perhaps they no longer liked each other.

John and Yoko were both fiercely rebellious artists who saw themselves as wounded children—not true of Paul, the well-adjusted young man from a happy home. Yoko encouraged John's creative and political inclinations that had been stifled and stunted within the confines of the band. She validated him as a creative communicator, irrespective of medium, and helped him articulate what that could mean in practice. She helped him envision a feasible, satisfying, and meaningful alternative to the boredom and stagnation of life as Beatle John. He needed and wanted to be with Yoko for his well-being and growth as a person.

Not all fans disliked Yoko at the time, or now. A female fan (b. '50) recalls, "I was happy for John when they got together, and I liked that she was an artist. He was so young when the Beatles started, he needed her to help him be an individual." Another female fan (b. '48) said, "Yoko was never a big deal to me. Who am I to begrudge him after he brought joy to so many people?" A male fan, age eighteen at the time, said, "I didn't think she belonged in the studio, but if John loved her so much, there must have been something special about her."

The conversation about why the Beatles broke up will likely continue for a very long time, and for some fans who grew up with them the issue still has an emotional tinge. Even those who disliked Yoko and see her as the primary reason for the band's disintegration recognize there were many other factors. A female fan, age sixteen at the time, said, "I didn't like her, but why blame her for the breakup? The business aspects took a toll on them. It was time. All good things must come to an end."

The most uplifting scene in *Let It Be* was of course the unannounced rooftop concert. Performing live, which all four loved, had become unpleasant and unwieldy on the road. The plan was for the *Get Back* project to culminate in a live show, but they couldn't identify a venue all could agree to.

The rooftop was convenient and would be free and open to all. There'd be no elaborate security ruses required for the large audience that would assemble, and they'd be able to hear themselves. The element of bad boy prank added to the fun, especially when the Blue Meanies, in an almost perfunctory way, came to shut it down. A female fan, age twenty-three at the time, thought the rooftop concert was very significant: "The older generation had dismissed the Beatles, but the people who gathered were very diverse in age and appearance. They were obviously impressed and acted like this was a momentous occasion. That was startling. Just as the Beatles were becoming widely acclaimed, even by the over thirties, they were splitting up. And the impromptu nature of the event, sort of like contemporary flash mobs, had really not been seen before."

In the rooftop scene, fans saw them playing on the big screen for the first time since *Help!*, and everyone on the screen and in the audience was five years older. Getting lost in this footage, it was easy to forget that this glimpse into Beatleworld is fifteen months old and *Abbey Road* didn't exist yet. John and Paul are not yet married, no one had thought about giving peace a chance, and most fans had never heard of Allen Klein or Lee Eastman, key figures in their contentious split.

The winter wind blew their hair and numbed their fingers, but they delivered. Their passion for rock and roll was rarely more visible than here. They exuded Beatleness, but the exuberance was tempered by maturity and the comfort of knowing they didn't have to answer to anyone ever again.

There was joy in this scene, and the warm smiles and connective glances between John and Paul were reassuring. Amid all the palpable tension, they ascended to the literal and metaphorical top of their empire, cohesion and synergy intact, and sent Beatlemusic into the firmament.

End of the Journey

The last new Beatle single fans could ever buy, "The Long and Winding Road" b/w "For You Blue" was released in mid-May, a few days before the *Let It Be* album, on which both songs appear. The A-side was Paul's second song to his estranged partner, making his partner's secret tampering with it even more of a personal and professional affront. The song hit number one in mid-June and held the position for two weeks. It was displaced by the Jackson 5's "The Love You Save," the third number one hit for little Michael and his brothers.

After over a year of delay, and a month after Paul's announcement, the Beatles' "roots" album, *Let It Be*, was finally released, and it quickly replaced *McCartney* at number one on the album charts. The cover's separate photos, with the simple words "Let It Be," stark white against the thick black border, seemed fitting. The sprinkling of ad libs and chatter, even though inserted out of place, gave the record a fun, playful feel, balancing the gravity of the two ballads, and the bittersweet knowledge that the journey was over. A male fan, age fifteen at the time, said, "It's like they were saying 'the seventies are starting, you're on your own.'" Another fan put it this way: "I was heartbroken when they broke up. I was graduating high school and going off to college. I was starting a new chapter of my life, and the thing I had to hang on to was gone. I had to grow up, but I continued to carry them inside me. They are part of me and always will be" (Male, b. '52).

CHAPTER EIGHT
Beatleness Abounds

I still think about the Beatles every day. They helped me get through my youth. I'm thankful to them for being an outlet for my frustration and anger, and a way to share joy and happiness with others.

Male, b. '60

FANS BELIEVE GOING THROUGH SIX YEARS of childhood and adolescence with the Beatles' constant, ubiquitous presence, as described in the preceding chapters, had a profound and lasting impact on the people they grew up to be.

Many said the Beatles were "imprinted" on their "spirit" or their "souls," part of their "DNA." One male fan (b. '54) said they are "interwoven" into his personality and that nothing in his life influenced him more. Another male fan (b. '50) said, "I'm a product of all of them. It's in my blood, still vital and important." A female fan (b. '55) put it this way: "They informed how I thought about the world. I was framing an identity for myself, and they were validating it and informing it."

Fans "can't imagine having lived life without the Beatles." A male fan (b. '54) said, "I would not be the same person. They helped me develop into what I am today; they opened my eyes to many things." A female fan (b. '52) said, "The Beatles have enlightened me, cheered me, challenged me, saddened me, and taught me. My life would be vastly altered if they had never been."

Of course, such "what if" statements are imponderable hypotheticals, and to imagine no Beatles is to imagine a completely different world— as several fiction writers have done. But such statements arise because the importance, magnitude, and peculiarity of the Beatle effect is hard to quantify and put into words.

Similarly, there is no word for the unique role they came to play in fans' lives. Many said "they were like cool older brothers." A male fan (b. '54) said, "They taught me about life; like a set of four older brothers who could do no wrong." A female fan the same age said, "They were like the crazy relatives you only see once in a while, but when you see them you know you're going to have a good time with them. Like family you can hardly wait to see."

Many said the Beatles were not merely "like" family but were as important to them as family. A male fan (b. '50) said, "they were more than a band, they were like your relatives. You felt close to them and knew so much about them. They were family. I identified with them intensely, and trusted them." Another male fan, five years younger, said, "They had as big or maybe even bigger impact on me than close family members."

Filling Special Needs

The Beatles earned fans' trust, telling them things that made them feel better and smarter. A female fan (b. '50) said, "They put their arms around me with their music." A male fan, the same age, said, "They helped me put up with the world." A male fan (b. '55) said, "We took comfort in knowing the Beatles were in the world."

Many said the Beatles "had more interesting and useful things to say" than anyone else in their lives. And "they were always there for you" as a source of consistent, reliable comfort and support. As one fan put it: "Their music helped me through some of those rough bumps we all go through during our lives. I could always turn to some Beatles music to pick me up when I was down" (Male, b. '61).

The Beatles effectiveness as communicators meant that they could also be a source of strength for fans twelve years older than the one quoted above: "They helped keep me sane during a turbulent period in which my family suffered several deaths and illnesses. I internalized qualities I admired in them and drew great strength from my identification with them" (Male, b. '49).

When we consider the age range and broad swath of the population moved by "In My Life" or "Eight Days a Week," for example, or the millions who played the Paul Is Dead game, or young people across a sixteen-year age range buying records in rural general stores, suburban shopping plazas, or at Woolworth's and card shops in downtowns across America, indeed, across the world, the magnitude of the phenomenon becomes vivid.

A Different Kind of Nurturing

One of the comments I heard most frequently in talking with fans is, "I grew up with them." This simple observation describes a process that was actually quite complex, with profound, lifelong impact—and three levels of meaning. First, the Beatles were a constant presence during fans' childhood and adolescence; they were there when fans were growing up.

At a deeper level, "I grew up with them" captures the feeling of having grown up alongside them, as one does with brothers and sisters. Everyone starts at a different place and eventually finds their own path, but the process is shared and everyone changes.

The third sense of "I grew up with them" captures the "nutritional" character of a relationship that stimulated fans' intellectual, emotional, social, aesthetic, and spiritual growth. As one female fan (b. '56) put it, "I grew up with them and because of them. They'd put something out there and I was ready to receive it." Another female fan (b. '61) said, "As a Beatle fan, your mind is open to possibilities, more and sooner." And another (b. '54) said, "The Beatles brought me along."

The Beatles gave fans a kind of nurturing or sustenance they weren't finding anywhere else. Growing up an engaged fan provided multifaceted enrichment from one constant, reliable source. It was comprehensive, holistic, and transformative. The Beatles consistently fired fans' young brains on all cylinders, creating synapses, making them smarter.

This space-age generation, growing up with television yet attending schools designed for the industrial age, could not resist the pleasure of this persistent and decidedly modern stimulus. George Harrison was on to something when he said the Beatles saved the world from boredom.

The Beatles taught what was then the largest demographic group in human history about the palette of human emotion, in all its breadth and nuance. From the beginning, they told these young people it was okay to be reflective and to think about big ideas. Through their songs and their own high-profile adventures, they encouraged fans to question and quest. Several fans said, "They made us think about things in different ways."

And, of course, they enhanced fans' aesthetic sensibilities with their compelling and always-evolving music and presentation of themselves. A male fan (b. '57) described the experience as "An endless flow of new," suggesting again Pauline Kael's "pleasure of constant surprise." Others describe it like this:

They enhanced my childhood. They gave me something to hope for. They entertained me, but they also made my little bubble bigger—more worldly and attractive. They made us feel cool and bigger and older than we were, like we could be part of this. Female, b. '55

The Beatles are special to me because they came along at what was probably the most impressionable junction of my life. They were cooler than anything before or since. Male, b. '53

Born at the Right Time

Fans of all ages say they feel "fortunate" to have grown up with the Beatles and "wouldn't trade having lived through 1964 to 1970 for anything." They all say they were at "the perfect age to be part of it." Prepubescent fans describe the joy of being young enough "to embrace it in a childlike way." But those who were teenagers, male or female, think they were the luckiest:

> I have always felt that I couldn't have been luckier than to be born in the summer of 1951. Being fully into them was a teenage, adolescent experience that was unique to our generation. The Beatles were and still are the biggest and best thing that has ever happened in my life. Male, b. '51

> Being thirteen, I was old enough to experience and understand the Beatles and their music as it happened. Female, b '51

Although fans know their experience would have been different had they been a few years older or younger, they are no less appreciative of the experience they had:

> It all seemed to happen at the right time for me, although I wasn't a teenager and couldn't go to concerts or be as involved as I would have wanted to be. . . . As I progressed through school, their music kept me going. At certain times we all need some sort of guidance and it came to me in their music. . . . I thought of the Beatles as my brothers and soul mates. Male, b. '55

> They have always been there for me in good times and bad. And like everyone else's lives they affected, their songs meant a great deal to me. The Beatles have always been and always will be a part of my life. They are very important to me. . . . It's a loyalty that will never die and I will never outgrow them. Female, b. '54

The music, images, and ideas fans encountered were complicated and compelling, regardless of what stage the band or fans were at. The Beatles created a fun and uniquely stimulating environment where fans of any age could partake as much as they needed or wanted, any time they wanted, and always be satisfied. Fans "never outgrew them" because the music is heard with different ears at different ages and is new again; or it's heard with the same ears and still pleases in the same way.

Based on the interviews I've conducted, fans born between 1953 and 1961 seem to have experienced the deepest Beatle impact. While the youngest fans in this group may not have the clear memories of "before and after," as do fans only a few years older, their very earliest memories are infused with Beatles.

As one female fan (b. '61) put it, "I have a powerful attachment to them because I was becoming a conscious human being at the time when they were everywhere." Fans in this eight-year age range, more or less prepubescent, were the least fully formed and the most impressionable when the Beatles arrived, which remained relatively true even as they grew up over the six Beatle years.

These are the fans most likely to say the Beatles are woven into their personalities and identities; these are the fans on whom the Beatles had the greatest cumulative impact. Ironically, these are also the fans who expressed regret about being "too young to be part of it," too young to go to concerts or be "real hippies." These fans may have felt too young to be "with it," but "it" was with them. Recall that in 1968, Hunter Davies's publisher thought his authorized Beatle biography would be purchased and read by twenty-year-olds, when, in fact, it was read by teens, preteens, and children barely old enough to decipher the words.

Fans born between 1945 and 1952, adolescents and teens during the Beatlemania years, were already listening to music, perhaps dating, and involved in other social activities when the Beatles came on the scene. Many had been young Elvis or Ricky Nelson fans; some were already in college and started smoking pot around the same time the Beatles did. Certainly, the Beatles were hugely important to them and influenced them in many ways, as discussed throughout this book. But because they hadn't known the Beatles since childhood, the impact was less primordial; their feelings for the band are a bit less gushy. That said, the Beatles' impact on older fans was no less real. A male fan (b. '47) said, "They made me question accomplishment without fulfillment."

Though Lennon said, "We don't give instructions on how to live your life," fans of all ages identified with the Beatles in various ways and emulated some of their behavior. A few male fans said making the Beatles into role models led them to delay decision making and planning for their own futures: "I clung to them and didn't want to focus on practical matters. They helped me in a lot of ways, but they slowed me down from finding what I needed to do to make a living" (Male b. '48).

When Lennon was asked to comment on achieving wealth and fame at such a young age, he said the Beatles "chose a modern form of success."[1] Many male fans wanted to make the same choice, but had unrealistic expectations about the real possibility of earning a living in the music industry:

> It's fine on one hand, within reason, to copy the accent or the clothing or the musical style of someone you like and find joy in. Screwing with your livelihood and so on . . . not so much. Male b. '49

> Twenty years ago my mom said the Beatles ruined my life. What she meant was that they awoke my musical talent and passion and I spent my whole life pursuing a recording contract. I gambled on the Beatles dream. I became a musician and went to art school; I wanted to be like them. Male, b. '55

Looking back on the Beatle years, a female fan (b. '54) said, "They grabbed my soul or some part of me, and they owned me." Consistent with this, several fans said they and their friends "followed the Beatles like Pied Pipers." Although the comparison has some resonance, it implies a mindless following that doesn't describe the Beatle fan experience. There was certainly peer pressure to be a fan, and some male fans may have over-identified with them, but as shown by the Beatle break at the start of the psychedelic period, or the young listeners who didn't like the *White Album*, fans didn't follow blindly; they thought for themselves. When the Beatles "no longer provided comfort" or when they "became disturbing," some young fans stopped following—for a while.

Older fans also "went through phases with them." A female fan (b. '47) recalled, "I followed them through high school, college, and graduate school. I had different attitudes at different times. Sometimes I was annoyed with them."

The band had established a solid foundation of trust over the first two years or so, and as many said, "You never completely abandon the Beatles." Like family members, they're trusted and forgiven.

A Coherent Philosophy

When asked if there is an overarching "Beatle message" or "philoso-phy," many stated the obvious: "All you need is love." A small number rejected the question as "pretentious" or "overblown." A male fan (b. '57), echoing comments Lennon and others have made in efforts to keep things in perspective, said, "Let's remember that these are just four kids that started a band and brought joy and happiness to a lot of people."

That the Beatles were about "peace and love" has become a cliché, and while this positive message is an important part of their legacy—along with freedom, authenticity, and questioning authority—they were also strong advocates of self-actualization. This significant aspect of Beatleness has been overlooked in fifty years of Beatle commentary, but it becomes apparent when we hear fan's voices.

A male fan (b. '57) who listened to no other music from the age of ten all through high school, said their message to him was, "It's okay to take chances and push the envelope." A female fan of the same age heard, "Stand up for what you believe." Another female fan, six years older (b.

'51), heard something similar: "They gave you a sense of what's possible; that you can find what you do well and express yourself doing it." Fans heard the Beatles saying, "Be yourself," "Be confident in who you are," "Follow your dreams," and "Don't let the world drag you down." Said one male fan (b. '51): "The message was, don't be afraid to be different. I grew up Jewish in a conservative town in the Midwest. If the Beatles could do it, I could do it. They were independent and did what they wanted to do."

Beyond messages about the self, the Beatles advocated maximizing human potential at the collective level as well. Hallucinogenics and TM, which they explored on the world stage, were two possible paths to that goal. But these were not required for changing one's consciousness.

Simply rethinking the mundane and commonplace, questioning received wisdom, enabled one to see a clearer, bigger picture and the essential commonality and connectedness within the diversity of human experience. A common takeaway was "to be a good, ethical person" and, as one female fan (b. '51) put it, "To be engaged and care about things; don't go through life with blinders on, because we're all in this together."

Invoking the Pied Piper metaphor, a male fan (b. '50) observed, "If the people in charge had been competent, ran the world better, and provided guidance to me, I wouldn't have felt the need to make them Pied Pipers. But all the institutions were broken. The Beatles presented a morality and a code of conduct."

Never before in human history were so many people, for a period of years, enthusiastically awaiting and responding to the same messages at the same time from a single source. Making the Beatles even more epochal is that the recipients of this communication were children and adolescents.

Gratitude and Bliss

For young people grappling with loneliness and insecurity, the Beatles provided a vehicle for connection with others. Many felt "accepted into a group for the first time" and for that they "still feel grateful."

For some, the Beatles were the friends or peer group that accepts you as you are and "never judges you." As one female fan (b. '54) said, "They were my salvation until I could find real people who would make me feel like they made me feel." And how did they make her feel? "Understood; that I was okay the way I was." Even though the Beatles were loved by millions and liking them was in no way nonconformist, they still made fans feel validated as individuals: "The Beatles have had a huge impact on my life. Everything I did, all the phases I went through, I followed and I actually learned from them. I think they were my friends when I was growing up. They made me feel special. Even though I didn't know them personally, it was like they were right there" (Female, b. '52).

In some ways, the band's impact on their fans was equal to if not greater than that of their parents during those years. Several said the Beatles were like "surrogate parents," often more reliable and nurturing than their real ones. Fans talked of the Beatles filling emotional voids, providing comfort not available from depressed, alcoholic, or insensitive parents:

My parents were alcoholics and there was lots of stress in the house. The Beatles took me away and made me happy. Female, b. '49

I was learning more from them than I was from my father, who always called me a schmuck. They were guys older than me who understood things I was trying to understand. Male, b '49

A female fan (b. '58) whose mother was "a career woman at a time when nobody's mom worked" said she and her siblings raised themselves, and "spent a lot of time alone listening to the Beatles."

Fans were also grateful for the hope the Beatles provided when they were seriously depressed. Several said the Beatles and their music gave them something to live for:

They came along when circumstances in my family were pretty dismal and looking back on it now, I clearly clung to them as a comfort and refuge from the disappointments of my adolescence. I think they got me through some very tough times in my life. I'm very glad they were there for me. Female, b. '55

My sister and I were so depressed after our mother died and we got a real bitch of a stepmother. I'm grateful to them for giving me something to live for, something to look forward to—something to help me get on with the horrible task of living the life I had. I endured a lot of pain and sadness, and they made me feel happiness and joy. Female, b. '53

They saved my life by filling it with joy and hope. When I was young and I wanted to harm myself, they made me so glad and happy. I wanted to be alive so I could hear them. . . . If not for them, life would have been horrible for me. Male, b. '50

In addition to the feelings of gratitude and comfort discussed above, the Beatles elicited joy, a feeling deeper and more enduring than happiness. Many say they "can't overestimate" or "express" the amount of joy the Beatles brought them. It's a feeling they "never want to let go of." One female fan (b. '57) said she was "hardwired for joy with the Beatles." An older female fan (b. '51) said, "They brought me so much joy when I was growing up, and still do." This male fan (b. '56) talked about how the Beatles brought forth a range of new, positive emotion: "I always felt in my heart that they were very special and meaningful to me. They sparked something in me that was new—inspiration, excitement, joy, happiness."

Looking back over the band's evolution, fans cite moments that, for them, capture what one female fan (b. '61) called "the shimmer of joy" in their music: the cowbell on "A Hard Day's Night," the hand claps on "Eight Days a Week," the feedback on "I Feel Fine," the fuzz bass on "Think For Yourself," the count-in on "Taxman," the alarm clock on "A Day in the Life," the harmony on "Because," or, back to the beginning, John and Paul singing unison on the chorus of "She Loves You"—a record described by one female fan (b. '54) as "pure joy on a piece of plastic." Those moments of shimmering joy evoke—and are themselves—Beatleness.

Writer and sixties icon Kurt Vonnegut said "a plausible mission of artists is to make people appreciate being alive at least a little bit." When asked if he knows of any artists able to do that, he replied, "The Beatles did."

A Singular Relationship

Even after the Beatles broke up, they remained an important presence in fans' lives. Regardless of age, fans continue to find new meaning in the music, approaching it with more life experience, wisdom, and maturity as they've grown older. At times, they may think about how they felt the first time they first heard a song or associate it with a particular place or group of friends. But because the Beatles have been so internalized, bringing them to mind or listening to their music doesn't necessarily recall the past. Rather, fans have carried the Beatles with them into the present.

To dismiss the feelings of first-generation Beatle fans as mere "nostalgia" is to trivialize an extraordinary relationship that has endured for a half century. Fans hang images of the Beatles in their homes and workplaces not to evoke bittersweet feelings of nostalgia or to relive their youth, but for the same reasons they display family photos: the images represent relationships that have been and continue to be important, meaningful, and, most of all, joyful. One fan (b. '53) talked about her Beatle decor as her "personal Feng Shui" and arranges her house so that she can see Beatles in any direction she looks.

The Beatles' constant presence in fans' lives, the perennial richness of their music and the ready enthusiasm with which first-generation fans engaged with them during their most formative years—and the joy this engagement reliably brought—created an historically unprecedented relationship analogous to nothing. As we saw in the discussion of the Beatles and the Kennedy era earlier in the book, the factors that created the Beatles as a phenomenon were historically unique.

These fans—often described as "Beatle people"—still feel attached to the Beatles and think about them often. Some people, especially nonfans, might find this strange. But given their experience growing up, it would be more strange if fans *didn't* still have these strong family-like feelings of attachment. A female fan (b. '54) said, "Their impact is hard to explain. . . . They've been part of my life since age nine. I can't describe it. It's part of who I am." A male fan, seven years younger, put it this way: "The Beatles to me are far more than a favorite group. It is almost an inner part of me. They are one of the most important things in my life."

All Together Now

In addition to recognizing the enormous impact the Beatles had on them personally, first-generation fans take it as a given that the Beatles were agents of change on the grandest scale and that they, as one male fan (b. '52) put it, "changed the way the world thinks":

Everybody was so stifled in their emotions before the Beatles hit. Not that they were solely responsible, but everybody did a one-eighty after 1964. Female, b. '51

I probably would be somewhat different today if it weren't for John, Paul, George, and Ringo. But then again, everybody would be different! Male, b. '57

The Beatle phenomenon illustrates how shared experiences at the individual level can trickle up and change the culture. To the extent that the Beatles "changed everything," they did it one fan at a time. Collectively, those fans—in suburban rec rooms, on school playgrounds, on college quads, in Haight-Ashbury, and at the Democratic convention in Chicago—brought about the changes referred to as "the sixties."

At the time, the socially conservative establishment, those who feared modernity, didn't appreciate this new world order. Likewise, when today's ultraright wing talks about "taking our country back," they are talking about a pre-Beatle America.

The Beatles had been questioning authority—and showing fans how to do it—since *A Hard Day's Night.* The politics in their music emerged explicitly with "Revolution" in the summer of '68, but it was there in chrysalis form two years earlier. The Nowhere Man questioned himself in relation to the world in February of that year, and three months later, that world itself was questioned in "Rain."

To question petty conventions and assert the power of the mind is to engage in politics. With changing consciousness, people begin to question how society is organized and the values that underlie its foundation. The values and priorities of those in power—the Establishment—are immediately called into question, and the personal becomes political.

With "Rain," the Beatles reified an unenlightened "they" along with the generational identity and power of "us." It is with this song that the Beatles and political currents began to converge and four pop musicians began to consolidate their power as agents of change—a process that started with their hair and the other essential attributes they showed up with in 1964.

This convergence continued, gradually, through 1967 with the band's high-profile role in the spread of the counterculture and generational identity. It was completed with "Revolution" in the summer of '68 and further symbolized by Harrison's appearance on the *Smothers Brothers Comedy Hour* that fall.

A Joyful Trauma

Fans often use metaphors to describe the impact of growing up with the Beatles. Some say it was like a drug; some say it was like a virus or a spell. Others see it as a journey or a ride, or brain rewiring. Earlier in the book I referred to it as an alternative, spiraling curriculum, and an odyssey. What all these metaphors have in common is the experience of transformation—you're different when it's over.

Just as the relationship between first-generation fans and the Beatles is historically unique, the collective, generational experience is similarly unique, and left a mark.

Of course, there have been other historical events that transformed the population that lived through them, but most such transformational events looked at in this way—what social historians call cohort events—have been horrible, traumatic experiences, such as wars and natural disasters.

The impact of these experiences are personal and can be difficult to describe. Decades later, it still pervades consciousness. People take comfort in sharing their feelings and reviewing the experience with others who went through it. The experience is a large enough component of identity to serve as the basis for lifelong friendship.

Now let's imagine a traumatic experience with lifelong impact on a large segment of the population, an experience whose emotional impact is as extreme as wars or natural disasters, but in the opposite emotional direction; in some sense, a positive, or joyful trauma.

The fans I spoke with, and millions like them, experienced just such a joyful trauma—a life-altering disturbance that was uplifting rather than destructive. It enriched fans' journey to adulthood, adding excitement, challenges, inspiration, and joy:

> They taught me to speak out on things, motivated me to look at what was going on around me, the war, civil rights, and to write. Female, b. '50

> They got the sixties revolution going by being different and opening people's minds to what could be. Personally, I think there's no more important event in human history. Male, b. '56

The media's obsession with teenagers, hippies, the generation gap, and student protestors between 1964 and 1970 ensured that people who came of age in this period would be aware of themselves as a cohesive group with a unique experience. But baby boomers' strong generational identity began early on, when the media targeted them as a population of young consumers easily reached through radio and the new medium of television. Today there is concern about "the commercialization of childhood," but this is when it all began.

Generational awareness was further enhanced by their exposure to unique historical events and circumstances within a narrow time frame: political assassinations that quickly gave rise to conspiracy theories in an increasingly cynical age; a military policy of mutual assured destruction that fueled the arms race and increased the threat of nuclear annihilation; an unpopular war; the violence of the civil rights movement; and the proud achievement of the moon landing.

This generation would have developed a strong generational consciousness even if the Beatles had never been part of the equation. But they weren't merely an additional factor—they became a broad, positive unifier.

The joyful trauma of the Beatles was experienced by millions, and so the culture itself was traumatized. The collaborative and reciprocal relationship between the Beatles and the fans, amplified and activated the social change slowly emerging from pre-Beatles culture.

Perpetual Beatleness

In a world where things don't always work out as planned, the Beatles continue to be a reliable source of comfort and joy, and they continue to not disappoint; indeed, they continue to delight. "For No One" sounds just as beautiful as it did when fans first heard it, but they're appreciating it anew, again and again. "Please Please Me" or "And Your Bird Can Sing" still cause a rush of excitement because, as a female fan (b. '60) said, she "associates them with joy and charm." The Beatles continue to provide a sense of constancy and continuity—a familiar anchor in a faster-and-faster-paced world that can often seem harsh and unkind:

I can't separate them out from the rest of my life. I rely on them when I feel bad. Their music still brings joy and makes you feel good. Female, b. '51

I do think about the Beatles often. I still find them to be a comfort in my life. Female, b. '51

Some fans I spoke with "didn't have much to do with the Beatles" for long stretches of time over the years, as work and family commitments took center stage. Some "rediscovered them" with their kids when the *Beatles Anthology* series was released in the nineties. Others started listening closely again at other points since then.

These fans realized how important the Beatles still were to them and that an important source of joy had been missing from their lives. A male fan (b. '53) said he started collecting Beatle memorabilia about ten years ago, and "got pretty excited about them again; it was like a whole new lease on life." A female fan (b. '50) said, "It was rather shocking to discover that hearing those albums brought back all kinds of feelings."

Interestingly, several female fans said their feelings about the Beatles have a kind of "clandestine quality" because their husbands don't approve:

My fascination with the Beatles has waxed and waned over the years. In fact, my recent reentry into the Beatle world, which came about three years ago, felt as strong as it did when I was a teenager. My husband doesn't even know the extent of it. It embarrasses me to talk about them with him. Female, b. '51

My husband gets exasperated with me due to my renewed interest over the past five years or so. Female, b. '53

The reaction of these men parallels the attitude of the Beatle-resistant boys and fathers at the dawn of Beatlemania. It's unfortunate that these women have to deny or defend the fact that the Beatles still bring joy to their lives.

Many fans said they "still think about the Beatles fairly often" and engage with them in some way every day, whether it be listening to music or talking about them with other fans, often through social media: "The Beatles have made my life joyous. My children listen to the Beatles, my home is filled with Beatles memorabilia as well as music. They taught me about love and kindness and how music can touch my heart. The internet has connected me to other fans and a world of new friends" (Female, b. '56).

As the golden anniversary of the Beatles arrival in America unfolds, there are numerous Beatle fan groups on Facebook, with active participants from all over the world. Beatle fans have been a global community for half a century, but with Facebook and other social networking sites members of this community can "come together" in cyberspace for interactive Beatleing.

Whenever the urge strikes, a fan can go online and discuss any and all aspects of the Beatles with other members of the global siblinghood. Provocative posts can elicit hundreds of comments in minutes. Photos of the Beatles, their former wives and girlfriends, and their families are posted and commented on 24/7. A steady stream of "Beatle news," including items about John, Paul, George, and Ringo's children, wives, ex-wives, widows, and anyone with a connection to the band, is reported, shared, and discussed.

Some may see this behavior as extreme, but we can understand fans' ongoing feelings of familial connection with people who have been providing joy, enrichment, and comfort to them throughout their lives. Similarly, it's understandable that fans express genuine concern for the happiness of the surviving Beatles and their families, as one would for an extended family.

Fans of all ages attend Beatle meet-ups to play music, discuss Beatle books, have trivia contests, and otherwise hang out, Beatleing with other fans. But the most important "Beatle meet-up" is a celebration that began, with John Lennon's blessing, four years after the band broke up.

Since 1974, Mark Lapidos has been convening fans for three days of serious Beatle fun at the Fest for Beatle Fans, originally called Beatlefest, which takes place annually in New York and Chicago. The Fest, enthusiastically endorsed by Lennon at its inception, is a place to luxuriate in Beatleness and spend time with others who experienced first-hand the deep impact, "the joyful trauma," as well as with younger fans of all ages. Fest attendees describe it as "three of the best days of the year," and many say they "can't ask for a better vacation." Fans say it's not only about the Beatles but about sharing their love of the Beatles with others. For those who attend regularly, it's like a family reunion.

The Beatles and the Cosmos

Several fans described the entire Beatle phenomenon as "magic." A male fan (b. '57) said, "I don't believe in magic but they're as close to magic as you can get." A female fan (b. '51) who said, "the Beatles were the most positive influence in my life" said, "the word miracle explains it best." A female fan (b. '61) said, "As a Christian, I liked that their music seemed to be in touch with something beyond."

It's not uncommon to hear fans say "the Beatles are like a religion to me." And while most don't mean this literally, Beatle fandom seems to serve a function in fans' lives that is similar to the function religion serves in the lives of believers.

Beatle fans are a global community whose members share feelings of appreciation, inspiration, and reverence for a charismatic communicator who brought and continues to bring joy and spiritual satisfaction to their lives. Liverpool, Abbey Road, the Dakota, and Strawberry Fields in Central Park are pilgrimage destinations, and fans note Beatle birthdays and other special days on the calendar. There is a Beatles creation story that is passionately retold and discussed, and there is a generally agreed upon set of principles. Fans analyze and interpret Beatle texts—songs, recordings, images, histories, commentaries—with a passion and appetite for nuance like that of biblical scholars.

The Beatles' ability to elicit joy and elevate people of all ages, across cultures, for a half-century, suggests something transcendent and universal. The uniqueness of the phenomenon and fans' feelings of joy and gratitude lead more than a few to attach a spiritual component to Beatleness, whether it's the "spiritual joy of a great melody" or believing "they were sent by Gods or angels to bring us music." A male fan (b. '55) described them as "messengers from the universe," telling people "to be bold enough to be themselves so they'll attract more love."

Fans unabashedly continue to celebrate the Beatles and perpetuate their legacy among friends, family, and coworkers. Many describe the great pleasure of introducing children, grandchildren, and other young people to the Beatles. It is through this process of transmission to the next generation—also structurally similar to religion—that Beatleness continues to permeate the culture. In addition, many first-generation fans brought Beatleness to careers as writers, designers, musicians, educators, therapists, social workers, and entrepreneurs, infusing their communication with Beatle references and sensibilities.

Fans often ponder the many moments of serendipity in the Beatles story—the luck and coincidence that brought them into existence. With every new Beatle history or biography, longer and more minutiae-filled than those that came before, comes the promise of really, finally, understanding what happened. Every retelling evokes feelings of awe and affirms fans' belief that they experienced something truly extraordinary. As one male fan (b. '49) put it:

When I think about them, it's more like a feeling of wonder. I wonder how all of us were so lucky that something as great as the Beatles occurred in our lifetime.

Notes

Chapter 1: Setting the Stage

1. John F. Kennedy, 1960 Democratic National Convention, July 15, 1960.
2. Students for a Democratic Society, *The Port Huron Statement*. Draft by Tom Hayden, revised by SDS National Convention, Port Huron, Michigan, June 11–15, 1962.
3. William G. Thomas III, *Television News and the Civil Rights Struggle*. November 3, 2004. http://southernspaces.org/2004/television-news-and-civil-rights-struggle-views-virginia-and-mississippi#section6. Accessed June 14, 2013.
4. "Students: A Matter of Attitude," *Time*, November 8, 1963.
5. Helen Gurly Brown, *Sex and the Single Girl* (New York: Bernard Geis Associates, 1962).
6. Betty Friedan, *The Feminine Mystique* (New York: W. W. Norton, 1963).
7. Joshua Meyrowitz, *No Sense of Place: The Impact of Electronic Media on Social Behavior* (New York: Oxford University Press, 1985).
8. Jonathan Cott, "The Good Dr. Seuss." *Pipers at the Gates of Dawn: The Wisdom of Children's Literature.* Reprint (New York: Random House, 1984). *The Sneetches* (1961) was about racial equality; *The Butter Battle Book* (1950s) was about the arms race; *Yertle the Turtle* (1958) was about Hitler and anti-authoritarianism; *How the Grinch Stole Christmas* (1957) criticized materialism and consumerism; and *Horton Hears a Who!* (1950) was about anti-isolationism.

9. Susan Karlin, "The Ascent of 'MAD'": see "60 Years of Comic Subversion," http://www.fastcompany.com. Accessed June 10, 2013.
10. "Times Topics: MAD Magazine," *New York Times*, April 13, 2009.
11. "Nightclubs: The Sickniks," *Time*, July 13, 1959, 42.
12. "Selling: The Children's Market," *Time*, July 12, 1963.
13. "Martin Luther King Jr., Time Man of the Year 1963," *Time*, January 4, 1964.
14. The group photo on the back of *Meet the Beatles*, where George has his arm extended to Ringo's shoulder; the group photo where the other three hover around a seated Ringo, suggesting a four-headed creature; and the photo with Ringo seated in the chair and the others standing.

Chapter 2: Something New

1. "I Want To Hold Your Hand" held the number one spot for seven weeks before being pushed out by "She Loves You." Leslie Gore's "You Don't Own Me," a teenage girl's manifesto for gender equality in the dating world had been climbing the charts throughout the new year and was number two the week of the first Sullivan broadcast. The song's forward-looking message was lost in the din and dazzle of Beatlemania. Dusty Springfield's "Wishin' and Hopin'" offered a very different message to teenage girls (and boys) a few months later.
2. In some of the early photos and footage, Paul's bangs are at a length that hits his eyebrows in a way that seems to alter their shape, giving him a strange expression.
3. Jack Gould, "The Beatles and Their Audience," *New York Times*, February 10, 1964, 53.
4. "The Beatles Bomb on TV," *New York Herald Tribune*, February 10, 1964; *Newsweek*, February 11, 1964.
5. David Elkind, "Egocentrism in Adolescence," *Child Development* 38 (1967): 1025–1034.
6. John Cloud, "Why Girls Have BFFs and Boys Hang Out in Packs," *Time*, July 17, 2009.
7. The "everybody tells me so" of "Can't Buy Me Love" suggests the importance of love over money is well-known and obvious,

foreshadowing "The Word," where the importance of love is asserted in both good and bad books.

8. Pat Boone, *Twixt Twelve and Twenty* (Englewood Cliffs, NJ: Prentice-Hall, 1958); Connie Francis, *For Every Young Heart* (Prentice-Hall, Inc., 1962).

9. Barbara Ehrenreich, Elizabeth Hess, and Gloria Jacobs, "Beatlemania: Girls Just Want to Have Fun," in Lisa A. Lewis, ed., *The Adoring Audience: Fan Culture and Popular Media* (London: Routledge, 1992), 102.

10. Editorial, *Saturday Evening Post*, March 21, 1964.

Chapter 3: British Boys

1. http://www.rogerebert.com/reviews/great-movie-a-hard-days-night-1964. Retrieved October 23, 2013.

2. "Yeah? Yeah. Yeah!" *Time*, August 14, 1964, 67.

3. Constantine FitzGibbon, *Life*, "A Hard Day's Night," August 7, 1964.

4. Andrew Sarris, "A Hard Day's Night," in Elizabeth Thomson and David Gutman, *The Lennon Companion* (New York: Da Capo, 2004), 50.

5. Larry Kane, *Ticket to Ride* (Philadelphia: Running Press, 2003); Judith Kristen, *A Date with a Beatle* (Pennsauken, NJ: Aquinas and Krone Publishing, 2011).

6. Shawn Levy, *Ready, Steady, Go: The Smashing Rise and Giddy Fall of Swinging London* (New York: Doubleday, 2002), 134–135.

7. The word "country*men*" accurately describes it. The women most associated with the "British Invasion" in the minds of Beatle fans are Pattie Boyd and Jane Asher. Some female fans knew about the first supermodel, Jean Shrimpton. British Invasion singers Cilla Black, Dusty Springfield, and Petula Clark didn't get the attention or airplay enjoyed by Beatle-inspired guitar bands and duos. "Downtown" and "I Know a Place" were big hits for Petula Clark in 1965, and she had four more top ten hits through 1967. Beatle gal-pal and Liverpool native Cilla Black had only one top ten hit, despite being managed by Brian Epstein and appearing on *Sullivan*. After a rebranding, Dusty Springfield went on to have two more top ten hits after "Wishin' and Hopin.'"

8. http://www.pophistorydig.com/?tag=rock-music-1960s Retrieved July 24, 2013. In 2004, *Rolling Stone* named "Satisfaction" the second-greatest song of all time, coming in second to Bob Dylan's "Like a Rolling Stone." And while *Newsweek* has called the opening riff "five notes that shook the world," Keith Richards said the song's riff could be heard in half of the songs his band had produced.

9. Andy Gill, *Don't Think Twice, It's All Right* (New York: Thunder's Mouth, 1998), 83.

10. Steven D. Stark, *Meet the Beatles* (New York: Harper Collins, 2005), 29.

11. *Time*, Cinema, September 3, 1965, 84.

12. Bosley Crowther, "Beatles Star in *Help!*, a Film of the Absurd," *New York Times*, August 25, 1965, 25.

13. The broadcast was taped on August 14, the day before the tour kickoff at Shea Stadium.

14. Shawn Levy, *Ready Steady Go*, 133, 135.

15. David DiMartino, "Matchstick Men" in *Mojo Special Edition: The Psychedelic Beatles*, February 2002, 23.

16. Eric Nuzum, *Parental Advisory* (New York: Perennial, 2001), 171. Stated reasons for the ban were that the song was an aid to the enemy in Vietnam and that the song's nihilistic lyrics would upset young people.

17. There was a lot of backlash against the song by conservatives, most notably Sgt. Barry Sadler's "Ballad of the Green Berets."

18. Domenic Priore, *Riot on Sunset Strip* (London, England: Jawbone Press, 2007) 197.

19. *Morley Safer Report*, CBS Evening News, August 5, 1965.

20. David A. Noebel, *Communism, Hypnotism, and the Beatles: An Analysis of the Communist Use of Music* (Tulsa, OK: Christian Crusade Publications, 1965).

Chapter 4: The Embodiment of Cool

1. Lennon used the line in a way that made it sound like more of a threat than in Presley's version.

2. David Sheff, *The Playboy Interviews with John Lennon and Yoko Ono* (New York: Playboy Press, 1981).

3. "Bards of Pop," *Newsweek,* March 24, 1966, 102.

4. I'm not a neurologist, and this is just a theory based on my reading of some relevant literature and my knowledge of the Beatles. However, it may be that a simple experiment could provide a scientific explanation for our positive emotional response to Beatle music.

5. Peter G. Christenson and Donald F. Roberts, *It's Not Only Rock and Roll: Popular Music in the Lives of Adolescents* (Cresskill, NJ: Hamilton Press, 1993), 121–122.

6. Sheff, *The Playboy Interviews with John Lennon and Yoko Ono.*

7. Francis J. Rigney and L. Douglas Smith, *The Real Bohemia* (New York: Basic Books, 1961).

8. Christenson and Roberts, *It's Not Only Rock and Roll,* 11.

9. The April 8, 1966, cover marks the first time the magazine ran a cover with text and no accompanying image. The *Los Angeles Times* named the "Is God Dead?" issue among "10 Magazine Covers that Shook the World." http://www.latimes.com/entertainment/news/la-et-10magazinecovers14-july14-pg,0,5472017.photogallery.

10. "Swinging London," *Time,* April 15, 1966.

11. "4th Time Around" was intended as a snarky response to "Norwegian Wood."

12. Priore, *Riot on Sunset Strip,* 76.

13. Robert Shelton, "Son of Suzy, Creamcheese," *New York Times,* December 25, 1966, D11.

14. Ibid., D11.

15. This song was written for Gerry Goffin, who descended into depression and drug abuse when bands started writing and performing their own songs and there was less of a need for Brill Building talent.

16. Richard R. Lingeman, "Offerings at the Psychedelicatessen," *New York Times,* July 10, 1966, 182.

17. Ibid.

18. Christenson and Roberts, *It's Not Only Rock and Roll,* 11; 121–122.

19. There are three explanations for the custom of putting coins on the eyes of the dead. Going back to antiquity, the coins were to pay Charon, the boatman on the river Styx, so that the deceased could cross over and start their next life. More recently, coins were wedged

into the eye sockets to keep out the evil spirits and worms. Another explanation is that the coins are used to weigh down the eyelids, ensuring they stay closed.

20. George Harrison, *I Me Mine* (New York: Simon and Schuster, 1980), 96.
21. Dan Sullivan, "Beatles: More than a Mania," *New York Times*, March 5, 1967, 141. The review gives a lot of credit to George Martin, saying that his "delicate hand insures that each track will have a particular electronic focus and atmosphere" and that this is "one reason Beatle LPs generally avoid monotony." Also, Sullivan errs in implying that McCartney writes the music and that Lennon is the lyricist.
22. Judy Stone, "The Monkees Let Down Their Hair," *New York Times*, October 2, 1966, 135.
23. Barney Huskins, *Waiting for the Sun: Strange Days, Weird Scenes, and the Sound of Los Angeles* (New York: Penguin, 1996), 134.
24. Jack Gould, "The Unpredictable Monkees Arrive on N.B.C.," *New York Times*, September 13, 1966, 95; Jack Gould, "September Song: The Same Old Tune," *New York Times*, September 18, 1966, 139. Gould also noted, in passing, that the lyrics on the Beatle Cartoons were "a little advanced for Saturday morning viewers."
25. Mickey Dolenz, *I'm a Believer: My Life of Monkees, Music, and Madness* (New York: Hyperion, 1993), 85.
26. Stone, "The Monkees Let Down Their Hair," 135.
27. Leonard Gross, "John Lennon: A Shorn Beatle Tries It on His Own," *Look*, December 13, 1966.
28. "Paul McCartney Predicts Breakup of Beatles Soon," *New York Times*, January 23, 1967, 29.

Chapter 5: I'd Love to Turn You On

1. Leroy F. Aarons, "LSD Is Taking a Trip Uptown," *Washington Post*, February 19, 1967, E3.
2. Benjamin Spock, *Rebuilding American Family Values: A Better World for Our Children* (Bethesda, MD: National Press Books, 1994); Thomas Maier. *Dr. Spock: An American Life* (New York: Harcourt Brace, 1998).
3. *Toledo Blade*, "Rev. Peale v. Dr. Spock," February 26, 1968, 8.

4. PBS, *American Experience: Summer of Love* program transcript. http://www.pbs.org/wgbh/amex/love/filmmore/pt.html.

5. Ibid.

6. CBS News, "Inside Pop: The Rock Revolution," April 1967.

7. Geoffrey Stokes, *The Beatles* (New York: Rolling Stone Press, 1980), i.

8. Mark Ellen, "The Complete Picture" in *Mojo Special Edition: The Psychedelic Beatles*, 2002, 105.

9. Derek Taylor, *It Was Twenty Years Ago Today: An Anniversary Celebration of 1967* (New York: Simon and Schuster, 1987), 35.

10. James Miller, *Flowers in the Dustbin: The Rise of Rock and Roll 1947–1977* (New York: Fireside, 1999), 258.

11. That there were no singles from *Sgt. Pepper*, yet it was played on AM radio—several songs at a time—also made it seem more special. According to Jim Kerr of New York's classic rock station Q104.3, "Top 40 stations just didn't do that. The Beatles forced their hand," cited in David Hinckley, "How 'Pepper' Shook Things Up," *New York Daily News*, May 31, 2007. Retrieved August 31, 2013.

12. Taylor, *It Was Twenty Years Ago Today*, 48.

13. Mark Hertsgaard, *A Day in the Life: The Music and Artistry of the Beatles* (New York: Delta, 1995), 199.

14. Ibid.

15. Thomas Thompson, *Life*, June 16, 1967.

16. *Time*, "The Hippies: The Philosophy of a Subculture," July 7, 1967.

17. *Time*, "Pop Music: The Messengers," September 22, 1967.

18. Ibid.

19. Miller, *Flowers in the Dustbin*, 265.

20. http://latimesblogs.latimes.com/thedailymirror/2009/05/crowd-battles-lapd-as-war-protest-turns-violent-.html. Retrieved August 27, 2013.

21. http://latimesblogs.latimes.com/thedailymirror/2009/05/crowd-battles-lapd-as-war-protest-turns-violent-.html. Retrieved August 27, 2013.

22. *Time*, "Youth: The Runaways," September 15, 1967.

23. Dave Marsh, "Introduction," in Randi Reisfeld and Danny Fields, *Who's Your Fave Rave?* (Berkley Trade, 1997).

24. William Klomen, *Saturday Evening Post*, "Meet Gloria Stavers," November 14, 1967, 80.

25. Robert Draper, *Rolling Stone Magazine: The Uncensored History* (New York: Doubleday, 1990).

26. Richard Goldstein, "Are They Waning?" *New York Times*, December 31, 1967, 62.

27. Richard Corliss, "The Censors Are Bothered," *New York Times*, November 26, 1967, J8.

28. David P. McAllester, "To Understand Our Children," *New York Times*, October 1, 1967, 123.

Chapter 6: We All Want to Change the World

1. Ringo made a guest appearance on the show in January 1970 when in LA to promote *The Magic Christian*.

2. Todd Gitlin, *The Sixties: Years of Hope, Days of Rage* (New York: Bantam, 1993), 300.

3. Norman MacAfee, *The Gospel According to RFK: Why It Matters Now* (Boulder, CO: Westview Press, 2004), 19.

4. Charles Kaiser, *1968 in America* (New York: Grove Press, 1988), 78.

5. *Time*, "Yeah? Yeah. Yeah!" August 14, 1964, 67.

6. George Gent, "TV: Another Look at Draft Resistance," *New York Times*, May 4, 1968, 79.

7. Paul Weiss, "Topics: Why College Students Revolt," *New York Times*, May 18, 1968, 32.

8. Judy Klemesrud, "An Arrangement: Living Together for Convenience, Security, Sex," *New York Times*, March 4, 1968, 40.

9. Ibid.

10. Kaiser, *1968 in America*, 83.

11. "McCarthy's Appeal to Youth," *New York Times*, March 14, 1968, 42.

12. *New York Times*, "David Rockefeller Bids Business Heed Disaffection Among Youth," March 14, 1968, 23.

13. *New York Times*, "Dr. Kirk Urges US To Leave Vietnam: Columbia Head Finds War Delays Nation's Advance," April 13, 1968, 5.

14. Students for a Democratic Society, 4.

15. Donal Henahan, "Stokowski, 86, Keeps Time for Youths—In Their Protest and Their Playing," *New York Times*, May 10, 1968, 53.

16. *New York Times*, "Student Graduation Speakers Stress Concern Over Vietnam and Racial Justice," June 17, 1968, 34.

17. Kaiser, *1968 in America*, 137.

18. Stark, *Meet the Beatles*, 28–29.

19. Ibid., 29.

20. Benjamin DeMott, "Rock as Salvation," *New York Times Magazine*, August 25, 1968, 30.

21. http://www.beatlesinterviews.org/db1968.0514pc.beatles.html Press conference, May 14, 1968, New York's Americana Hotel.

22. Peter Brown and Steven Gaines, *The Love You Make: An Insider's Story of the Beatles* (New York: McGraw Hill, 1985), 313.

23. It is often said that James Taylor's career was launched by Apple, but the poster from *Sweet Baby James* was hanging on the wall by the time Taylor fans learned of and then acquired the excellent but unpromoted first James Taylor record, *James Taylor*.

24. *Time*, "Essay: Why Those Students Are Protesting," May 3, 1968.

25. Anthony Lewis, "Londoners Cool to *Hair*'s Nudity: Four Letter Words Shock Few at Musical's Debut," *New York Times*, September 29, 1968.

26. http://www.theguardian.com/theguardian/2013/sep/12/hair-musical-nudity-west-end. Retrieved September 14, 2013.

27. Clive Barnes, "Theater: *Hair* – It's Fresh and Frank; Likable Rock Musical Moves to Broadway," *New York Times*, April 30, 1968, 40.

28. John O'Connor, "The Theater: *Hair*," *Wall Street Journal*, May 1, 1968.

29. Richard Watts, Jr., "Two on the Aisle—Broadway Theater Review—Music of the American Tribe." *New York Post*, April 30, 1968.

30. Evan Thomas, *Robert Kennedy: His Life* (New York: Simon and Schuster, 2000), 300.

31. http://www.boston.com/news/nation/articles/2003/10/21/shock_over_plan_to_sell_rfk_home/. Retrieved September 14, 2013.

32. *New York Times*, "Kennedy Gave View on Students' Spirit," June 8, 1968, 13.

33. Donal Henahan, *New York Times*, "Young Campaign Workers 'Lost': Volunteers Seeking New Hero, Sadly Ponder Future," June 7, 1968, 26.

34. *New York Times*, "Reagan, Scoring Courts, Links Shooting to Permissive Attitude," June 6, 1968, 29.

35. Martin Arnold, "Experts Link Attack on Kennedy to a Strain of Violence in US," *New York Times*, June 6, 1968, 23.

36. Bernard Weinraub, *New York Times*, "In Vietnam, G.I.'s Express Grief, with a Touch of Bitterness," June 7, 1968, 28.

37. *New York Times*, "Pope's Vicar Arrives with a Plea for Love," June 8, 1968, 12.

38. *Teen Screen*, "Hippies: Sinners or Saviors," June 1968, 22.

39. Robert Sam Anson, *Gone Crazy and Back Again* (New York: Doubleday, 1981), 172.

40. Michael R. Frontani, *The Beatles: Image and the Media* (Jackson, MS: University Press of Mississippi, 2007), 180.

41. Gitlin, *The Sixties: Years of Hope, Days of Rage*, 285.

42. Ibid., 331.

43. Ibid., 327.

44. Ibid., 317.

45. Ibid., 318.

46. Ibid.; Jon Wiener, *Come Together: John Lennon in His Time* (Chicago: University of Illinois Press), 60.

47. Kaiser, *1968 in America*, 234.

48. Wiener, *Come Together: John Lennon in His Time*, 61.

49. Kaiser, *1968 in America*, 213.

50. Forty years after the song's release, Yoko wanted to explain the ambiguity: "John was simply saying his spirit was 'in' but his body was 'out.'" She called the lyric, "A confession of a truly conceptual guy" and affirmed that "His idea of revolution was without violence." John Harris, "Music from a Doll's House," *Mojo*, September 2008, 83.

51. Jann Wenner, "The Beatles: On the Occasion of Their Authorized Biography," in Ben Fong-Torres, ed., *The Rolling Stone Rock 'n' Roll Reader* (New York: Bantam, 1974), 73.

52. Ibid., 71.

53. Harry Gilroy, "Two Biographies of the Beatles Rushed to Stores," August 17, 1968, 25.

54. Renata Adler, "Beatles, Comic Strip Style," *New York Times*, November 17, 1968, D1.

55. Renata Adler, "Screen: 'Yellow Submarine' Emerges: Songs of the Beatles Pepper Cartoon," *New York Times*, November 14, 1968, 56.

56. Pauline Kael, "The Metamorphosis of the Beatles," *The New Yorker*, November 30, 1968.

57. George Harrison, Smothers Brothers, *Smothers Brothers Comedy Hour*, November 17, 1968. http://www.beatlesinterviews.org/db1968.1117.beatles.html.

58. Richard Shepard, "Disks Wear Art on Their Sleeves to Woo Buyers," *New York Times*, March 12, 1968, 50.

59. Frontani, *The Beatles: Image and the Media*, ebook edition Loc 2738.

60. Nick Bromell, *Tomorrow Never Knows* (Chicago: University of Chicago Press, 2000), 184.

61. Frontani, *The Beatles: Image and the Media*, ebook edition Loc 2756.

62. *Time*, "Recordings: The Mannerist Phase," December 6, 1968.

63. http://www.rollingstone.com/music/news/john-lennon-the-rolling-stone-interview-19681123?page=3.

Chapter 7: The Last Leg

1. *New York Times*, "A Jersey Prosecutor Bans Sales of a Beatles' Album," January 25, 1969, 24.

2. Betty Rollin, "Top Pop Merger: Lennon/Ono Inc.," *Look*, March 18, 1967, 37.

3. Geoffrey Giuliano, *The Beatles: A Celebration* (Sunburst Books, 1993), 144.

4. Gitlin, *The Sixties*, 342–343.

5. Jacqueline Edmondson, *John Lennon: A Biography* (Santa Barbara, CA: Greenwood, 2010) 122; Phillip Norman, *John Lennon: The Life* (Doubleday Canada, 2008) 603.

6. *Rolling Stone*, "Beatles: No Discernible Pattern," May 3, 1969, 10.

7. Norman, *John Lennon*, 605.

8. Wiener, *Come Together*, 92.

9. Peter Doggett, *There's a Riot Going On: Revolutionaries, Rock Stars, and the Rise and Fall of the 60s* (Edinburgh: Canongate, 2008).

10. Interview with John Lennon and Paul McCartney, May 14, 1968, WNDT, New York. http://www.beatlesinterviews.org/db1968.0514.beatles.html.

11. *New York Times*, "WMCA Bans New Single, 'Ballad,' by Beatle Lennon," May 24, 1969, 70.

12. Ian McDonald, *Revolution in the Head* (New York: Henry Holt and Company, 1994), 277.

13. Phillip Norman, *John Lennon: The Life* (Doubleday Canada, 2008), 608.

14. David Sheff, *All We Are Saying* (New York: St. Martin's Press), 166.

15. Jon Wiener, *Come Together: John Lennon in His Time* (Urbana and Chicago: University of Illinois Press, 1984), 104.

16. John Lennon "Man of the Decade Interview," December 2, 1969, http://www.beatlesinterviews.org/db1969.1202.beatles.html.

17. *Rolling Stone*, "Beatles 'Get Back' Track by Track," September 20, 1969, 8.

18. *Rolling Stone*, "John and Yoko on a Peace Cruise," September 20, 1969, 8.

19. Allen J. Wiener, *The Beatles; The Ultimate Recording Guide*, 3rd edition, (Holbrook, MA: Bob Adams Inc, 1994), 472.

20. Nik Cohen, "The Beatles: For 15 Minutes, Tremendous," *New York Times*, October 5, 1969, HF13. http://www.nytimes.com/library/music/100569lennon-beat.html.

21. Mike Jahn, "'Abbey Road' by Beatles Marked by Moderation," *New York Times*, October 4, 1969, 25.

22. David Fricke, "Road to Nowhere," *Mojo Special Edition: The Beatles Final Years*, February 2003, 110.

23. http://www.huffingtonpost.com/john-w-whitehead/john-lennon-antiwar-activist_b_1948185.html.

24. *New York Times*, "Beatle Spokesman Calls Rumor of McCartney's Death 'Rubbish,'" October 22, 1969, 8.

25. Jack Doyle, "The Paul-Is-Dead Saga, 1969–1970," *PopHistoryDig.com*.

26. *Rolling Stone*, "One and One and One Is Three?" November 15, 1969.

27. J. Marks, "No, No, No, Paul McCartney Is Not Dead," *New York Times*, November 2, 1969, D13.

28. McCartney interview: *Life*, November 7, 1969. http://www.beatlesinterviews.org/db1969.1107.beatles.html.

29. John Burks, "Rock & Roll's Worst Day," *Rolling Stone*, February 7, 1970.

30. Martha Ann Bari, *Mass Media is the Message: Yoko Ono and John Lennon's 1969 Year of Peace*, doctoral dissertation, Graduate School of the University of Maryland, College Park, 2007.

31. Jann Wenner, "Man of the Year," *Rolling Stone*, February 7, 1970, 24.

32. Joan Cook, "In the 60's, Hair Was a Fighting Word," *New York Times*, December 31, 1969, 29.

33. Wenner, "Man of the Year," 24.

34. Ritchie Yorke, "John, Yoko, and Year One," *Rolling Stone*, February 7, 1970, 19.

35. *Rolling Stone*, "John, Yoko, Kyoko Get Trimmed," February 21, 1970, 7.

36. Neil Young, *Decade* (Reprise Records, 1977).

37. *New York Times*, "Film: Beatles Together: 'Let It Be' Documents Recording Sessions," May 29, 1970, 11.

Chapter 8: Beatleness Abounds

1. Interview with John Lennon and Paul McCartney, May 14, 1968, WNDT, New York. http://www.beatlesinterviews.org/db1968.0514.beatles.html.

Bibliography

Aarons, Leroy F. "LSD Is Taking a Trip Uptown." *Washington Post*, February 19, 1967.

Adler, Renata. "Beatles, Comic Strip Style." *New York Times*, November 17, 1968.

Adler, Renata. "Screen: 'Yellow Submarine' Emerges: Songs of the Beatles Pepper Cartoon." *New York Times*, November 14, 1968.

Anson, Robert Sam. *Gone Crazy and Back Again*. New York: Doubleday, 1981.

Arnold, Martin. "Experts Link Attack on Kennedy To a Strain of Violence in US." *New York Times*, June 6, 1968.

Bari, Martha Ann. "Mass Media is the Message: Yoko Ono and John Lennon's 1969 Year of Peace." PhD diss., Graduate School of the University of Maryland, College Park, 2007.

Barnes, Clive. "Theater: Hair—It's Fresh and Frank; Likable Rock Musical Moves to Broadway." *New York Times*, April 30, 1968.

Bianculli, David. *Dangerously Funny: The Uncensored Story of the Smothers Brothers Comedy Hour*. New York: Touchstone, 2009.

Boone, Pat. *Twixt Twelve and Twenty*. Englewood Cliffs, NJ: Prentice-Hall, 1958.

Bromell, Nick. *Tomorrow Never Knows*. Chicago: University of Chicago Press, 2000.

Brown, Peter and Steven Gaines. *The Love You Make: An Insider's Story of the Beatles*. New York: McGraw Hill, 1985.

Burks, John. "Rock & Roll's Worst Day." *Rolling Stone*, February 7, 1970.

CBS Evening News, *Morley Safer Report*, August 5, 1965.

CBS News, "Inside Pop: The Rock Revolution," April 1967.

Christenson, Peter G. and Donald F. Roberts. *It's Not Only Rock and Roll: Popular Music in the Lives of Adolescents*. Cresskill, NJ: Hamilton Press, 1993.

Cloud, John. "Why Girls Have BFFs and Boys Hang Out in Packs." *Time*, July 17, 2009.

Cohen, Nik. "The Beatles: For 15 Minutes, Tremendous." *New York Times*, October 5, 1969.

Coleman, Terry. "Nudity in *Hair* Only Brief." *Guardian*, September 12, 1968. http://www.theguardian.com/theguardian/2013/sep/12/hair-musical-nudity-west-end. Retrieved September 14, 2013.

Cook, Joan. "In the 60's, Hair Was a Fighting Word." *New York Times*, December 31, 1969.

Corliss, Richard. "The Censors Are Bothered." *New York Times*, November 26, 1967.

Cott, Jonathan. "John Lennon: The Rolling Stone Interview." *Rolling Stone*. November 23, 1968. http://www.rollingstone.com/music/news/john-lennon-the-rolling-stone-interview-19681123.

Cott, Jonathan. *Pipers at the Gates of Dawn: The Wisdom of Children's Literature*. New York: McGraw-Hill, 1984.

Crowther, Bosley. "Beatles Star in *Help!*, A Film of the Absurd." *New York Times*, August 25, 1965.

DeMott, Benjamin. "Rock as Salvation." *New York Times*, August 25, 1968.

DiMartino, David. "Matchstick Men." *Mojo Special Edition: The Psychedelic Beatles*, February 2002.

Doggett, Peter. *There's a Riot Going on: Revolutionaries, Rock Stars, and the Rise and Fall of the 60s*. Edinburgh: Canongate, 2008.

Dolenz, Mickey. *I'm a Believer: My Life of Monkees, Music, and Madness*. New York: Hyperion, 1993.

Doyle, Jack. "The Paul-Is-Dead Saga, 1969–1970." PopHistoryDig.com. March 7, 2011.

Draper, Robert. *Rolling Stone Magazine: The Uncensored History*. New York: Doubleday, 1990.

Ebert, Roger. "A Hard Day's Night" movie review. http://www.rogerebert.com/reviews/great-movie-a-hard-days-night-1964. Retrieved October 23, 2013.

Edmondson, Jacqueline. *John Lennon: A Biography*. Santa Barbara, CA: Greenwood, 2010.

Elkind, David. "Egocentrism in Adolescence." *Child Development* 38 (1967).

Ellen, Mark. "The Complete Picture." *Mojo Special Edition: The Psychedelic Beatles*, 2002.

FitzGibbon, Constantine. "A Hard Day's Night." *Life*. August 7, 1964.

Francis, Connie. *For Every Young Heart*. Englewood, NJ: Prentice-Hall,1962.

Fricke, David. "Road to Nowhere." *Mojo Special Edition: The Beatles Final Years*, February 2003.

Friedan, Betty. *The Feminine Mystique*. New York: W. W. Norton, 1963.

Frontani, Michael R. *The Beatles: Image and the Media*. University Press of Mississippi, 2007.

Gent, Geoffrey. "TV: Another Look at Draft Resistance." *New York Times*, May 4, 1968.

Gill, Andy. *Don't Think Twice, It's All Right*. New York: Thunder's Mouth, 1998.

Gitlin, Todd. *The Sixties: Years of Hope, Days of Rage*. New York: Bantam, 1993.

Giuliano, Geoffrey. *The Beatles: A Celebration*. Sunburst Books, 1993.

Goldsmith, Martin. *The Beatles Come to America*. New York: Wiley, 2004.

Goldstein, Richard. "Are They Waning?" *New York Times,* December 31, 1967.

Gould, Jack. "September Song: The Same Old Tune." *New York Times*, September 18, 1966.

Gould, Jack. "The Beatles and Their Audience." *New York Times*, February 10, 1964.

Gould, Jack. "The Unpredictable Monkees Arrive on N.B.C." *New York Times*, September 13, 1966.

Gross, Leonard. "John Lennon: A Shorn Beatle Tries It on His Own." *Look,* December 13, 1966.

Gurly Brown, Helen. *Sex and the Single Girl*. New York: Bernard Geis Associates, 1962.

Harris, James F. *Philosophy At 33 1/3 rpm*. Chicago: Open Court: 1993.

Harris, John. "Music from a Doll's House." *Mojo*, September, 2008.

Harrison, George. *I Me Mine*. New York: Simon and Schuster, 1980.

Harrison, George. "George Harrison Interview: Smothers Brothers, November 17, 1968." Beatles Interviews Data Base. http://www.beatlesinterviews.org/db1968.1117.beatles.html. Retrieved September 23, 2013.

Harry, Bill. *The Ultimate Beatles Encyclopedia*. New York: Hyperion, 1992.

Henahan, Donal. "Stokowski, 86, Keeps Time for Youths—In Their Protest and Their Playing." *New York Times*, May 10, 1968.

Henahan, Donal. "Young Campaign Workers 'Lost': Volunteers Seeking New Hero, Sadly Ponder Future." *New York Times*, June 7, 1968.

Hertsgaard, Mark. *A Day in the Life: The Music and Artistry of the Beatles*. New York: Delta, 1995.

Hinckley, David. "How 'Pepper' Shook Things Up." *New York Daily News*, May 31, 2007. Retrieved August 31, 2013.

Huskins, Barney. *Waiting for the Sun: Strange Days, Weird Scenes, and the Sound of Los Angeles*. New York: Penguin, 1996.

Jahn, Mike. "'Abbey Road' by Beatles Marked by Moderation." *New York Times*, October 4, 1969.

Kael, Pauline. "The Metamorphosis of the Beatles." *The New Yorker*, November 30, 1968.

Kaiser, Charles. *1968 in America*. New York: Grove Press, 1988.

Kane, Larry. *Ticket to Ride*. Philadelphia: Running Press, 2003.

Karlin, Susan. "The Ascent of 'MAD': See 60 Years of Comic Subversion." http://www.fastcompany.com. Accessed June 10, 2013.

Klemesrud, Judy. "An Arrangement: Living Together for Convenience, Security, Sex." *New York Times*, March 4, 1968.

Klomen, William. "Meet Gloria Stavers." *Saturday Evening Post*, November 14, 1967.

Kristen, Judith. *A Date with a Beatle*. Pennsauken, NJ: Aquinas and Krone Publishing, 2011.

Lennon, John. "Man of the Decade Interview December 2, 1969." Beatles Interviews Data Base. http://www.beatlesinterviews.org/db1969.1202.beatles.html.

Lennon, John and Paul McCartney. "Interview with WNDT, New York. May 14, 1968." Beatles Interviews Data Base. http://www.beatlesinterviews.org/db1968.0514.beatles.html.

Leonard, Mary. "Shock Over Plan to Sell RFK Home." *Boston Globe*, October 23, 2003. http://www.boston.com/news/nation/articles/2003/10/21/shock_over_plan_to_sell_rfk_home/. Retrieved September 14, 2013.

Levy, Shawn. *Ready, Steady, Go: The Smashing Rise and Giddy Fall of Swinging London*. New York: Doubleday, 2002.

Lewis, Anthony. "Londoners Cool to *Hair*'s Nudity: Four Letter Words Shock Few at Musical's Debut." *The New York Times*, September 29, 1968.

Lewis, Lisa A., editor. *The Adoring Audience: Fan Culture and Popular Media*. London: Routledge, 1992.

Lingeman, Richard R. "Offerings At the Psychedelicatessen." *New York Times*, July 10, 1966.

McCartney, Paul. "Interview: *Life*, November 7, 1969." Beatles Interviews Data Base: http://www.beatlesinterviews.org/db1969.1107.beatles.html.

MacAfee, Norman. *The Gospel According to RFK: Why It Matters Now*. Boulder, CO: Westview Press, 2004.

Maier, Thomas. *Dr. Spock: An American Life*. New York: Harcourt Brace, 1998.

Margulis, Elizabeth Hellmuth. *On Repeat: How Music Plays the Mind*. New York: Oxford University Press, 2014.

Marks, J. "No, No, No, Paul McCartney Is Not Dead." *New York Times*, November 2, 1969.

McAllester, David P. "To Understand Our Children." *New York Times*, October 1, 1967.

McDonald, Ian. *Revolution in the Head*. New York: Henry Holt, 1994.

Meyrowitz, Joshua. *No Sense of Place: The Impact of Electronic Media on Social Behavior*. New York: Oxford University Press, 1985.

Miles, Barry. *The British Invasion: The Music, the Times, the Era*. New York: Sterling Publishers, 2009.

Miller, James. *Flowers in the Dustbin: The Rise of Rock and Roll 1947–1977*. New York: Fireside, 1999.

Newsweek. "Bards of Pop." March 24, 1966.

New York Herald Tribune. "The Beatles Bomb on TV." February 10, 1964.

New York Times. "Paul McCartney Predicts Breakup of Beatles Soon." January 23, 1967.

New York Times. "David Rockefeller Bids Business Heed Disaffection Among Youth." March 14, 1968.

New York Times. "McCarthy's Appeal to Youth." March 14, 1968.

New York Times. "Dr. Kirk Urges US to Leave Vietnam: Columbia Head Finds War Delays Nation's Advance." April 13, 1968.

New York Times. "Reagan, Scoring Courts, Links Shooting to Permissive Attitude." June 6, 1968.

New York Times. "Kennedy Gave View on Students' Spirit." June 8, 1968.

New York Times. "Pope's Vicar Arrives with a Plea for Love." June 8, 1968.

New York Times. "Student Graduation Speakers Stress Concern over Vietnam and Racial Justice." June 17, 1968.

New York Times. "A Jersey Prosecutor Bans Sales of a Beatles Album." January 25, 1969.

New York Times. "WMCA Bans New Single, 'Ballad,' by Beatle Lennon." May 24, 1969.

New York Times. "Beatle Spokesman Calls Rumor of McCartney's Death 'Rubbish.'" October 22, 1969.

New York Times. "Times Topics: MAD Magazine." April 13, 2009.

Noebel, David A., *Communism, Hypnotism, and the Beatles: An Analysis of the Communist Use of Music.* Tulsa, OK: Christian Crusade Publications, 1965.

Norman, Phillip. *John Lennon: The Life.* Doubleday Canada, 2008.

Nuzum, Eric. *Parental Advisory: Music Censorship in America.* New York: Perennial, 2001.

O'Connor, John. "The Theater: *Hair.*" *Wall Street Journal,* May 1, 1968.

PBS, *American Experience.* "Summer of Love" program transcript. http://www.pbs.org/wgbh/amex/love/filmmore/pt.html.

Pop History Dig. "No Satisfaction." http://www.pophistorydig.com/?tag=rock-music-1960s. Retrieved July 24, 2013.

Priore, Domenic. *Riot on Sunset Strip.* London, England: Jawbone Press, 2007.

Reich, Kenneth. The Bloody March That Shook LA. http://latimesblogs. latimes.com/thedailymirror/2009/05/crowd-battles-lapd-as-war-protest-turns-violent-.html. Retrieved August 27, 2013.

Reisfeld, Randi and Danny Fields. "Who's Your Fave Rave?" New York: Berkley, 1997.

Rigney, Francis J. and L. Douglas Smith. *The Real Bohemia*. New York: Basic Books, 1961.

Riley, Tim. *Lennon: The Man, the Myth, the Music, the Definitive Life.* New York: Hyperion, 2011.

Rollin, Betty. "Top Pop Merger: Lennon/Ono Inc." *Look*, March 18, 1967.

Rolling Stone. "Beatles 'Get Back' Track by Track." September 20, 1969.

Rolling Stone. "Beatles: No Discernable Pattern." May 3, 1969.

Rolling Stone. "John and Yoko on a Peace Cruise." September 20, 1969.

Rolling Stone. "John, Yoko, Kyoko Get Trimmed." February 21, 1970.

Rolling Stone. "One and One and One Is Three?" November 15, 1969.

Sawyers, June Skinner, editor. *Read the Beatles.* New York: Penguin, 2006.

Sheff, David. *All We Are Saying.* New York: St. Martin's, 2010.

Sheff, David. *The Playboy Interviews with John Lennon and Yoko Ono.* New York: Playboy Press, 1981.

Shelton, Robert. "Son of Suzy, Creamcheese." *New York Times*, December 25, 1966.

Shepard, Richard. "Disks Wear Art on Their Sleeves to Woo Buyers." *New York Times*, March 12, 1968.

Sounes, Howard. *Fab: An Intimate Life of Paul McCartney*. Philadelphia, PA: DaCapo, 2010.

Spitz, Bob. *The Beatles: The Biography.* New York: Little, Brown, 2005.

Stark, Steven D. *Meet the Beatles.* New York: Harper Collins, 2005.

Stokes, Geoffrey. *The Beatles.* New York: Rolling Stone Press, 1980.

Stone, Judy. "The Monkees Let Down Their Hair." *New York Times*, October 2, 1966.

Students for a Democratic Society. *The Port Huron Statement.* Draft by Tom Hayden, revised by SDS National Convention, Port Huron, Michigan, June 11–15, 1962.

Sullivan, Dan. "Beatles: More than a Mania." *New York Times*, March 5, 1967.

Taylor, Derek. *It Was Twenty Years Ago Today: An Anniversary Celebration of 1967*. New York: Simon and Schuster, 1987.

Teen Screen, "Hippies: Sinners or Saviors." June 1968.

Thomas, Evan. *Robert Kennedy: His Life*. New York: Simon and Schuster, 2000.

Thomas, William G., III. "Television News and the Civil Rights Struggle." November 3, 2004. http://southernspaces.org/2004/television-news-and-civil-rights-struggle-views-virginia-and-mississippi#section6. Retrieved June 14, 2013.

Thompson, Howard. "Film: Beatles Together: 'Let It Be' Documents Recording Sessions." *New York Times*. May 29, 1970.

Thompson, Thomas. *Life* magazine, June 16, 1967.

Thomson, Elizabeth and David Gutman, *The Lennon Companion*, New York: Da Capo, 2004.

Time. "Nightclubs: The Sickniks." July 13, 1959. http://content.time.com/time/subscriber/article/0,33009,869153,00.html.

Time. "Selling: The Children's Market." July 12, 1963. http://content.time.com/time/subscriber/article/0,33009,940326,00.html.

Time. "Students: A Matter of Attitude." November 8, 1963. http://content.time.com/time/subscriber/article/0,33009,897042,00.html.

Time. "America's Gandhi: Rev. Martin Luther King, Jr." January 4, 1964. http://content.time.com/time/subscriber/article/0,33009,940759,00.html.

Time. "Yeah? Yeah. Yeah!" August 14, 1964. http://content.time.com/time/subscriber/article/0,33009,897286,00.html.

Time. "Cinema: Chase and Super Chase." September 3, 1965. http://content.time.com/time/subscriber/article/0,33009,842079,00.html.

Time. "Great Britain: You Can Walk Across It On the Grass." April 15, 1966. http://content.time.com/time/subscriber/article/0,33009,835349-1,00.html.

Time. "Youth: The Runaways." September 15, 1967. http://content.time.com/time/subscriber/article/0,33009,941149,00.html.

Time. "Pop Music: The Messengers." September 22, 1967. http://content.time.com/time/subscriber/article/0,33009,837319-1,00.html.

Time. "Essay: Why Those Students are Protesting." May 3, 1968. http://content.time.com/time/subscriber/article/0,33009,841240-1,00.html.

Time. "Recordings: The Mannerist Phase." December 6, 1968. http://content.time.com/time/subscriber/article/0,33009,844646,00.html.

Time. "Youth: The Hippies: Philosophy of a Subculture. July 7, 1967. http://content.time.com/time/subscriber/article/0,33009,899555,00.html.

Toledo Blade. "Rev. Peale v. Dr. Spock." February 26, 1968, 8.

Watts, Richard, Jr., "Two on the Aisle—Broadway Theater Review—Music of the American Tribe." *New York Post*, April 30, 1968.

Weinraub, Bernard. "In Vietnam, G.I.'s Express Grief, with a Touch of Bitterness." *New York Times*, June 7, 1968.

Weiss, Paul. "Topics: Why College Students Revolt." *New York Times*, May 18, 1968.

Wenner, Jann. "Man of the Year." *Rolling Stone*, February 7, 1970.

Wenner, Jann. "The Beatles: On the Occasion of Their Authorized Biography." In *The Rolling Stone Rock 'n' Roll Reader*. Ben Fong-Torres, ed. New York: Bantam, 1974.

Whitehead, John W. "John Lennon: The Last Great Anti-War Activist." Huffington Post, October 15, 2012. http://www.huffingtonpost.com/john-w-whitehead/john-lennon-antiwar-activist_b_1948185.html. Retrieved September 18, 2013.

Wiener, Allen J. *The Beatles; The Ultimate Recording Guide*, 3rd edition. Holbrook, MA: Bob Adams Inc., 1994.

Wiener, Jon. *Come Together: John Lennon in His Time.* Urbana and Chicago: University of Illinois Press, 1984.

Womack, Kenneth, and Todd F. Davis. *Reading the Beatles: Cultural Studies, Literary Criticism, and the Fab Four.* Albany, NY: State University of New York Press, 2006.

Yorke, Ritchie. "John, Yoko, and Year One." *Rolling Stone*, February 7, 1970.

Young, Neil. *Decade.* Reprise Records, 1977.

Index

Note: Songs performed and albums recorded by The Beatles are marked as (song) and (album). Songs and albums by other musicians are marked with the musician's name.

Discussion Questions

FOR SOME READERS, the story in *Beatleness* is long-ago history; for others, some parts are faintly remembered. And for first-generation fans, it remains a vivid, living memory. Readers of different ages experience the book very differently, and appreciate it for different reasons.

The questions below are designed to stimulate discussion of the ideas and themes presented in the book, while drawing on the reader's experience. One set of questions is for readers of all ages, another set is especially for first-generation fans, and another set is intended for younger readers. I hope these questions generate not only good conversation but good "Beatleing," too.

For All Ages

- The author claims that the relationship between the Beatles and their fans was, and continues to be, historically unique. Do you agree or disagree with this claim? Why?
- Were the Beatles agents of change or were they a reflection of changes already happening in the culture?
- Half the population was under age twenty-five in the 1960s. How did this demographic fact fuel Beatlemania?

- What are some similarities and differences between the Beatle fandom and the fandoms that surrounds the Rolling Stones and Bob Dylan, the Harry Potter books, and the Star Trek series, or other large and enduring fandoms?

- The Beatles were role models for young people in the 1960s. In what ways were they "good" role models? In what ways were they "bad" role models?

- The author discusses several factors that made the Beatles phenomenon possible. Do you think anything like the Beatles could happen again? Why or why not?

- Boys who grew their hair long to emulate the Beatles faced resistance and sometimes punishment from parents and teachers. Why? What does this say about conformity and gender roles in the 1960s?

- In addition to their music, what do you think is the Beatles' most enduring legacy?

- The author claims that the Beatles phenomenon is important to postwar American history. Do you agree? Why or why not?

For First-Generation Fans

- The author suggests that the Beatles in some sense replaced John F. Kennedy in the hearts of young people. Do you agree? In what ways were the Beatles and Kennedy similar?

- Baby boomers have a very strong sense of generation identity. What factors, other than the Beatles, contribute to that generational identity?

- Did the Beatles have an impact on your childhood or teenage years? How so? What are some of your most vivid Beatle memories?

- Did you consider yourself a hippie? What did that mean at the time? In what ways have "hippie values" endured? How do you see the Beatles' role in the hippie movement?

- Recreational drugs started becoming mainstream in the sixties. Do you think the Beatles and other popular artists inspired some first-generation fans to smoke marijuana and use LSD?
- Did John and Yoko's peace campaign affect the way you and your friends thought about the war in Vietnam?
- Young people discovering the Beatles today are intrigued by the Paul-Is-Dead frenzy that gripped Beatle fans in 1969. Did you and your friends look for clues? Did you believe Paul was really dead?

For Younger Fans

- Do you remember when you first "discovered" or became interested in the Beatles? How did your experience differ from the experience of the fans interviewed in *Beatleness*?
- Do you think the Beatles story can still inspire people? Why or why not?
- After reading *Beatleness*, what aspects of growing up in the sixties do you find most interesting or surprising?
- If you could go back in time and experience any Beatles album or song for the first time in real time, which one would it be? Why?
- *Beatleness* shows how males and females experienced the Beatles differently. Are there bands or performers today that are experienced in gendered ways?
- Are there bands or performers that have affected your generation in the way that the Beatles affected the baby boom generation?